hugo

Arabic
in Three Months

Mohammad Asfour

A DK Publishing Book
www.dk.com

A DK PUBLISHING BOOK

www.dk.com

First American Edition, 1999
10 9 8 7 6 5 4 3 2 1

Published in the United States by
DK Publishing, Inc.
95 Madison Avenue
New York, New York 10016

Published in Great Britain by Dorling Kindersley Limited.

Library of Congress Cataloging-in-Publication Data
Asfour, Mohammad.
Arabic in three months / Mohammad Asfour.-- 1st American ed.
p. cm. -- (Hugo's simplified system)
Includes index.
ISBN 0–7894–4398–8 (alk. paper). -- ISBN 0–7894–4432–1 (w/cassette)
1. Arabic language--Textbooks for foreign speakers--English. I. Title. II. Series.
Pj 6307.A776 1999
492.7'82421 -- dc21 98–31746
CIP

Set in 10/12pt Palatino by
Andrew Burrell
Printed and bound by LegoPrint, Italy

Preface

'Arabic in Three Months' has been written for us by Professor Mohammad Asfour, at the University of Jordan in Amman. He has drawn on his considerable experience as a poet, teacher and translator to produce a simple yet complete course for students aiming to acquire a good working knowledge of Arabic in a short time, and who will probably be studying at home. The 'Three Months' series as a whole is renowned for its success in self-tuition, with some titles proving to be equally useful in supporting teacher-led classes; this book is no exception.

The course is intended to serve the needs of those whose aim is not to read Arabic books and newspapers, or to write letters in Arabic, but to *speak* a variety of Arabic that will serve them well in almost any Arab country. We therefore asked the author to prepare his text in the spoken form of Arabic, not the written form. The spoken language is more practical, for while written Arabic is understood by ordinary people in the Arab world, nobody uses it for everyday oral transactions.

In view of all this, there was no point in setting any of the text in Arabic script. Instead, we have transcribed the Arabic into roman characters. This entailed modifying some letters by means of dots and short lines, and using certain combinations of letters to represent Arabic sounds that are not heard in English. You should master these thoroughly before proceeding to study the structure of the language; the book begins with a detailed study of its pronunciation and how we have transliterated certain sounds.

Working without a teacher, you'll find that using the book together with our audio cassettes (allowing you to hear much of the Arabic text at the same time that you read it) is an ideal combination, giving another dimension to the course. Ask for the Hugo Arabic Cassette Course, which consists of this book plus four audio tapes.

It has always been a principle of the Hugo method to teach only what is really essential. We assume that the student wants to learn Arabic from a practical angle; the chapters contain those rules of grammar that will be of most use in this respect. Constructions are clearly explained, and the order in which everything is presented takes into consideration the need for rapid progress. Chapter 1 concentrates on pronunciation. Chapters 2–12 include exercises as well as detailed tuition on points of grammar and construction. A series of conversations follows Chapter 12. Answers to the exercises, and a full vocabulary list, appear at the back of the book.

Ideally, you should spend about an hour a day on your work (slightly less, maybe, if you do not use the cassette recordings), although there is no hard and fast rule on this. Do as much as you feel capable of doing; it is much better to learn a little at a time, and to learn that thoroughly. However, ideally you should try to complete one chapter each week.

In studying the chapters, first read each rule or numbered section carefully and re-read it to ensure that you have fully understood the grammar, then work through any following exercise(s) as they occur by writing down the answers. Check these by referring to the key at the back of the book; if you have made too many mistakes, go back over the instruction before attempting the same questions again. Any conversational exercises and conversations should be read aloud and their constructions carefully noted. If you have the cassette recordings, you should listen to these at the same time as you read. After you have listened to the conversations and read them aloud, see how closely you can imitate the voices on the recording.

When you think you have completed a section satisfactorily (alternatively, just before your daily study period is over) go back over what you have recently done, to ensure that it is firmly committed to memory. When the course is completed, you should have a very good understanding of the spoken language – more than sufficient for general holiday or business purposes. If you want to see what written Arabic looks like, or if you need to decipher public signs and so on, our Arabic Phrase Book will help you further.

Contents

Chapter 1: The sounds of Arabic

This first chapter introduces you to the sounds you will hear in Arabic, wherever it is spoken. They include:

- *vowels and diphthongs, fewer than in English*
- *the consonants that are also found in English, and the few that are not*
- *the* **hamza** *or glottal stop*

1 Vowels

The vowel system in Arabic is much simpler than in English. Regional differences exist, but this course recognizes only eight vowels, representing the vowel sounds least likely to sound peculiar to speakers of Arabic everywhere. The short vowels, three in number, correspond to the vowels in Southern English *but, bit* and *put*, and these will be transliterated with **a, i** and **u** respectively. The long vowels correspond to the vowels in *bad, bean* and *boon,* and these will be transliterated as **ā, ī** and **ū** respectively. The other two vowels do not exist in Standard or Classical Arabic (the written form of the language); these are undiphthongized forms (that is, single, 'pure' sounds) of the *a* in *cane* and the *o* in *cone.* They will be transliterated simply as **ai** and **ō** respectively. The vague vowel at the end of feminine nouns and adjectives will be represented by **eh**, where the **h** is given only to remind you that this is not a silent *e* as is often the case in English. The **h** must not be pronounced at all.

Symbol	*English example*	*Arabic example*
a	but	**bard** (cold weather)
ā	bad	**kān** (was)
ai	bait	**bait** (house)
i	bit	**bint** (girl, daughter)
ī	beat	**mīn** (who?)
ō	home	**yōm** (day)
u	put	**funduq** (hotel)
ū	fruit	**sūq** (market)

Four diphthongs (combinations of vowels) also occur, as follows:

Symbol	*English example*	*Arabic example*
aw		**law** (if); pronounce like the *-low* in *allow*, but with a much shorter *a* sound
āw	now	**ṭāwleh** (table)
ay	stay	**fayy** (shade)
āy	why	**nāy** (flute)

Diphthongs, however, are much less frequent in Arabic than they are in English: there are very few diphthongs in which vowels other than the **a** and the **ā** are involved.

2 Consonants found in English

The consonant system, on the other hand, is richer in Arabic than in English. Many consonants are common to both languages, but some occur in one and not in the other. We give the consonants of English first.

Symbol	*Remarks and Arabic examples*
b	Same in both languages: **bait** (house), **ibin** (son).
d	Same in both languages: **dīn** (religion), **mudīr** (manager).
f	Same in both languages: **funduq** (hotel), **ghurfeh** (room).

g When soft (e.g. in *age) g* is identical with the *j* sound. The hard *g* (e.g. in *game)* occurs in colloquial Arabic but not in Standard Arabic. However, the hard **g** is substituted for the normal **j** sounds in many parts of Egypt and Southern Arabia; it also replaces the **q** sound in many parts of the Eastern Arab countries. Where used in the transliteration, it will always stand for the hard **g: gōl** (goal), **Ingilīzi** (English).

h Much more important in Arabic than in English. Should ALWAYS be pronounced as in *he* and *prohibit,* except sometimes at the end of words, where it represents a lengthening of the preceding vowel, and in the feminine ending **-eh: haram** (pyramid), **shahar** (month).

j Same in both languages; sometimes pronounced as in French *je* or *Georges* (cf. the *s* in English *measure):* **jaish** (army), **ujra** (fare).

k Same in both languages: **kursi** (chair), **malik** (king).

l Same in both languages; in the neighbourhood of 'emphatic sounds' (see below) pronounced positively as in *lull;* otherwise as in *lend:* **lail** (night), **ẓulum** (injustice).

m Same in both languages: **Maṣri** (Egyptian), **yōm** (day).

n Same in both languages: **nāyim** (asleep), **bint** (girl, daughter).

p Does not exist in Arabic.

q English *q* is pronounced as *k* (often in the combination *kw,* because invariably followed by the letter *u*). The letter **q** will be used in the transliteration to stand for the emphatic form of **k** (see below).

r Always trilled in Arabic somewhat in the Scottish or Spanish manner: **rās** (head), **@arab** (Arabs).

s Always as in *see;* never as in *as* or *is:* **si@ir** (price), **isim** (name).

t Same in both languages: **tārīkh** (date), **kitāb** (book).

v Does not exist in Arabic except in words borrowed from other languages.

w In Arabic always rounded as in *we* and *win:* **walad** (boy), **ṭawīl** (tall).

y In Arabic always equivalent to its sound in *yes:* **yōm** (day), **nāyim** (asleep).

z Same in both languages: **zaman** (time), **wazīr** (minister).

ch This sound (English *church)* occurs in colloquial (rural) Arabic mainly as a variant of the **k** sound. It will be disregarded in this course.

sh (English *shoe.)* Same in both languages: **shams** (sun), **jaish** (army). When the two letters are meant to be pronounced separately, they will be separated by a hyphen to avoid confusion.

th In English this combination of letters represents two different sounds, both of which exist in Arabic. The sound in *thin* will be represented by the same combination: **thaman** (price), **thamānyeh** (eight), but the sound in *this* will be transliterated as **dh** to avoid confusion: **dharra** (atom), **ladhīdh** (delicious). When the two letters are meant to be pronounced separately, they will be separated by a hyphen.

3 Further consonants

Now, in addition to these consonants, Arabic has nine more which do not normally occur in English and require, therefore, some extra effort on the part of the learner. Except for the **ḥ**, the **kh**, the **@** and the **gh**, they are conventionally referred to as the emphatic sounds. There is no question really of emphasis here; the sounds are simply different.

Symbol *Remarks and Arabic examples*

ḥ Produced by expelling the air through a narrowed throat in much the same way as when one tries to clear one's throat: **ḥall** (solution), **muḥāmi** (lawyer).

kh The sound of *ch* in Scottish *loch,* but rougher: **khaṭar** (danger), **tārīkh** (date).

ṣ Emphatic form of **s**; nearest English equivalent in *bustle* or *bus.* Start with normal **s**, then raise your tongue as much as possible to produce the **ṣ**: **ṣōt** (sound, vote), **Maṣri** (Egyptian).

ḍ Emphatic form of **d**; nearest English equivalent in *dull* or *double.* Start with normal **d**, then raise your tongue as much as possible to produce the **ḍ**: **ḍarar** (damage), **abyaḍ** (white).

ṭ Emphatic form of **t**; nearest English equivalent in *tumble.* Start with normal **t**, then raise your tongue as much as possible to produce the **ṭ**: **ṭāwleh** (table), **khaṭar** (danger).

ẓ Emphatic form of **dh**, not **z**; nearest English equivalent in *mother.* Start with the **dh** sound *(th* in *mother),* then raise your tongue as much possible to produce the **ẓ**: **ẓulum** (injustice), **naẓar** (sight). Many speakers of Arabic use this sound instead of the **ḍ** which has all but disappeared from the Arabic of Iraq, the Arabian Gulf and Saudi Arabia.

@ This arbitrary sign will be used for the sake of convenience to represent a sound that has no equivalent in English. It is produced by expelling the air through a much narrowed throat and causing the vocal chords to vibrate. Say a long *a-a-a-ah* and try as you are doing so to raise the lower part of your throat in order to narrow the passage through which the air is expelled, and you will find that you are pronouncing the @ (called **@ayn**): **@arab** (Arabs), **si@ir** (price).

gh The sound of *r* in French *Paris:* **gharb** (west), **maghrūr** (snobbish).

q Emphatic form of **k**; nearest English equivalent in *car,* but the 'click' of the *k* is produced further back by the uvula, the soft membrane hanging from the back of the roof of the mouth: **qamar** (moon), **el-ḥaqīqa** (truth). Now this sound is used in formal speech and in words that retain their Standard-Arabic flavour. In normal conversation the **q** is usually replaced by either the **hamza** (see below) or the hard **g**. Both are heard on the cassettes. Generally speaking, the **hamza** as a substitute for the **q** is used in urban areas, the **g** in rural areas, although because of increased social mobility this division is no longer clear-cut. Whichever you choose to use, try to be consistent and not use both varieties.

4 hamza

Another feature of Arabic is the frequent use of the **hamza,** which we may describe as a glottal stop, i.e., a sound requiring momentary stoppage of the air stream in the glottis, followed by sudden release. It is the sound that makes the pronunciation of a vowel at the beginning of a syllable possible and it corresponds to the explosive sound that enables an English speaker to pronounce the initial vowels in *on, in, an, end* and *under*. It is this sound that replaces the h's in Henry Higgins' name in Eliza Dolittle's dialect. In this course we shall use the sign " to symbolize this sound, which should be pronounced wherever it appears. To simplify, we shall drop all initial hamzas in the transliteration, since the vowel that remains cannot be pronounced without it anyway: **ab** (father), **umm** (mother), **su"āl** (question), **ra"īs** (president), **sayyi"** (bad), **jarī"** (bold).

5 Doubling

Doubling in Arabic is also to be noted carefully. Whenever double letters appear in the transliteration, the two letters must be given full value. Most speakers of English pronounce *immortal* as if it were *i-mortal,* but the doubling may be heard in *unnerve, unnatural, unknown,* etc., where the *n* is given extra length. Now doubling in Arabic is not only reflected in the pronunciation but also makes a difference to the meaning: **@alam** means 'flag', but **@allam** means 'he taught'; **katab** means 'he wrote', but **kattab** means 'he caused someone to write'; **thaman** 'price', but **thamman** 'he valued'; **dafa@** 'he paid', but **daffa@** 'he made someone pay'.

6 Distinguishing sounds

Since we are dealing here with the spoken form of the language, we must bear in mind that the fixity of the written form (Classical Arabic) is lost and a degree of fluidity, especially in the vowel system, creeps in. (On this see Section 14, 'Some Observations on the Vowels', below.) But even the consonants show some degree of unfixity, as we have seen.

You are advised to pay particular attention to long and short vowels, for the difference in the length of the vowel may result in a difference in meaning. Here are some examples:

min from	**mīn** who?
malik king	**mālik** owner
ḍarabu he hit him	**ḍarabū** they hit him
@alam flag	**@ālam** world

And finally, there is a tendency among most foreign learners of Arabic to confuse certain pairs of consonants. The following 'minimal pairs' (pairs, that is, in which only one element is different) are given to help you learn to distinguish between the problematic sounds.

hamza (")/@ayn (@)

alam pain (initial hamza dropped)	**@alam** flag
sa"al he asked	**sa@al** he sneezed
masā"i nightly	**masā@i** efforts, attempts

dāl (d)/ḍad (ḍ)

damm blood	**ḍamm** annexation, embracing
mada scope	**maḍa** he/it went away
radd answer, response	**raḍḍ** bruise

dhāl (dh)/ẓā" (ẓ)

nadhar he vowed	**naẓar** sight; he looked
dhalīl (of a person:) humiliated	**ẓalīl** (of a place:) shady
maḥdhūr something expected and feared	**maḥẓūr** prohibited

hā" (h)/ḥā" (ḥ)

sāhir wakeful — **sāḥir** magician
hadd he pulled down — **ḥadd** boundary
fāhim understanding — **fāḥim** pitch black

kāf (k)/qāf (q)

kās cup — **qās** he measured
makfūl guaranteed — **maqfūl** locked
shōk thorns — **shōq** yearning

(Note: the **q** is often replaced by either the **hamza** or the hard **g**.)

kāf (k)/khā" (kh)

kān was — **khān** inn; he betrayed
kāmil perfect — **khāmil** idle
sākin quiet — **sākhin** hot, feverish

sīn (s)/ṣād (ṣ)

sār he walked — **ṣār** he became
fasīḥ spacious — **faṣīḥ** eloquent
sadd he closed; dam — **ṣadd** he repulsed; repulsion

tā" (t)/ṭā" (ṭ)

tīn figs — **ṭīn** mud
tāb he repented — **ṭāb** (of a sick person:) he recovered; (of life:) it is pleasant

amtār metres — **amṭār** rains

Chapter 2

In this chapter you will learn some useful nouns: names of people, things and concepts. You will discover that:

- *the definite article is regarded as part of the noun or adjective*
- *possession is expressed by a construction called* **iḍāfa**, *which is very important in Arabic*
- *nouns may be either masculine or feminine*
- *not all sentences need a verb*

7 The definite article

Indefiniteness in Arabic is expressed by the absence of the definite article (in English, 'the'), not by a separate word; definiteness is expressed by the article **el-**, which is considered part of the noun or adjective it is attached to, not, as in English, a separate word. In spoken Arabic, **el-** is pronounced as a combination of a vague vowel (called in English the 'schwa', found in 'moth*er*' and represented in phonetic script by /ə/) and the **l** sound. But the vowel of **el-** is dropped if the preceding word ends with a vowel, and the **l** sound itself is assimilated into the next sound if the word it is attached to begins with one of the following letters or sounds: **t, th, d, dh, r, z, s, sh, ṣ, ḍ, ṭ, ẓ, l** and **n**. These fourteen letters are conventionally called 'sun letters' because the word **shams** ('sun') illustrates the point: the **el-** becomes **esh-** when the article is attached to the word, as in **esh-shams** ('the sun'). The other fourteen letters or sounds are called 'moon letters' because the word **qamar** ('moon') illustrates the point: the **el-** retains its **l** sound when it is attached to the word, as in **el-qamar** ('the moon'). Notice that the sun letters are doubled in transliteration; this is done in order to indicate that the sound is to be pronounced with the kind of emphasis accorded to all doubled letters in Arabic.

Words beginning with moon letters:

ab father	**el-ab** the father
umm mother	**el-umm** the mother
ibin son	**el-ibin** the son
bait house	**el-bait** the house
jaish army	**el-jaish** the army (but the **j** sound is a borderline case; **ej-jaish** is also heard)
ḥall solution	**el-ḥall** the solution
khaṭar danger	**el-khaṭar** the danger
@arab Arabs	**el-@arab** the Arabs
gharb west	**el-gharb** the West
funduq hotel	**el-funduq** the hotel
qalam pen	**el-qalam** the pen
kursi chair	**el-kursi** the chair
Maṣri Egyptian	**el-Maṣri** the Egyptian
haram pyramid	**el-haram** the pyramid
walad boy	**el-walad** the boy
yōm day	**el-yōm** the day; today

Words beginning with sun letters:

tārīkh date (of an event)	**et-tārīkh** the date; history
thaman price	**eth-thaman** the price
dīn religion	**ed-dīn** the religion; religion in the abstract
dharra atom	**edh-dharra** the atom
rās head	**er-rās** the head
zaman time	**ez-zaman** the time; Time as an abstract concept
si@ir price	**es-si@ir** the price
shaqqa apartment	**esh-shaqqa** the apartment
ṣōt sound, voice, vote	**eṣ-ṣōt** the sound, etc.
ḍarar damage	**eḍ-ḍarar** the damage
ṭūl length	**eṭ-ṭūl** the length
ẓulum injustice	**eẓ-ẓulum** the injustice
lail night	**el-lail** the night
nō@ kind, species	**en-nō@** the kind, the species

You may have noticed that words that in English do not take the definite article, such as the abstract nouns 'religion', 'time' and 'injustice', do take the definite article in Arabic. This is a peculiarity well worth remembering.

As we explained above, the vowel of the definite article is dropped when the preceding word ends with a vowel. Thus:

fi 'l-bank *in the bank* (pronounced with a much shorter 'a' than in English)
muḥāmi 'sh-sharikeh *the company's lawyer*
waddi 'l-maktūb *send the letter*
iṭfi 'n-nūr *switch off the light*
akhu 'l-mudīr *the director's brother*
aja 's-sāyiq *the driver has come*
@ala 'r-raff *on the shelf*

8 iḍāfa

Definiteness is also achieved by what is called in Arabic **iḍāfa.** This construction indicates possession, like 'of' in English. In a phrase containing **iḍāfa,** we normally have an indefinite noun followed by a definite one:

ṣāḥib ed-dār (the) owner (of) the house
ism el-walad (the) name (of) the boy
@inwān el-kitāb (the) title (of) the book
lōn es-sayyāra (the) colour (of) the car

In all of these phrases, there is no equivalent to the English word 'of', but the construction conveys this meaning, and the indefinite first noun in each phrase becomes definite by being placed in this **iḍāfa** relationship with the second. This is a very important construction in Arabic, and you are well advised to be alert to it. Furthermore, **iḍāfa** may consist of more than two elements:

isim ṣāḥib ed-dār (the) name (of) (the) owner (of) the house

isim ṣadīq ṣāḥib ed-dār (the) name (of) (the) friend (of) (the) owner (of) the house

Needless to say, such constructions can be even longer than that, but long **iḍāfa** constructions can look as cumbersome in Arabic as does the equivalent accumulation of 'of's in English. In the translations given above, the parentheses indicate elements that do not appear in Arabic but are implied by the construction. If the last element in the construction is indefinite, however, every other noun in it remains indefinite as well.

Since all pronouns are, by definition, definite, indefinite nouns acquire definiteness by being attached to them:

isim name	**ismi** my name (on vowel shifts and vowel elisions see Section 14 below)
ibin son	**ibnu** his son
bait house	**bait-hum** their house
sayyāra car	**sayyārit-ha** her car

As this last example shows, the feminine suffix **-a** or, more frequently, **-eh** is transformed into **-(i)t** in **iḍāfa** constructions. The presence or absence of the vowel of this suffix is determined by factors that will be explained in Section 14. Here are a few more examples:

sā@a watch	**sā@ti** my watch
minshafeh towel	**minshafit-ha** her towel
blūzeh blouse	**blūzit Fadwa** Fadwa's blouse

The pronouns are covered in greater detail in Section 13.

Exercise 1

Make the following nouns definite by adding the definite article to them. Make sure that you are able to pronounce the new words correctly. The definite article is never stressed.

1 sadd
2 faṣīḥ
3 naẓar
4 @alam
5 malik
6 kāmil
7 fāhim
8 damm
9 alam
10 bait

Exercise 2

For each of the words in column A choose a suitable word from column B to form a meaningful phrase. Make all necessary changes, and use all the words.

A	B
kitāb *(book)*	haram
qalam	shita / shitā" *(winter)*
khaṭar	Nuha *(female's name)*
ghurfeh *(room)*	ḥarb *(war)*
ṣōt	kīlu *(kilogramme)*
ujra *(fare)*	Shawqi *(male's name)*
ṭūl *(length, height)*	ab
thaman	walad
amṭār	sayyāra
shaqqa	Aḥmad *(male's name)*

9 Gender

Arabic has only two genders, masculine and feminine; there is no neuter gender. Therefore, those nouns or adjectives which do not clearly refer to masculine or feminine beings must be learnt together with their grammatical gender, which is given in the mini-dictionary at the end. The presence of a vowel (with or without a final **h**) is usually, but not always, a sign that the word is feminine. Thus the nouns **qalam** and **bait** and the adjective **qaşīr** ('short') are masculine (*m.*), while **waraqa** ('sheet of paper'), **ghurfeh** and **jarīdeh** ('newspaper') are feminine (*f.*). Another feminine marker is the suffix **-t**, which reappears in feminine nouns in the **iḍāfa** construction.

Although some masculine nouns can be made feminine by adding the feminine suffix to them, it is in the adjectives that the process seems to be consistently possible. In some cases, the addition of the suffix entails some other changes within the word, usually involving the vowels. Nouns made feminine by the addition of the feminine suffix include:

zōj/zawj husband	**zōjeh/zawjeh** wife
ṭabīb physician	**ṭabībeh**
@amm paternal uncle	**@ammeh** paternal aunt
malik king	**malikeh** queen

And here is a handful of adjectives to illustrate the process:

qaşīr short	**qaşīreh**
ṭawīl tall, long	**ṭawīleh**
ḥilw sweet, handsome	**ḥilweh** sweet, beautiful
nāyim asleep	**nāymeh**
ghanī rich	**ghaniyyeh**
aḥmar red	**ḥamra** (somewhat irregular)
abyaḍ white	**baiḍa** (somewhat irregular)

As for the verbs, we shall see how gender affects them later in this course.

10 The simple verbless sentence

Although verbs are no less important in Arabic than they are in English, it is not always grammatically necessary for the Arabic sentence to contain a verb. This is particularly true if the idea of the verb is that of 'being':

Samīr nāyim.
Samīr (is) asleep.
Samīra nāymeh.
Samīra (is) asleep.
el-kitāb ṣa@b.
The book (is) difficult.
el-qalam maksūr.
The pen (is) broken.
lōn el-qamīs abyaḍ.
(The) colour (of) the shirt (is) white.
sayyārit mudīr el-bank min Almānya.
(The) car (of) (the) manager (of) the bank (is) from Germany.

Notice that the subject of the sentence (in these examples **Samīr, Samīra, el-kitāb,** etc.) is always definite (is a proper noun, has the definite article prefixed to it, or is made definite by being in an **iḍāfa** construction) and that the predicate (what is said about the subject: **nāyim, nāymeh, ṣa@b,** etc.) is often adjectival or adverbial in nature.

Exercise 3

Translate into English:
1 mudīr el-bank nāyim.
2 sayyārit Samīra min Almānya.
3 qamīs Aḥmad abyaḍ.
4 lōn sayyārit Ṣubḥi aḥmar *(red).*
5 kitāb Maḥmūd min Faransa *(France).*
6 umm Nāyif qaṣīreh.
7 kursi ibni maksūr.
8 shaqqit el-Maṣri zghīreh *(small).*
9 el-ḥall ṣa@b.
10 thaman el-kitāb khamis dūlārāt *(five dollars).*

Exercise 4

Translate into Arabic:

1 The bank manager's apartment is large (**wās@a**).
2 His son is in (**fi**) Germany.
3 My son is the bank manager.
4 My son is a bank manager.
5 War time is a difficult time.
6 Army Day is a holiday (**@uṭleh**).
7 The hotel owner's name is Ḥāmid.
8 The history of Egypt is long (**ṭawīl**).
9 The father is in France.
10 Huda's room is large.

Chapter 3

By the end of this chapter you will be able to make some simple Arabic sentences. The chapter covers:

- *adjectives and their relationship with nouns*
- *how adjectives are used in* **iḍāfa** *constructions*
- *personal pronouns (I, you, his, them, etc.)*
- *how the different forms of pronouns are used in sentences*

11 Adjectives

In Arabic, adjectives are treated as nouns; in fact, Arab grammarians do not recognize a separate part of speech called 'adjective'. They do speak, of course, about a grammatical function of that nature. In this course we shall use the term in its English sense of a word which describes a noun. Unlike their English counterparts, however, Arabic adjectives follow the nouns they qualify, take the definite article when needed, may be feminine or masculine, and can be put in the plural. Adjectives also agree with the nouns they qualify in definiteness or indefiniteness, gender and (usually) number:

qamīṣ abyaḍ a white shirt
(indef. m. sing. n., indef. m. sing. adj.)
el-qamīṣ el-abyaḍ the white shirt
(def. m. sing. n., def. m. sing. adj.)
el-bint el-ḥilweh the pretty girl
(def. f. sing. n., def. f. sing. adj.)
el-banāt el-ḥilwāt the pretty girls
(def. f. pl. n., def. f. pl. adj.)

Inanimate plural nouns are usually treated as feminine in gender regardless of the gender of the singular and can be qualified by singular or, less frequently, plural adjectives:

el-qumṣān el-bīḍ the white shirts
(def. f. pl. n., def. f. pl. adj.)
el-khuṭūṭ el-jawwiyyeh 'l-Urduniyyeh The Jordanian Airlines

Here we have a definite plural noun, **el-khuṭūṭ** (*sing.* **khaṭṭ**, 'line') followed by two definite singular adjectives: **el-jawwiyyeh** (lit., 'of the atmosphere, of the upper space') and **el-Urduniyyeh** ('the Jordanian'). This latter pattern is the predominant one:

kutub (*pl. of* **kitāb,** 'book') **thamīneh** (*sing. adj.*, 'valuable')
manāṭiq (*pl. of* **manṭiqa**, 'area, district') **rāqyeh** (*sing. adj.*, 'posh, upper-class')
afkār (*pl. of* **fikra**, 'idea') **@amīqa** (*sing. adj.*, 'deep, profound')

Now the construction **el-banāt el-ḥilwāt** is simply a noun and an adjective, i.e., not a sentence, but **el-banāt ḥilwāt** is a complete sentence: 'The girls (are) pretty'. Similarly, if we drop the definite article from some of the adjectives in the phrases given above, we come up with perfectly grammatical sentences:

el-qamīṣ abyaḍ.
The shirt (is) white.
kutub thamīneh
valuable books
el-kutub eth-thamīneh
the valuable books
el-kutub thamīneh.
The books (are) valuable.

Vocabulary (exercise 5)

Note: In the vocabulary lists, letters in brackets are optional. Following the oblique line, the feminine suffix is given or, if adding this suffix involves some change within the word, the whole word is repeated.

abu	father of
Almāni/yyeh	German
ḥamra	red
maghrūr/a	snobbish; conceited

Exercise 5

Translate the following into English. Which are sentences, which are not?

1 sayyārit Huda el-ḥamra
2 es-sayyāra 'l-Almāniyyeh 'l-ḥamra
3 es-sayyāra 'l-ḥamra Almāniyyeh
4 bint mudīr el-bank el-ḥilweh maghrūra
5 Huda 'l-maghrūra
6 Huda maghrūra
7 Huda, bint mudīr el-bank el-maghrūra, ḥilweh
8 mudīr el-bank abu Huda 'l-maghrūra
9 es-sayyāra 'l-ḥamra sayyārit mudīr el-bank
10 es-sayyarāt el-Almāniyyeh el-ḥamra

12 Adjectives in 'iḍāfa' constructions

When an adjective follows a noun which is itself part of an **iḍāfa** construction, there may be some ambiguity about which noun the adjective applies to. In sentence no. 1 in Exercise 5 above, only common sense prevents the adjective **el-ḥamra** from applying to Huda. Put a male's name instead of Huda's and you will have the ambiguity removed. Put an adjective like **el-ḥilweh** instead of **el-ḥamra** and you will have the ambiguity increased. Larger contexts usually remove all possibility of misunderstanding, but such ambiguities are inevitable in all languages. Your best guide in such matters is common sense.

Exercise 6

Complete each of the following sentences with the Arabic equivalent of the English word in parentheses:

1 **mudīrit esh-sharikeh** (asleep).
2 **sayyārit Aḥmad** (white).
3 **abu Nāyif** (short).
4 **bait** [*m.*] **shawqi** (small).
5 **el-mas"aleh** *(problem, question)* (difficult).
6 **el-ghurfeh** (locked).
7 **el-ghuraf** [*pl.*] (locked).
8 **Samīra** (obnoxious, hated).
9 **Sāmi** *(male's name)* (conceited).
10 **ṣadīqit Nuha** (tall).

13 Personal pronouns

There are two kinds of pronouns in Arabic, detached and attached. Detached pronouns are always in the nominative case (the case used principally for the subject of a sentence); attached pronouns can be in the nominative, accusative (used for the object of a sentence) or possessive case. The following table puts the whole thing in a nutshell.

	Detached	*Attached to perfect verbs*		*Attached to nouns*
Person	*Nominative*	*Nominative*	*Accusative*	*Possessive*
Singular:				
1	**ana** (I)	**-t** (I)	**-ni** (me)	**-i** (my)
2 m.	**inta** (you)	**-t** (you)	**-ak** (you)	**-ak** (your)
2 f.	**inti** (you)	**-ti** (you)	**-ik*** (you)	**-ik*** (your)
3 m.	**hū** *or* **huwweh** (he)	—	**-u** (him)	**-u** (his)
3 f.	**hī** *or* **hiyyeh** (she)	**-at** (she)	**-ha** (her)	**-ha** (her)
Plural:				
1	**iḥna** *or* **niḥna** (we)	**-na** (we)	**-na** (us)	**-na** (our)
2 m.	**intu** (you)	**-tu** (you)	**-ku** *or* **-kum** (you)	**-ku** *or* **-kum** (you)
2 f.	**intin** (you)	**-tin** (you)	**-kin** (you)	**-kin** (your)
2 m.	**hummeh** (they)	**-u** (they)	**-hum** (them)	**-hum** (their)
3 f.	**hinneh** (they)	**-in** (they)	**-hin** (them)	**-hin** (their)

* **-ki** if preceded by a vowel

Notes:

1 The alternatives given are of more or less equal status among Jordanian speakers of Arabic.

2 The fact that the same nominative attached pronoun **-t** is used for both first and second person singular is due to the loss of the final vowel of Standard Arabic. Differentiation in cases of possible confusion is achieved by using the appropriate detached form of the pronoun as well as this one.

3 The possessive pronouns are identical with those of the accusative case (object) except for the presence of an extra **n** in the first person singular accusative pronoun, originally intended to safeguard verbs from ending with the vowel **-i**.

4 Nothing is attached to the perfect verb when the subject

is the third person singular, masculine gender.

5 When a detached pronoun is followed by a perfect verb, the verb carries the appropriate attached form of the nominative case of the pronoun as well.

6 A perfect verb may have two attached pronouns, one functioning as a subject and the other as an object, in that order.

7 There is a growing tendency among urban speakers of Arabic to use **intu** ('you', *pl.*) and **hummeh** ('they') for both masculine and feminine genders.

Study the following sentences carefully.

A. Detached pronouns: verbless sentences

ana sā"iḥ Barīṭānī. *I (am) a British tourist.*
inta mudīr nājiḥ. *You (m.) (are) a successful manager.*
inti umm nājḥa. *You (f.) (are) a successful mother* (i.e., you take good care of your children).
hū ibn el-mudīr. *He (is) the manager's son.*
hiyyeh eṭ-ṭabībeh 'l-waḥīdeh fi 'l-manṭiqa.
She (is) the only physician in the area.
iḥna suwwāḥ min Awrubba. *We (are) tourists from Europe.*
hummeh mnain? *Where are they from?* (**mnain?** *from where?)*
hummeh suwwāḥ min Amairka.
They (are) tourists from America.
intu Barīṭāniyyīn? *(Are) you (m. pl.) British?*
hinneh Barīṭāniyyāt. *They (f.) (are) British.*
intin sā"iḥāt Amrīkiyyāt? *(Are) you (f. pl.) American tourists?*

B. Detached pronouns with perfect verbs

ana kunt hunāk. *I was there.*
inta kunt hunāk. *You (m. sing.) were there.*
inti kunti hunāk. *You (f. sing.) were there.*
huwweh kān hunāk. *He was there.*
hiyyeh kānat hunāk. *She was there.*
iḥna kunna hunāk. *We were there.*
intu kuntu hunāk. *You (m. pl.) were there.*

intin kuntin hunāk. *You (f. pl.) were there.*
hummeh kānu hunāk. *They (m.) were there.*
hinneh kānin hunāk. *They (f.) were there.*

Variations within the verb **kān** ('was') and similar verbs will be explained later. The point here is that, although the detached pronoun is used, the appropriate attached form is also used along with it. As you can see, there is no attached form in the case of the third person singular, masculine gender. The very form of the verb indicates this person; this is the purest form of the word, from which the Arabs derive all other related words. Is it like the 'root' in English.

C. Attached pronouns, nominative case

katabt imbāriḥ maktūb la Aḥmad.
Yesterday, I wrote a letter to Aḥmad.
katabt la abūk?
Did you (m. sing.) write to your father? (**abūk: abu** plus possessive pronoun **-ak**)
katabti la ummik?
Did you (f. sing.) write to your mother?
Aḥmad katab la abū.
Aḥmad wrote to his father. (**abū: abu** plus possessive pronoun **-u**)
Huda katbat la Samīra.
Huda wrote to Samīra.
katabna 'l-yōm khamis rasā"il.
Today, we wrote five letters.
katabtu la 'l-wazīr?
Did you (m. pl.) write to the minister?
katabtin la mudīr el-bank?
Did you (f. pl.) write to the bank manager?
aṣdiqā"i katabū li khamis rasā"il.
My friends wrote me five letters. (**katabu** and all similar verbs ending in a vowel lengthen the final vowel if followed by **li**, 'for me', **lu**, 'for him', **lha**, 'for her', etc.)
el-banāt katabin la mudīrit el-madraseh.
The girls wrote to the school's headmistress.

D. Attached pronouns, accusative case

These can come only after another attached pronoun functioning as a subject (except in the case of the third person singular, masculine gender, which as you know has no attached pronoun in the nominative case).

shuftu mbāriḫ. *I saw him yesterday.*
shuftu mbāriḫ? *Did you (m. sing.) see him yesterday?*
inta shuftu mbāriḫ. *You (m. sing.) saw him yesterday.*
inti shuftī mbāriḫ. *You (f. sing.) saw him yesterday.*
hū shāfu/shāfni/shāfha/shāfhin . . .
He saw him/me/her/them (f.) . . .
hī shāfat-hum/shāfatna/shāfatak . . .
She saw them (m.)/us/you (m. sing.) . . .
shāfūni/shāfūna/shāfūk/shāfūhin/shāfū . . .
They (m.) saw me/us/you (m. sing.) /them (f.)/him . . .
shāfinni/shāfinnu/shāfinna/shāfinhum/shāfinnak/ shāfinkum . . .
They (f.) saw me/him/us/them (m.)/you (m. sing.)/ you (m. pl.) . . .
shufnā/shufnāk/shufnāhin . . .
We saw him/you (m. sing.)/ them (f.) . . .

Notice in these sentences that when the attached pronoun in the nominative case ends in a vowel, the vowel becomes long if it is followed by another pronoun in the accusative case; when the latter begins with a vowel or is itself a vowel, the vowel of the last pronoun is assimilated into the preceding one of the pronoun in the nominative case:

shufti *you (f. sing.) saw* (**shāf + -ti**)
shuftī *you (f. sing.) saw him* (**shāf + -ti + -u**; assimilation of vowel of accusative pron. into vowel of nominative pron.)
shuftīhum *you (f. sing.) saw them (m.)* (**shāf + -ti + -hum**; lengthening of vowel of nominative pron. before accusative pron. beginning with a consonant)
shufnāk *we saw you (f. sing.)* (**shāf + -na + -ak**; assimilation and lengthening of vowels of nominative and accusative pronouns)

When the pronoun in the accusative case is or begins with a vowel and is attached to the pronoun in the nominative case of the second and third person plural, feminine gender, the **n** of the latter is doubled:

shuftinnu *you (f. pl.) saw him* (**shāf + -tin + -u**)
shāfinnak *they (f.) saw you (m. sing.)* **(shāf + -in + -ak)**

In the second person singular, the attached pronoun of the feminine gender shifts its vowel to the final position to avoid any possible confusion with the masculine gender:

shufnāk *we saw you (m. sing.)* **(shāf + -na + -ak**)
shufnāki *we saw you (f. sing.)* (**shāf + -na + -ik**, becoming **-ki)**

Needless to say, this shift is unnecessary when the pronoun of the nominative case ends with a consonant (why?):

shāfatik *she saw you (f. sing.)* **(shāf + -at + -ik**)

E. Attached pronouns, possessive case

These pronouns are attached to nouns to form what we have called **iḍāfa** (Section 8). The nouns they are attached to must always be indefinite; they acquire definiteness by being attached to the pronouns:

kitābi my book (more naturally pronounced **ktābi;** see the rule of short-vowel elision discussed in Section 14)
ktābak your (*m. sing.*) book
ktābik your (*f. sing.*) book
ktābu his book
ktābha her book
ktābna our book
ktābkum your (*m. pl.*) book
ktābkin your (*f. pl.*) book
ktābhum their (*m.*) book
ktābhin their (*f.*) book

Feminine nouns (usually ending in **-a** or **-eh**) take on the letter **-t** before the possessive pronoun:

mara woman	**marati** my wife
(in contexts requiring more educated speech: **mar"a**)	
bajāma pyjamas	**bajāmtu** his pyjamas
	bajāmit-ha her pyjamas
badleh suit	**badlitu** his suit
	(**badiltu** is also heard)
sayyāra car	**sayyārti** my car
	sayyārit-ha her car
	sayyārit-hum their (*m.*) car
	sayyārtak your (*m. sing.*) car

In these examples, the hyphen has been used to separate the **t** and the **h** when they are meant to be pronounced separately. Notice, too, that the **i** before the **t** in **sayyārit-ha** and **sayyārit-hum** prevents the occurrence of a three-consonant cluster.

There are, however, some nouns that do end in a vowel but do not take the **-t** when the possessive pronoun is attached to them. The reason is either that the nouns in question are masculine in gender and do not, therefore, take the feminine marker **-t**, or that the original vowel in Standard Arabic is long. Since this is beyond the scope of the present course, we shall have to make do with a few examples:

hawa air (*m.*)	**hawākum** your air
	hawākum laṭīf. Your air is balmy.
sama sky (*f.*, but originally **samā"**)	**samāna** our sky
jaza reward, punishment (*m.*)	**jazā** his reward, his punishment (notice the lengthening of the final vowel: **jaza + -u**, with **-u** assimilated into previous vowel)
qura villages (*f.; sing.* **qaryeh**)	**qurāna** our villages
wādi valley (*m.*)	**wādīkum** your valley

F. Attached pronouns governed by prepositions

Since pronouns function as substitutes for nouns, they can be governed by prepositions just like the nouns. Detached pronouns in Arabic cannot be so governed, but the attached ones can. We shall illustrate here with one preposition: **min** ('from').*

minni from me	**minna** from us
minnak from you	**minkum** from you
minnik from you	**minkin** from you
minnu from him	**minhum** from them
minha from her	**minhin** from them

Notice how the consonant of the preposition is doubled if the pronoun begins with a vowel.

Exercise 7

Translate the following into English. The verb ***zār*** *means 'he visited' and is similar in its internal vowelling to the verb* ***shāf*** *'he saw' (cf. page 30).*

1 zārūna	12 zurtīni	23 zārūha
2 zurnāhum	13 zārūki	24 zurtī
3 zārinna	14 zurnāk	25 zurtūhum
4 zurtu	15 zārinni	26 zurtīha
5 zāratna	16 zurtūhum	27 zārat-hum
6 zurtak	17 zārinkum	28 zāratkin
7 zurt-hum	18 zurtik	29 zārat-hin
8 zārūni	19 zurtinna	30 zāratak
9 zurtīhum	20 zurtinni	31 zurt-ha
10 zurtinhin	21 zurnākin	32 zārat-ha
11 zārūk	22 zurnāhin	33 zurnāki

* Here and from now on, the order of the pronouns will be that given on p. 27, i.e. singular (1, 2m., 2f., 3m., 3f.) and plural (1, 2m., 2f., 3m., 3f.).

Vocabulary (exercises 8–10)

aḥsan min	better than
akhadh (I.4, but irregular; see Ex. 46)	took
el-Batra	Petra
fōq	on; above
ishtara (VIII.2)	bought
mīn?	who?

Exercise 8

Translate the following into Arabic:

1 Yesterday we saw Maḥmūd in the hotel (**fi 'l-funduq**).
2 Today (**el-yōm**) I saw Huda in the bank.
3 Huda saw me there.
4 She took five dollars from me.
5 I took five dollars from her.
6 Where is she from?
7 Maḥmūd paid me a visit yesterday.
8 We visited Ghānim at (**fi**) the hotel.
9 I took Maḥmūd's book from him.
10 His book is better than Ghānim's.

Exercise 9

Translate the following into English:

1 Salma akhdhat minni sayyārti.
2 shuft imbāriḥ khamis suwwāḥ Amairkān fi 'l-Batra.
3 sayyārtak min Almānya?
4 mīn akhadh-ha minnak?
5 shuftu ktābi?
6 ktābak fōq er-raff.
7 mīn akhadh kitāb Ghānim? *(Note:* akhadh ktāb *would give us a three-consonant cluster, hence* kitāb *here.)*
8 Ḥāmid ishtara khamis kutub.
9 kutbu fōq er-raff.
10 kutub Salma fi sayyārit-ha.

Exercise 10

Replace the italic nouns with the appropriate pronouns.

1 akhadht el-kitāb min *Ghānim*.
2 shuft *Salma* fi 'l-bank.
3 *el-banāt* fi 'l-madraseh.
4 mīn akhadh *el-kitāb*?
5 shuftu *'s-suwwāḥ*?
6 zurt *Huda*?
7 Huda zārat *Ghānim*.
8 *Huda* zārat Ghānim.
9 ana zurt @amm *Huda*.
10 inta zurt abu *Ghānim*.

Chapter 4

This chapter introduces the important concept of consonant roots and shows how these remain the same, while the vowels change to create different words or word forms. You will learn:

- *how short vowels may be dropped in certain combinations and long vowels may be shortened*
- *where the stress (the emphasized syllable) falls in Arabic*
- *how regular plurals of nouns and some irregular plurals are formed*
- *the demonstrative pronouns (this, that, these and those)*
- *some common prepositions (in, by, with, etc.)*

14 Some observations on the vowels

It must have become abundantly clear by now that vowels in Arabic play a vital role in determining meaning. Not only does a change from one vowel to another change the meaning of a word, it can also change the class to which it belongs: **katab** ('he wrote') is a verb, but **kutub** ('books') is a noun. If the class is not changed, at least the meaning is modified: **katab** and **kātab** are both verbs, but the latter means 'he corresponded' with somebody, and the action is reciprocal.

In this section, however, we shall point out what happens to certain vowels in certain situations, where no change in meaning or word class is involved.

To begin with, it is necessary to reiterate that the most important elements in any Arabic word are the consonants. If **k-t-b** are kept in that order, the idea of writing will be retained, whatever elements are introduced within this root or outside it. Another overriding rule in Arabic is the inadmissibility of having a consonant cluster of more than two consonants; in fact, there is a general tendency in Arabic to avoid having even two consonants together unless the second is immediately followed by a vowel. (See, however, pp. 42 and 59 below.) The word 'English', which has a cluster of three consonants (**-ngl-**), is often pronounced **ingilīzi** in Arabic; since it is the consonants that sound important to the Arab in this word, a shift in the vowel **i** makes no real difference: **iniglīzi** is also heard.

Now what we earlier called the fluidity of the vowel system in modern spoken Arabic seems to affect only the short vowels, and of these the short **a** is less likely to be affected than the **i** and the **u**.

A. Short vowel after initial consonant

This is usually dropped in normal speech if it is not an **a** and if its elision does not result in a three-consonant cluster: **kitāb** ('book') → **ktāb, ḥiṣān** ('horse') → **ḥṣān, dhirā@** ('arm') → **dhrā@.** The pattern is observed in many plural forms:

jamal camel	**jimāl/jmāl**
balad country	**bilād/blād**
nijmeh star	**nujūm/njūm**
baḥar sea	**buḥūr/bhūr**
jabal mountain	**jibāl/jbāl**
dars lesson	**durūs/drūs**
jundi soldier	**junūd/jnūd**

B. Short vowel before last consonant

This is usually dropped if a suffix that either is a vowel or begins with a vowel is attached to the word, but if the vowel is a short **a**, the **a** is sometimes retained:

nāzil descending	**nāzlīn** (m. pl. suff.)
nāyim asleep	**nāymāt** (f. pl. suff.)
kutub books	**kutbi** (1st pers. sing. poss. pron.)

si@ir price	**si@ru** (3rd pers. sing. poss. pron.)
shāri@ street	**shār@ak** (2nd pers. sing. poss. pron.)
maṣna@ factory	**maṣna@ak** (same suff.; **a** retained)
sha@ar hair	**sha@rak** (same suff.; **a** dropped)
qadar fate	**qadarak** (same suff.; **a** retained)

*C. The vowel of the feminine ending (**-a, -eh**)*

As was mentioned above, this ending is transformed into **-(i)t** in **iḍāfa** constructions:

sayyāra car	**sayyārit Huda**
sā@a watch	**sā@it Aḥmad**

In both these examples, the **i** is retained because its omission would result in an unacceptable three-consonant cluster. But

sayyārti my car
ṣā@tu his watch

illustrate the rule of short-vowel elision when a suffix that either is or begins with a vowel is attached to the word. The word **ghurfeh** behaves slightly differently. We have **ghurfit Aḥmad,** but **ghuruftu,** where a short **u** is inserted to avoid having a cluster of **rft,** exists in addition to **ghurfitu,** the normal form. This example illustrates well the fluidity that is possible in the vowel system in Arabic when there is no danger of changing the meaning or word class of a word.

D. Vowel changes in word groups

But this short-vowel elision rule, together with the one concerning consonant clusters, applies even beyond the boundaries of the single word. When the definite article **el-** is prefixed to a word like **blād** (*pl. of* **balad,** 'country') it becomes **li-blād** because the form **el-blād** contains three consonants in proximity and the alternative **el-bilād** sounds literary or unduly emphatic. Similarly, **khamis** ('five' in **iḍāfa** constructions) keeps its last short vowel (against the rule of short-vowel elision) in a phrase like **khamis kutub** ('five books') because the elision of the **i** would result in the inadmissible consonant cluster **msk. Sinīn** (*pl. of* **saneh**, 'year') gives us **snīn** according to the rule of short-vowel elision, but application of this rule requires that we have something like **khamsi snīn** ('five years'), where the **-i** in **khamsi** is merely a means of avoiding the occurrence of a cluster of three consonants. The same result is achieved if the speaker says, as some do, **khamis sinīn** or even **khamis sanīn.** The alternative plural **sanawāt** keeps the first short **a** (as often with this vowel), and so **khamis sanawāt** poses no problem. Words that begin with a **hamza** (") simply drop the **hamza** to allow the vowel that invariably follows it to act as a buffer against the third consonant: **khams asabī@** ('five weeks'; **"usbū@,** 'week'); articulation of the hamza in **"asabī@** would give us the equally acceptable **khamis "asabī@.**

E. Vowel before double consonants

Finally, we observe that long vowels are shortened if, for any reason, such vowels are followed by double letters or two different consonants. Thus **kān** ('was') becomes **kunna** ('we were'), **kunt** ('I was'), etc. It seems that the presence of two consonants, whether similar or dissimilar, compensates for the length of the vowel that precedes them.

15 A note on stress patterns

In Arabic, as in English, some syllables are pronounced with greater force (or stress) than others. Stress patterns in Arabic are very simple. The following rules cover practically all cases:

1 Never stress the definite article.
2 Never stress feminine endings.
3 Stress the first syllable of any word that lacks a long syllable (i.e., a long vowel followed by a single consonant or a short vowel followed by a consonant cluster).
4 Stress any syllable that has a long vowel.
5 Stress any syllable that ends in a consonant cluster, unless it is followed by a long vowel.
6 In general, first syllables in prefixes are not stressed even when they end in a consonant cluster.
7 If, for any reason, a word has more than one stressed syllable, the last receives greater emphasis than the other(s).
8 The stress patterns of the imperative and imperfect verbs follow that of the perfect.
9 Derived forms keep the stress pattern of the root from which they have been derived.

Vocabulary (exercise 11)

b@īd/eh	distant
ḩadīqa (*pl.* **ḩadā"iq** or **ḩadāyiq**)	garden
ḩāleh	case; state
qarīb/eh	near
thāni/thānyeh	second

Exercise 11

Translate the following into Arabic:

1 Huda's school is distant.
2 My school is near.
3 Your (*m. pl.*) bank is distant.
4 Their (*f.*) house is near.
5 Their (*m.*) garden is beautiful.
6 Salma's room is large.
7 My hotel is a five-star hotel.
8 Her book is difficult.
9 His case is difficult.
10 Britain's queen is Elizabeth II.

Exercise 12

Attach all the nominative pronominal suffixes to the following verbs:

qāl he said
rāḥ he went
@ād he returned

Exercise 13

Attach all the possessive pronominal suffixes to the following nouns:

maktabeh library
maktab office
makātib offices
ḥṣān stallion
isim name
waḍi@ state, situation

16 Plural forms: regular

As we said in Section 9, nouns and adjectives in Arabic are either masculine or feminine. Now if a noun or an adjective indicates a human being or a human attribute, it often has two regular plural forms, one for the masculine and another for the feminine. 'Regular' in this case means that the plural suffix is simply added to the word without necessitating any internal changes, very much like the addition of **-s** or **-es** to English nouns. The regular plural suffix for masculine nouns and adjectives is **-īn**, for feminine ones, **-āt**.

Masculine	*Feminine*
nāyim (asleep); **nāymīn**	**nāymeh; nāymāt**
m@allim (teacher); **m@allmīn**	**m@allmeh; m@allmāt**
mudarris (teacher); **mudarrsīn**	**mudarriseh; mudarrisāt**
fallāḥ (peasant); **fallaḥīn**	**fallāḥa; fallaḥāt**
siyāsi (politician, political); **siyasiyyīn**	**siyāsiyyeh; siyasiyyāt**
muhandis (engineer); **muhandisīn**	**muhandiseh; muhandisāt**
riyāḍi (athlete); **riyāḍiyyīn**	**riyāḍiyyeh; riyādiyyāt**
masjūn (imprisoned); **masjunīn**	**masjūneh; masjunāt**
Faransi (French); **Faranisyyīn**	**Faransiyyeh; Faransiyyāt**

Notes:

1 The addition of a suffix containing a long vowel often results in the shortening of the long vowel within the word.

2 The addition of a suffix sometimes results in the elision of the original last short vowel of the word.

3 The rule about the inadmissibility of the occurrence of a three-consonant cluster does not apply if two of the consonants are identical.

4 The addition of a suffix beginning with a vowel to a word that ends in an **-i** requires the addition of **-yy-** before the suffix can be added **(riyāḍi; riyāḍiyyīn).**

5 The shortening of the vowel within the word is a characteristic of normal speech; more emphatic or

deliberately educated speech keeps the full value of the vowels and even the otherwise omitted short vowels (see Section 14B).

17 Plural forms: irregular

Irregular plural forms (i.e. those requiring changes within the word itself) are very frequent. There are, to be sure, broad patterns under which nouns and adjectives can be classified, but these classifications cannot be depended on to enable a non-native speaker to predict the plural forms accurately. This is why we give in the Mini-dictionary the plural form of any noun or adjective whose plural is irregular, and you are advised to learn the meaning, the gender and the plural form all at the same time. Here, at any rate, are the major patterns, where **C** = consonant (**kh, sh, dh, gh** and **th** count as one consonant each), **v** = short vowel, **V** = long vowel, other elements = themselves.

Pattern I

Singular **CvCCVC**, plural **CvCVCVC** (or more specifically **CaCāCīC/CaCaCīC**; see notes 1 and 5 above).

Singular	*Plural*
dukkān (*m.*) shop	**dakakīn** (*f.*)
mandīl (*m.*) handkerchief	**manadīl** (*f.*)
muftāḥ/miftāḥ (*m.*) key	**mafatīḥ** (*f.*)
majnūn (*m.*) mad person	**majanīn** (*m.*)
maktūb (*m.*) letter	**makatīb** (*f.*)
finjān (*m.*) small coffee cup	**fanajīn** (*f.*)
sulṭān (*m.*) sultan	**salaṭīn** (*m.*)
ṣandūq (*m.*) box	**ṣanadīq** (*f.*)
tilmīdh (*m.*) pupil	**talamīdh** (*m.*)
masjūn (*m.*) prisoner	**masajīn** (*m.*) (alternative plural)

Note that the plural form of inanimate, non-human nouns is

feminine although the singular may be masculine; this is a purely grammatical gender.

Now the same plural form is used when instead of **CvCCVC** for the singular we have **CVCVC**; as explained above (Section 14E), a long vowel is equal to two consonants in value:

shākūsh hammer	**shawakīsh**
ḥasūb computer	**ḥawasīb**
qāmūs dictionary	**qawamīs**
nāqūs church bell	**nawaqīs**

Here all the singular nouns are masculine, all plurals feminine.

Pattern II

Singular **CvCCvC** with or without feminine ending, plural **CvCVCvC** (or **CaCāCiC**).

funduq (*m.*) hotel	**fanādiq** (*f.*)
maṭ@am (*m.*) restaurant	**maṭā@im** (*f.*)
ma@mal (*m.*) factory	**ma@āmil** (*f.*)
maṣna@ (*m.*) factory	**maṣāni@** (*f.*)
maṭba@a (*f.*) printing press	**maṭābi@** (*f.*)
jawhara (*f.*) jewel	**jawāhir** (*f.*)
tha@lab (*m.*) fox	**tha@ālib** (*f.*)
"iṣba@ (*m.*) finger	**"aṣābi@** (*f.*)
mu@jam (*m.*) dictionary	**ma@ājim** (*f.*)

The same plural form is often used when instead of **CvCCvC** we have **CvCVC** with or without a feminine ending (here again we have a long vowel equalling two consonants):

qabīleh (*f.*) tribe	**qabā"il/qabāyil** (*f.*)
@ajūz (*f.*) old woman	**@ajā"iz/@ajāyiz** (*f.*)
rahīneh (*f.*) hostage	**rahā"in/rahāyin** (*m.*)
sitāra (*f.*) curtain	**satā"ir/satāyir** (*f.*)
ḥadīqa (*f.*) garden	**ḥadā"iq/ḥadāyiq** (*f.*)
ḥabīb (*m.*) lover	[not used] / **habāyib** (*m.*)

The plural form with **y** is the more colloquial of the two.

Pattern III

The singular pattern **CvCVC** we have seen in Pattern II above sometimes has a different plural form: **CvCvCv** (or **CuCaCa**).

wazīr (*m.*) minister	**wuzara** (*m.*)
safīr (*m.*) ambassador	**sufara** (*m.*)
"amīr (*m.*) prince	**"umara** (*m.*)
wasīṭ (*m.*) mediator	**wusaṭa** (*m.*)
ra"īs (*m.*) chief, president	**ru"asa** (*m.*)
sharīf (*m.*) honourable	**shurafa** (*m.*)
sa@īd (*m.*) happy	**su@ada** (*m.*)
za@īm (*m.*) leader	**zu@ama** (*m.*)
faqīr (*m.*) poor	**fuqara** (*m.*)

The more emphatic form of these plurals would be **CuCaCā"**, yielding **wuzarā", sufarā", "umarā",** etc.

Pattern IV

Singular **CvCvC**, plural **"aCCāC**; since the hamza (") is regular, it will be dropped.

qalam (*m.*) pen, pencil	**aqlām** (*f.*)
@alam (*m.*) flag	**a@lām** (*f.*)
waṭan (*m.*) homeland	**awṭān** (*f.*)
qamar (*m.*) moon	**aqmār** (*f.*)
si@ir (*m.*) price	**as@ār** (*f.*)
nagham (*m.*) tune	**anghām** (*f.*)
khaṭar (*m.*) danger	**akhṭār** (*f.*)
safar (*m.*) travel	**asfār** (*f.*)
walad (*m.*) boy	**awlād** (*m.*)

Pattern V

Singular **CVC**, plural **"aCwāC** or **"aCyāC**; since the hamza (") is regular, it will be dropped.

bāb (*m.*) door	**abwāb** (*f.*)
kūb (*m.*) cup	**akwāb** (*f.*)
māl (*m.*) wealth, possessions	**amwāl** (*f.*)

sūr (*m.*) wall surrounding a building	**aswār** (*f.*)
zōj (*m.*) husband	**azwāj** (*m.*)
ṣōt (*m.*) voice, vote	**aṣwāt** (*f.*)
nūr (*m.*) light	**anwār** (*f.*)
nō@ (*m.*) species	**anwā@** (*f.*)
@īd (*m.*) feast	**a@yād** (*f.*)
mīl (*m.*) mile	**amyāl** (*f.*)
fīl (*m.*) elephant	**afyāl** (*f.*)

This is really a variant of Pattern IV, but here the middle sound is a long vowel, which is kept in the plural form: **ī** and **ai** become **yā; ā, ū** and **ō** become **wā**; and a few words with medial **ā** take the form **yā** before the final consonant, e.g., **nāb** (*m.*) 'incisor' → **anyāb**.

Pattern VI

Singular **CvCC** (last two consonants identical), plural **CuCūC** (first short vowel often omitted except in emphatic or deliberately educated speech).

ḥadd (*m.*) boundary, border	**ḥudūd/ḥdūd** (*f.*)
khadd (*m.*) cheek	**khdūd** (*f.*)
radd (*m.*) answer, response	**rudūd** (*f.*)
khaṭṭ (*m.*) line	**khṭūṭ** (*f.*)
sadd (*m.*) dam	**sdūd** (*f.*)
hamm (*m.*) worry	**hmūm** (*f.*)
sharr (*m.*) evil	**shrūr** (*f.*)
ḥabbeh (*f.*) grain	**ḥbūb** (*f.*)

Vocabulary (exercises 14–16)

Note: Roman and Arabic numerals in brackets refer to verb classes (see Sections 21ff.)

afraj (IV.1)	released (from prison)
akl or **akil**	food
ḍayya@ (II.1)	lost; mislaid
ḥukūmeh	government

ḥuṭṭ (imperative of **ḥaṭṭ** (I.7))	put
malyān/eh	full (of)
min faḍlak	please (addressed to male)
qahweh	coffee
@āli/@ālyeh	high
akthar min	more (numerous) than
bidūn	without
gharīb/eh (*pl.* **ghuraba**)	stranger
jiddan	very
mustaqbal	future
zāl (I.10)	disappeared; is over
@arīḍ/a	wide; broad
bāb (*pl.* **abwāb**)	door
nādir/nādreh	rare
ṣinā@i/yyeh	manufactured
qamar ṣinā@i	lit., man-made moon, i.e., satellite
waṭani/yyeh	national
zōj (*pl.* **azwāj**)	husband

Exercise 14

Translate the following into English:

1 el-awlād nāymīn.
2 fallaḥāt baladna ḥilwāt.
3 et-talamīdh fi madrasitna nājḥīn.
4 shāri@ku malyān dakakīn.
5 el-ḥukūmeh afrajat @an el-masjunīn es-siyāsiyyīn.
6 Qadri ḍayya@ mafatīḥ el-bait.
7 ḥuṭṭ el-makatīb fi 'ṣ-ṣandūq.
8 es-su@ada hummeh 'l-majanīn.
9 khamis fanajīn qahweh min faḍlak.
10 akl el-bait aḥsan min akl el-maṭā@im.

Exercise 15

Translate the following into Arabic:

1 Successful female teachers are more plentiful than successful female engineers.
2 The Egyptian peasants (*m.*) are poor.
3 The leaders of the world are the engineers of the future.
4 Poor people are strangers in their own country.
5 Fathers are sultans in their own houses.
6 We are happy.
7 The dangers of war are over.
8 My maternal aunt's husband is an engineer.
9 Book prices are very high.
10 The future is a box without a key.

Exercise 16

Use the appropriate form of the adjective given in parentheses. Examples:

anghām (ḥilw): anghām ḥilweh (f. sing. adj. with inanimate pl.)
muhandisāt (ḥilw): muhandisāt ḥilwāt (f. pl. adj. with f. human pl.)
awlād (ḥilw): awlād ḥilwīn (m. pl. adj. with m. human pl.)

1 **abwāb (maqfūl)**
2 **azwāj (sa@īd)**
3 **zawjāt (sa@īd)**
4 **khuṭūṭ/khṭūṭ (@arīḍ)**
5 **a@yād (waṭani)**
6 **zu@amā" (waṭani)**
7 **siyāsiyyīn (majnūn)**
8 **aqmār (ṣinā@i)**
9 **anwā@ (nādir)**
10 **wusaṭa (Faransi)**
11 **wuzara (sharīf)**
12 **umara (faqīr)**
13 **mu@allimāt/m@allmāt (faqīr)**

Exercise 17

Rewrite the phrases obtained in the previous exercise so as to make each one a simple sentence.

18 Demonstrative pronouns

The main element in all demonstrative pronouns (in English: 'this, that, these, those') in spoken Arabic is **hā-,** which is sometimes found as an independent word, but is usually attached to other elements indicating gender, distance and number. When used alone, **ha** is invariably followed by a noun that has the definite article, and the vowel **a** is short; it is used with both genders and with singular and plural nouns:

ha 'l-walad this boy
ha 'l-mablagh this sum of money
ha 'l-bint this girl
ha 'd-dafātir these copybooks

The meaning often implies an apologetic attitude or a belittling of the thing mentioned. When other elements are attached to **hā-**, the **a** becomes long if the other vowel/s is/are short; otherwise, it is short:

hādha/hāda this (*m.*)
hadhāk/hadāk that (*m.*)
hadhōl/hadōl these (*m. & f.*)
hādhi/hādi/hāy this (*f.*)
hadhīk/hadīk that (*f.*)
hadhulāk/hadulāk those (*m. & f.*)

Vocabulary (exercise 18)

@ind	near
akhkh (*pl.* **ikhweh**)	brother
mablagh (*pl.* **mabāligh**)	sum of money
maftūḥ	open (*adj.*)
min	(one) of
yimkin	maybe

Exercise 18

Translate the following into English:

1 hāy binti.
2 hadhīk sayyārit-ha.
3 hadhōl el-banāt min madrasit-ha.
4 hadhāk el-walad akhūha.
5 ḥuṭṭ ha 'l-mablagh fi 'l-bank.
6 hādha 'l-funduq min el-fanādiq er-rāqyeh.
7 ḥuṭṭ hadhulāk el-kutub @a 'r-raff.
8 ḥuṭṭ hādha 'l-kitāb @ind hadhāk.
9 hādha 'l-bāb maqfūl; yimkin hadhāk maftūḥ.
10 hāy es-sayyāra aḥsan min hadhīk.

Exercise 19

Translate the following into Arabic:

1 this elephant
2 those elephants
3 this tribe
4 that tribe
5 these jewels
6 those keys
7 that door
8 these pencils
9 these dangers
10 that bank

19 Prepositions

Prepositions in Arabic are much simpler than their counterparts in English; they are fewer in number and not so much involved in idiomatic uses. Here are the ones in actual use in spoken Arabic:

fi in, into (the vowel is sometimes elided)

el-kitāb fi 'sh-shanṭā. *The book is in the briefcase.*

As a preposition **fi** always has a short vowel, but when the vowel is long, the word means 'there is' (or 'is there' in questions):

fī ma@ak qalam? (lit. *Is there a pen with you?) Have you a pen?*
fī ktāb @a 'r-raff. *There is a book on the shelf.*

bi by, by means of, at (the vowel is sometimes elided)

sāfar *(he travelled)* **bi 'ṭ-ṭayyāra.** *He went by plane.*
sāfar bi 'l-lail. *He went at night.*
hay el-ghurfeh mad-hūneh b' lōn azraq.
This room is painted with a blue colour/is painted blue.
uktub ib qalam aḥmar. *Write with a red pen.*
Here the vowel has preceded the consonant because its normal position would give us a first syllable with a short vowel **(bi qalam)** and the tendency is to omit such a vowel; its omission, however, would give us a consonant cluster of three consecutive consonants. The transposition of the vowel solves the problem.

Note: **fi** and **bi** are frequently interchangeable:
Salma b' ghurfit-ha.
Salma f' ghurfit-ha. *Salma is in her room.*
However, only **bi** is used to coin adverbs, as we shall see.

@ala (frequently shortened to **@a**) on, above, upon

el-kitāb @a/@ala 'r-raff. *The book is on the shelf.*

la/ila for, to

khudhni la 'l-maṭār. *Take me to the airport.*
hāy esh-shanṭa ili. *This suitcase is mine.*
(ili = ila + possessive pronoun **-i,** 'my')
iḥki la Salma. *Speak to Salma.*

ma@ with

es-sayyāra ma@ Ḥāmid. *The car is with Ḥāmid/Ḥāmid has it.*
ma@ i (*with me,* i.e., *I have)* **khamis kutub.** *I have five books.*
ma@ak flūs? *Do you have any money on you?*
A literal translation of this last phrase would be: *With you money?* But since an Arabic sentence does not have to have a verb, particularly if the verb expresses the idea of being, we may retranslate: *Is (there any) money with you?* or more idiomatically as above. The same usage may be observed with the preposition **fi:**
fī *(there are)* **fi** (*in*) **@ammān fanādiq rāqyeh.**
There are in Amman top-notch hotels.

@an about

hādha 'l-kitāb maktūb bi 'l-lugha 'l-ingilīziyyeh @an el-lugha 'l-@arabiyyeh.
This book is written in the English language about the Arabic language.

min from

khudh min Samīra kitāb el-lugha 'l-@arabiyyeh.
Take from Samīra the Arabic language book.

bala without

katab li kalām *(words, talk)* **bala ma@na** (*meaning*).
He wrote to me meaningless words/meaninglessly.
Note: Do not confuse the word **ma@na** (*meaning*) with the word **ma@na: ma@** (*with*) + **-na** (*us*) which is sometimes pronounced **ma@āna.**

bidūn without

hādha 'l-maktūb bidūn @inwān.
This letter is without an address.

The last two prepositions are often interchangeable.

20 Prepositions with pronouns

As some of the examples given above may have shown, prepositions can, of course, be followed by pronouns. When they are, some changes occur in their vowels. The following list gives all the possibilities.

bi: biyyeh, bīk, bīki, bī, bīha, bīna, bīkum, bīkin, bīhum, bīhin
fi: fiyyeh, fīk, fīki, fī, fīha, fīna, fīkum, fīkin, fīhum, fīhin
@ala: @alayy / @alayyeh, @alaik, @alaiki, @alai, @alaiha, @alaina, @alaikum, @alaikin, @alaihum, @alaihin
ila: ili, ilak, ilik, ilu, ilha, ilna, ikum, ilkin, ilhum, ilhin
ma@: ma@i, ma@ak, ma@ik, ma@u, ma@ha, ma@na, ma@kum, ma@kin, ma@hum, ma@hin
@an: @anni, @annak, @annik, @annu, @anha, @anna, @ankum, @ankin, @anhum, @anhin
min: minni, minnak, minnik, minnu, minha, minna, minkum, minkin, minhum, minhin
bala: balāy, balāk, balāki, balā, balāha, balāna, balākum, balākin, balāhum, balāhin
bidūn: bidūni, bidūnak, bidūnik, bidūnu, bidūnha, bidūnna, bidūnkum, bidūnkin, bidūnhum, bidūnhin

The preposition **la +** pronoun is only used as the indirect object of verbs such as **qāl,** 'he said', **@imil**, 'he made', etc. It is the equivalent of 'to me' and 'for me' in 'he said this to me', 'he made a chair for me', etc. The pattern is:

qal li	he said to me
qal lak	he said to you (*m. sing.*)
qal lik	he said to you (*f. sing.*)

qal lu	he said to him
qal lha/qāl ilha	he said to her
qal lna/qāl ilna	he said to us
qal lkum/qāl ilkum	he said to you (*m. pl.*)
qal lkin/qāl ilkin	he said to you (*f. pl.*)
qal lhum/qāl ilhum	he said to them (*m.*)
qal lhin/qāl ilhin	he said to them (*f.*)

(Try to apply our observations on the changes that occur to the vowels to the variations given above.)

When the verb ends in a vowel, whether it is part of the verb itself or belongs to an attached pronoun (pronominal suffix) in the nominative case, the vowel becomes long if the verb is followed by this complementary combination of preposition and pronoun: **ḥaka** ('he said, told') gives us **ḥakā li** ('he told me'); **qālu** ('they said') gives us **qalū lu** ('they said to him').

Vocabulary (exercises 20 and 21)

@ādatan	usually
@a 'l-bāb	at the door
@asha	supper
banām	I sleep
nām (I.12)	slept
biydill	it indicates
dall (I.8)	indicated
ḥada	someone
jāyib	bringing
muz@ij/eh	annoying
raṣīd (*pl.* **arṣideh**)	funds in bank account
Sāmi/yyeh	Semitic
shakk or **shīk**	cheque
ṣūra (*pl.* **ṣuwar**)	picture
thāni	second; other; else
id-han	paint (not in the artistic sense)
dahan (I.3)	painted

jumleh (*pl.* **jumal**)	sentence
mushkileh (*pl.* **mashākil**)	problem
tarjim	translate
tarjam (XI)	translated
ṭāwleh	table
w	and

Exercise 20

Translate the following into English:

1 Su@ād ḥakat li @annak.
2 el-lugha 'l-@arabiyyeh min el-lughāt es-Sāmiyyeh.
3 Nizār katab shakk bidūn raṣīd.
4 ana @ādatan banām bala @asha.
5 fī fi li-ktāb ṣuwar ḥilweh.
6 fī ḥada @a 'l-bāb.
7 hādha Aḥmad jāyib ma@u Ṣubḥi.
8 fī ma@hum ḥada thāni?
9 sayyārtak fīha ṣōt muz@ij.
10 ṣōt sayyārti biydill @alayy.

Exercise 21

Translate the following into Arabic:

1 Translate this sentence into Arabic.
2 Put the money in the box.
3 Has Ṣubḥi any money on him?
4 Put the book on the table.
5 Did he tell you (*m. sing.*) about me?
6 Did she tell him about you (*m. sing.*)?
7 Take the money from Huda and put it in the bank.
8 Who was Huda with?
9 Tell him about the problem in Huda's school.
10 Paint your room with a white colour.

Chapter 5

In this chapter you will learn some of the verbs in the first 'class' of Arabic verbs. You will find out:

- *that almost all verbs are based on three-consonant roots*
- *that the 'basic' form of a verb is its past tense*
- *how Class I verbs form their imperative (command form)*

21 Verbs

It is important to remember that Arabic is a Semitic language whose vocabulary is based on mostly triliteral roots (roots consisting of three consonants). Learning one root is the first step towards learning dozens of other words derived from it, all with predictable related meanings. These roots are mostly verbs in the past tense (henceforward called the perfect), third person singular, masculine gender. Thus, **katab** ('he wrote') consists of the three consonants **k-t-b** with vowels placed in between. These three consonants remain in the same order in any word derived from this root; variations in meaning result from changes in the internal vowels, from doubling one of the consonants, from affixes, or from any combination of these. The following is only a short list of possible derivations from **k-t-b**:

katab	he wrote
katbat	she wrote
kattabat	she caused someone to write
katabna	we wrote
tkātabu	they wrote to each other

kitāb	book
kutub	books
maktūb	written, a letter
kātib	writer
kuttāb	writers
maktab	office
maktabeh	library

In all of these words the letters of the root **k-t-b** occur in the same order, regardless of the elements (known as affixes) added to the beginning (prefixing), middle (infixing) or end (suffixing). Such additions follow certain patterns, which it is the business of a good deal of the rest of this course to explain.

In modern spoken Arabic, verbs fall into eleven different classes, the most important of which is the first, the triliteral root described above.

The eleventh class consists of quadrilateral (four-consonant) roots and is a class apart, while the other nine classes are all derived from the first, at least in theory. The reason for this last qualification is that while theoretically one can derive all the other nine classes from the first, it is rarely the case that all ten verbs are in actual use. This will become clearer in due course.

22 Class I verbs

This class is divided into twelve subclasses, which form four groups as follows:

CiCiC (truncated form **CiCi**) subclasses 1–2
CaCaC (truncated form **CaCa** subclasses 3–6
CaCC subclasses 7–9
CāC subclasses 10–12
(Note: Truncated forms are those in which the last consonant of the pattern is lacking.)

In what follows we shall give the root of the perfect followed by the imperative (command form), from which the imperfect (equivalent to the English present tense) will be easy to derive.

I.1 CiCiC – iCCaC

Perfect	*Imperative*
shirib he drank	**ishrab** drink!
simi@ he heard	**isma@** listen!
riji@ he came back	**irja@** come back!
@irif he knew	**i@raf** (**i@rif**) know!
li@ib he played	**il@ab** play!
ribiḫ he won	**irbaḫ** win!
nizil he descended	**inzal** (**inzil**) come down!

As we said before, there is a tendency among Arab speakers to omit the last short vowel of the word if a suffix is attached to it, a tendency that is also observed sometimes affecting the first short vowel (cf. **kitāb**; **ktāb**). This tendency seems to be most apparent when the vowel is either **i** or **u.** Now if we attach the pronominal suffixes to the imperative verbs given above, the **a**s will not be affected:

ishrabu drink! (addressed to a group of males)
il@abin play! (addressed to a group of females)
irbaḫi win! (addressed to a single female)

But if the variants with the **i** are used, we get **inizlu, i@irfi,** etc., since the omission of the last **i** in the root would give us **inzlu, i@rfi,** etc., with the unacceptable cluster of three consonants. It may be helpful to re-read Section 14 on the vowels before you proceed any further. To help you, however, here is how the verb **shirib** behaves when the pronominal suffixes are attached to it:

ana shribit	**shāy** (*m.*, tea)	**shribtu**
	qahweh (*f.*, coffee)	**shribt-ha**
inta shribit	**shāy**	**shribtu**
	qahweh	**shribt-ha**
inti shribti	**shāy**	**shribtī**
	qahweh	**shribtīha**

huwweh shirib shāy	**shirbu**
qahweh	**shiribha**
hiyyeh shirbat shāy	**shirbatu**
qahweh	**shirbat-ha**
iḫna shribna shāy	**shribnā**
qahweh	**shribnāha**
intu shribtu shāy	**shribtū**
qahweh	**shribtūha**
intin shribtin shāy	**shribtinnu**
qahweh	**shiribtinha**
hummeh shirbu shāy	**shirbū**
qahweh	**shirbūha**

Note: The first person singular and the second person singular in the above examples have yielded what amounts to an exception from the rule of the inadmissibility of consonant clusters of more than two consonants. The same result is obtained with a verb like **qāl** ('he said'), which gives us **qult lu** ('I said to him') or **qult-ha** ('I said it'). In either case this violation of the rule occurs only in words of foreign origin and at word boundaries. Besides, some speakers stick to the rule and say **shribit-ha** (Jordan), **shiribtaha** (Egypt), and **shrabit-ha** (Iraq). The power of the rule is also attested in the fact that most people say **intin ishribtin,** avoiding the three-consonant cluster even at word boundaries.

Exercise 22

Answer the following question affirmatively in Arabic, using each person in turn as subject, treating the word 'news' (a) as a singular **(khabar,** *m.) and (b) as a plural* (**akhbar,** *f.), and substituting the appropriate pronominal suffix for the word.*

Have you heard the news?

Example: (a) **ana smi@tu.** (I have heard it.)

(b) **ana smi@t-ha.** (I have heard them.)

Vocabulary (exercise 23)

dīnār (*pl.* **danānīr**)	(currency unit in several Arab countries varying in value from one country to another)
jā"izeh (*pl.* **jawā"iz**)	prize
qişşa (*pl.* **qişaş**)	story, novel
ūla	first
yā	(vocative particle:) hey!
za@lān/eh	angry; cross; 'hurt'

Exercise 23

Translate the following into English:

1 isma@ ha 'l-khabar: Aḥmad ribiḥ 10,000 dīnār.
2 ishrab shāyak.
3 Huda rij@at min Almānya.
4 ana @rifit mīn ribiḥ el-jā"izeh 'l-ūla.
5 Samīr, il@ab ma@ Sawsan fi 'l-ghurfeh 'th-thānyeh.
6 riji@ min Barīs?
7 si@r ed-dūlār nizil.
8 inzal @an es-sayyāra yā walad.
9 mīn shirib finjāni?
10 Aḥmad @irif bi 'l-qişşa w nizil za@lān.

I.2 CiCi – iCCa

Perfect	*Imperative*
nisi he forgot	**insa**
riḍi he felt satisfied	**irḍa**
şiḥi he woke up	**işḥa**
fiḍi he/it became empty	**ifḍa**
@ili he rose up high	**i@la**

The perfect verbs of this category take the following forms when attached to pronominal suffixes: **nsīt, nsīt, nsīti, nisi, nisyat, nsīna, nsītu, nsītin, nisyu, nisyin.** The imperatives take the forms **insa, insi, insu, insin.**

Vocabulary (exercise 24)

@amal (*pl.* **a@māl**)	work; business
dhahab	gold
kull	whole; entire; every
nōm	sleep (n.)
qabil	before; ago

Exercise 24

tarjim el-jumal et-tālyeh la 'l-lugha 'l-@arabiyyeh:

1 Your mother has forgotten me.
2 Aḥmad woke up from sleep an hour ago.
3 Huda was reconciled (use proper form of **riḍi**) with her husband and returned to him.
4 Ḥāmid's apartment became vacant when he left for America.
5 The price of gold has gone up.
6 Wake up, Huda; wake up, Munīr.
7 Forget the whole matter. I have forgotten it.
8 Was the bank manager satisfied with your work?

I.3 CaCaC – iCCaC

Perfect	*Imperative*
fataḥ he opened	**iftaḥ**
najaḥ he succeeded	**injaḥ**
sabaḥ he swam	**isbaḥ**
zara@ he planted	**izra@**
ba@ath he sent	**ib@ath**
mana@ he prohibited	**imna@**
sa"al he asked	**is"al**
dafa@ he paid, he pushed	**idfa@**

The imperatives of this category do not drop their last short vowel when pronominal suffixes are attached to them; and of the perfect ones, only the third person singular, feminine gender, nominative necessitates the elision of the second **a** of the verb.

Vocabulary (exercise 25)

baḥath (I.3)	looked for
idhin	permission
imtiḥān	examination; test; ordeal
Īṭālya	Italy
khuḍra or **khuḍrawāt**	vegetables
kull yōm	every day
lamma	when
nihā"i/yyeh	final
wiqif (I.1)	stood up; stopped; stalled

Exercise 25

tarjim el-jumal et-tālyeh la 'l-lugha 'l-ingilīziyyeh:

1 Huda fatḥat el-bāb bidūn idhin.
2 ibni najaḥ fi 'l-imtiḥān en-nihā"i.
3 najaḥna fi hādha 'l-imtiḥān eṣ-ṣa@b.
4 isbaḥ kull yōm sā@a.
5 zara@u khuḍrawāt fi ḥadīqit-hum.
6 akhūy ba@ath li maktūb min Īṭālya.
7 abuha mana@ha min ziyāritna.
8 Sawsan sa"lat @annak.
9 ḍafa@ū li sayyārti lamma wiqfat.
10 ibḥath @an el-mar"a.

I.4 CaCaC – uCCuC

Perfect	*Imperative*
katab he wrote	**uktub (iktib** is also heard)
daras he studied	**udrus**
qatal he killed	**uqtul**
harab he ran away	**uhrub**
ḍarab he hit	**uḍrub**
amar he ordered	**u"mur**
sakan he took for a dwelling	**uskun**
rakaḍ he ran	**urkuḍ**
nashar he published	**unshur**

Here the perfect verbs behave in exactly the same way as verbs in subclass 3 behave: only when the third person singular, feminine gender, nominative pronoun is attached to the verb does the rule of short-vowel elision in the final syllable come into force: **katab; katbat.** The imperatives, however, behave somewhat differently. The retention of the vowel of the last syllable of the verb sounds more formal than usual, and so the vowel is often shifted backwards one syllable: thus **udrus** becomes **udursi** instead of **udrusi.**

Vocabulary (exercise 26)

ijrā"	carrying out; conducting
sur@a	speed
b'sur@a	quickly; fast
taḥqīq	investigation

Exercise 26

tarjim el-jumal et-tālyeh la 'l-lugha 'l-@arabiyyeh:

1 Write a letter to your brother.
2 Study this problem for me.
3 Huda lived in her maternal aunt's apartment.
4 Maḥmūd published his book in Beirut.
5 The girl ran away from school when the headmistress hit her.
6 Here is a news item about a woman who has killed her husband.
7 Layla, run fast; Ḥāzim is at the door.
8 The minister ordered (the carrying out of) an investigation.

1.5 CaCaC – iCCiC

Perfect	*Imperative*
kasar he broke	**iksir**
sajan he incarcerated	**isjin**
rasam he drew	**irsim**
ghasal he washed	**ighsil**
hajam he attacked	**ihjim**
ḩaraq he burned	**iḩriq**

Here, too, the perfect verbs behave as in subclasses 3 and 4, while the imperatives behave as in 4, i.e., they shift their last original vowel one syllable backwards: **ikisru, ikisrin.**

Vocabulary (exercise 27)

@amāra	building
baladiyyeh	municipality
ḩubb	love (*n.*)
lawḩa	a painting
madīneh (*pl.* **mudun**)	city
māma	mother
maţar (*pl.* **amţār**)	rain
mithil or **mithl**	like (*prep.*)
qalb (*pl.* **q(u)lūb**)	heart
ẓulman	unjustly

Exercise 27

tarjim el-jumal et-tālyeh la 'l-lugha 'l-ingilīziyyeh:

1 māma kasrat finjān el-qahweh.
2 hādha 'l-bāb maqfūl; ikisrū.
3 sajanūni ẓulman.
4 Ghāda rasmat lawḩa mithil lawḩāt Picasso.
5 el-amţār ghaslat esh-shāri@.
6 el-jaish hajam @ala 'l-madīneh.
7 el-junūd haraqu @amārit el-baladiyyeh.
8 ighsil qalbak bi 'l-ḩubb.

I.6 CaCa – iCCi

Perfect	*Imperative*
masha he walked	**imshi**
wafa he fulfilled	**iwfi**
rama he threw	**irmi**
washa he informed upon	**iwshi**
saqa he gave a drink to	**isqi**
baka he cried, shed tears	**ibki**
kawa he ironed, cauterized	**ikwi**
ra@a he shepherded, patronized	**ir@a** (anomalous)

Pronominal suffixes give us the following forms with the perfect: **mashait, mashait, mashaiti, masha, mashat, mashaina, mashaitu, mashaitin, mashu, mashin.** With the imperative they give us **imshi** (for both 2nd persons singular), **imshu, imshin; ir@a,** however, gives us: **ir@a, ir@i, ir@u, ir@in.**

Vocabulary (exercise 28)

dakhal (I.4)	went in
faraḥ	joy
ḥafleh	ceremony; celebration; party
innu, inha, inhum (etc.)	that he, she, they (etc.)
jakait	jacket
mayy [*m* as in *mother*] (*pl.* **miyāh** [*m* as in *may*])	water
muddeh (*pl.* **mudad**)	period
mujrim	criminal
rajā"an	please
ṣōfa	sofa
wa@d or **wa@id** (*pl.* **w(u)@ūd**)	promise

Exercise 28

tarjim el-jumal et-tālyeh la 'l-lugha 'l-ingilīziyyeh:

1 mashait imbāriḥ muddit khamis sā@āt.
2 el-ḥukūmeh wafat ib *[transposition of vowel]* wa@id-ha.
3 rama 'l-jakait @a 'ṣ-ṣōfa w dakhal fi 'l-ghurfeh.
4 zōjit el-mujrim washat bī.
5 isqīni mayy, min faḍlak.
6 umm Ḥāzim bakat min el-faraḥ lamma sim@at innu ibinha ribiḥ el-jā"izeh 'l-ūla.
7 Salma, ikwī li 'l-qamīṣ el-ābyaḍ, rajā"an.
8 el-malik ra@a 'l-ḥafleh.

I.7 CaCC – CuCC

Perfect	*Imperative*
ḥaṭṭ he put	**ḥuṭṭ**
radd he responded	**rudd**
marr he passed	**murr**
ṣadd he repulsed	**ṣudd**
ẓann he supposed, surmised	**ẓunn**
ḍamm he embraced, annexed	**ḍumm**

When attached to pronominal suffixes, these verbs give us the pattern **ḥuṭṭ, ḥuṭṭi, ḥuṭṭu and ḥuṭṭin** in the imperative and **ḥaṭṭait, ḥaṭṭait, ḥaṭṭaiti, ḥaṭṭ, ḥaṭṭat, ḥaṭṭaina, ḥaṭṭaitu, ḥaṭṭaitin, ḥaṭṭu, ḥaṭṭin** in the perfect tense.

Vocabulary (exercise 29)

hujūm	attack
illi (*relative pronoun*)	who, which (etc.)
sahl/eh	easy
talafōn (*pl.* **talafōnāt**)	telephone

Exercise 29

tarjim el-jumal et-tālyeh la 'l-lugha 'l-ingilīziyyeh:

1 ḥaṭṭait el-kitāb @ala raff el-maktabeh.
2 Salma raddat @ala 't-talafōn; is"alha mīn illi ḥaka.
3 Shafīq w zōjtu marru @alayy imbāriḥ.
4 jnūdna ṣaddu 'l-hujūm.
5 inta ẓannait inn el-mushkileh sahleh.
6 Ṣāliḥ ḍamm sharikit ibnu la shariktu.

I.8 CaCC – CiCC

Perfect	*Imperative*
madd he extended	**midd**
sadd he closed	**sidd**
ḥabb he loved	**ḥibb**
tamm it became complete	**timm**
ḥathth he urged	**ḥithth**
ḥass he felt	**ḥiss**

These verbs behave like those in subclass 7 above when attached to pronominal suffixes.

Vocabulary (exercise 30)

ba@aḍ	each other
bass	but; only
dirāseh	study (*n.*)
ḍidd	against
ghiliṭ (I.1)	made a mistake
īd or **yad** (*pl.* **ayādi;** *dual* **idain**)	hand
lākin	but
muwāfaqa	approval
tjāhal (VI.1)	ignored

Exercise 30

tarjim el-jumal et-tālyeh la 'l-lugha 'l-ingilīziyyeh:

1 Fadwa maddat lu īd-ha bass huwweh tjāhalha.
2 sidd el-bāb min faḍlak.
3 ḥabbu ba@aḍ khamsi snīn, lākin el-qadar wiqif ḍidd-hum.
4 el-muwāfaqa tammat @ala 'l-ifrāj @an el-masjunīn es-siyāsiyyīn.
5 ḥithth ibnak @ala 'd-dirāseh.
6 ḥassu inhum ghilṭu.

I.9 CaCC – CaCC

Of this group, only the verb **ẓall** need be given. It means 'he stayed', but it is more frequently used in combination with imperfect verbs to give what in English would be the past continuous tense: **ẓall yiḥki** ('he kept on talking'); **ẓallait asā@du** ('I continued to help him').

I.10 CāC – CūC

Perfect	*Imperative*
shāf he saw	**shūf**
ṣām he fasted	**ṣūm**
māt he died	**mūt**
rāḥ he went	**rūḥ**
qāl he said	**qūl**
@ād he came back	**@ūd**
kān he was	**kūn**

The perfect verbs give us the following forms when attached to pronominal suffixes: **kunt, kunt, kunti, kān, kānat, kunna, kuntu, kuntin, kānu, kānin.** The imperatives give us **kūn, kūni, kūnu, kūnin.**

Vocabulary (exercise 31)

ḥādith (*pl.* **ḥawādith**)	accident
jār/a (*pl.* **jīrān**)	neighbour
quddām	in front of
Ramaḍān	9th month of the Hijra Year, Muslim month of fasting
ṣaraf (I.5)	cashed; spent
Turkiyya	Turkey
wain?	where?
wāqif/wāqfeh	standing

Exercise 31

tarjim el-jumal et-tālyeh la 'l-lugha 'l-ingilīziyyeh:

1 wain kuntu? kunna fi bait ṣadīqit Huda.
2 Huda ṣāmat shahar Ramaḍān kullu.
3 sīdi māt qabil khamsi snīn.
4 jīrānkum @ādu min Turkiyya?
5 el-banāt rāḥin la 'l-madraseh.
6 rūḥ iṣrif hādha 'sh-shakk min el-bank.
7 shuft el-ḥādith illi ṣār quddām bāb el-bank?
8 mīn ḥakā lak @annu?
9 Ḥusām qal li. māt ḥada?
10 mātat mara kānat wāqfeh fi 'sh-shāri@.

I.11 CāC – CīC

Perfect	*Imperative*
ṣār he became, it took place	**ṣīr**
sār he walked	**sīr**
ṭār he flew	**ṭīr**
māl he inclined	**mīl**
jāb he brought	**jīb**
@ād he repeated	**@īd**

Here the imperatives give us **ṭīr, ṭīri, ṭīru, ṭīrin,** and the perfect tense **ṭirt/ṭirit, ṭirt/ṭirit, ṭirti, ṭār, ṭarat, ṭirna, ṭirtu, ṭirtin, ṭāru, ṭārin.** But the verb **ṣār** and its derivatives behave irregularly in the perfect tense: **ṣurt/ṣurit, ṣurt/ṣurit, ṣurti, ṣār, ṣārat, ṣurna, ṣurtu, ṣurtin, ṣāru, ṣārin.** The **i** instead of the **u** in these verbs is also heard, however.

Vocabulary (exercise 32)

ba@(i)d	after
darb (*pl.* **d(u)rūb**)	road; path
fā"ideh	interest; usefulness
ḥatta	in order that; in order to; until
mu"akhkharan	lately; recently
musā@id	helper; assistant
naḥw	towards
raf(i)@	raising
shū?	what?
takharruj	graduation

Exercise 32

tarjim el-jumal et-tālyeh la 'l-lugha 'l-ingilīziyyeh:

1 ba@d et-takharruj, Luṭfi ṣār musā@id mudīr esh-sharikeh.
2 shū ṣār?
3 sīr @ala darb abūk.
4 Aḥmad ṭār min el-faraḥ lamma simi@ bi 'l-khabar.
5 jīb li ma@ak khamis kutub min el-maktabeh.
6 mālat el-ḥukūmeh mu"akhkharan naḥw rafi@ as@ār el-fā"ideh.
7 @īd illi qultu ḥatta nisma@.
8 shū jab li abūy min Faransa?

I.12 CāC – CāC

Perfect	*Imperative*
nām he went to bed	**nām**
bāt he spent the night	**bāt**
khāf he felt scared	**khāf**

This very small group of verbs gives us the pattern **nām, nāmi, nāmu** and **nāmin** in the imperative and **nimt/nimit, nimt/nimit, nimt/nimit, nimti, nām, nāmat, nimna, nimtu, nimtin, nāmu** and **nāmin** in the perfect tense. The verb **khāf**, however, behaves like **ṣār.**

Vocabulary (exercise 33)

aimta?	when?
alīf/eh	domesticated; harmless
bakkīr	early
kalb (*pl.* **k(i)lāb**)	dog
lail	night time
laileh	night
el-laileh	tonight
laish?	why?
nuṣṣ	half
nuṣṣ el-lail	midnight
ṣarakh (I.4)	screamed

Exercise 33

tarjim el-jumal et-tālyeh la 'l-lugha 'l-ingilīziyyeh:

1 Salwa nāmat ba@id nuṣṣ el-lail.
2 aimta nirntu mbāriḥ?
3 bitna @ind Sāmi w nimna ba@id nuṣṣ el-lail.
4 ana bitit fi 'l-funduq w nimit bakkīr.
5 Nādya khāfat min el-kalb w ṣarkhat.
6 laish khuftin? hādha 'l-kalb alīf.

Other Class I verbs

There remain three Class I verbs which are somewhat irregular: **akhadh** ('he took'), **akal** ('he ate') and **aja** ('he came'). As you can see, they all begin with a **hamza.** The first two drop the **hamza** in the imperative, giving us **khudh, khudhi,** etc., and **kul, kuli,** etc., but otherwise behave like other triliteral verbs of class I.6. The third verb, however, has for its imperative the phonetically unrelated verb **ta@āl, ta@āli,** etc., while in the perfect it takes the forms **jīt, jīt, jīti, aja, ajat, jīna, jītu, jītin, aju, ajin.** The irregularity of this verb is further compounded by the fact that, unlike all other verbs, its imperfect form is related not to its imperative but to its perfect (see p. 96).

Chapter 6

This chapter continues the theme of verbs. You will learn:

- *how the verbs of Classes II to X are derived from Class I verbs*
- *that Class XI verbs are the exception, and are based on four-consonant roots*
- *how all these verbs form their imperative*

23 Class II verbs

This class, which is derived like all the other classes except Class XI from Class I, doubles the middle consonant: **CaCCaC – CaCCiC**; truncated verbs give us **CaCCa – CaCCi**. The meaning is usually emphatic or causative. It is to be noted, however, that although Class II verbs are derived from Class I roots, not all the roots of Class I are in actual use. Some of the examples given below will be derived from the lists already given. When Class I verbs are not given, this means that they are no longer part of everyday language.

Perfect		*Imperative*
I	II	
simi@	**samma@** he caused (someone) to hear	**sammi@**
riji@	**rajja@** he returned (something)	**rajji@**
najaḥ	**najjaḥ** he caused (someone or something) to succeed	**najjiḥ**
daras	**darras** he taught	**darris**
harab	**harrab** he smuggled	**harrib**
kasar	**kassar** (emphatic use of root: indicates repetition and determination)	**kassir**

masha	**mashsha** he caused (someone) to walk or (something) to go through	**mashshi**
	sawwa he made	**sawwi**
baka	**bakka** he caused (someone) to cry	**bakki**
nisi	**nassa** he caused (someone) to forget	**nassi**
shāf	**shawwaf** he caused (someone) to see	**shawwif**
māt	**mawwat** he caused (someone) to die	**mawwit**
ṣār	**ṣayyar** he caused (someone or something) to become	**ṣayyir**
ṭār	**ṭayyar** he caused (something) to fly	**ṭayyir**
	haddad he threatened	**haddid**
	ḥarrar he liberated; he edited (i.e., made a text free of error)	**ḥarrir**

It is clear that the pattern here is fairly regular except where the middle vowel is a long **ā**, in which case the doubled consonant becomes either a **y** or a **w.** But these, too, follow a regular pattern. If the imperative of the root verb has a long middle **ī (ṭār: ṭīr),** the middle consonants in Class II are **yy;** if it has a long middle **ū (shāf: shūf)** the doubled consonants of Class II are **ww**.

Vocabulary (exercise 34)

@ilāqa	relation
aḥlām (*sing.* **ḥilim, ḥulum, ḥilmeh**)	dreams
albōm (*pl.* **albōmāt**)	album
ashwāk (*sing.* **shōkeh**)	thorns
daktōr	doctor; physician; Ph.D. holder
dukhkhān	smoke; cigarettes collectively
fassar (II.1)	explained
fil(i)m (*pl.* **aflām**)	film
illa	except
jū@	hunger
kthīr	much
khōf (*pl.* **makhāwif**)	fear
li"an(n)	because

ma@na	meaning
ma@nāsh	we don't have
min shān	in order to
mōsīqa	music
mukhaddirāt	drugs
muwaẓẓaf	employee
qāsi/qāsyeh	harsh
Rūsi/yyeh	Russian
Rūsya	Russia
sabab (*pl.* **asbāb**)	reason
safāra	embassy
shajara (*pl.* **shajar**)	tree
ṭalab	request; application
ṭard	dismissal
ṭarīq (*pl.* **ṭuruq**)	road
ṭayyāra	aeroplane; kite
thalj	snow; ice
pl. **thulūj**	snow (not ice)
vīza (sometimes **fīza**) (*pl.* **viyaz**)	visa
wāḍiḥ/wāḍḥa	clear

Exercise 34

tarjim el-jumal et-tālyeh la 'l-lugha 'l-ingilīziyyeh:

1 mudīrit el-madraseh samma@atna kalām qāsi.
2 Ḥusām, sammi@na mōsīqa ḥilweh.
3 Maḥmūd rajja@ el-badleh li"ann el-jakait zghīr.
4 rajja@ūna min el-maṭār li"anna ma@nāsh vīza.
5 el-mudarris najjaḥni li"anni darast kthīr.
6 mīn darrasak ingilīzi fi 'l-madraseh?
7 illi harrab ed-dukhkhān harrab el-mukhaddirāt.
8 eth-thalj kassar esh-shajar.
9 ez-zaman mashshāni @ala ṭarīq malyān ashwāk.
10 es-safāra mashshat li ṭalab el-vīza b'sur@a.
11 shufna mbāriḥ filim bakkāna.
12 kalāmik nassāni illi jīt min shān aḥkī lik @annu.
13 shawwifha 'ṣ-ṣuwar illi fi 'l-albōm.

14 mawwatūna mn el-jū@.
15 shū sawwāk mudīr illa abūk el-wazīr?
16 ţayyir ţayyārtak fi 'l-ḥadīqa.
17 mudīr esh-sharikeh haddad bi ţard nuşş el-muwaẓẓafīn bidūn sabab wāḍiḥ.
18 mīn illi ḥarrar el-Jazā"ir min Faransa?
19 Shawqi ḥarrar kitāb @an el-@ilāqāt er-Rūsiyyeh 'l-Amairkiyyeh.
20 ed-daktōr Ghāzi ḥarrarha mn el-khōf lamma fassar ilha ma@na aḥlāmha.

24 Class III verbs

This class is derived from Class I by infixing a long **ā** after the first consonant. The form suggests basically a prolonged or reciprocal action. The Class I verbs not given in the following list are no longer in use. The form is **CāCaC – CāCiC** or, for truncated verbs, **CāCa – CāCi**.

Perfect		*Imperative*
I	III	
wa@ad	**wā@ad** he promised to meet (someone); he 'dated'	**wā@id**
	nāda he called	**nādi**
	wāfaq he agreed	**wāfiq**
	ḥārab he fought	**ḥārib**
	@ālaj he treated (a patient, a situation)	**@ālij**
masha	**māsha** he walked with; he went along with	**māshi**
khalaţ	**khālaţ** he mixed with (usu. bad people)	**khāliţ**
hajar	**hājar** he emigrated	**hājir**

Vocabulary (exercise 35)

@ālami/yyeh	international; worldwide
@ayyan (II.1)	appointed
a@ṭa (IV.2)	he gave
ālāf (*sing.* **al(i)f**)	thousands
Atrāk (*sing.* **Turki**)	Turks
ba@id mā	after
es sā@a thamānyeh	it's eight o'clock
Libnān	Lebanon
nās	people collectively
qarḍ (*pl.* **qurūḍ**)	loan
sabab	cause
bi sabab	because
yi@ṭi	(3rd person m. sing. subjunctive of **a@ṭa**: he gave (IV.2))
yīju	(3rd person m. pl. subjunctive of **aja**: he came; see Ex. 46)

Exercise 35

Translate the following into Arabic:

1 They promised to come at eight o'clock.
2 Huda, call Salma from her room.
3 The bank manager agreed to give me a loan.
4 My father fought with the Turks in the First World War.
5 The government took care of the problem quickly.
6 Na@īm went along with the company's manager until he appointed him assistant manager.
7 We got to know them after we mixed with them.
8 Thousands of people emigrated from Lebanon because of the war.

25 Class IV verbs

Here the perfect tense always begins with a **hamza** (dropped in spelling because automatically pronounced) followed by a short **a**. The pattern is **aCCaC – iCCiC** or **aCCa – iCCi** for truncated verbs. The meaning is often causative, and the form makes intransitive verbs transitive (i.e., they can have an object).

Perfect			*Imperative*
I	IV		
nizil	**anzal**	he got (sthg) down	**inzil** (but identical with the imp. of Class I, so not used; **nazzil** of Class II used instead)
tilif	**atlaf**	he damaged (sthg)	**itlif**
	aslam	he converted to Islam	**islim**
kharaj	**akhraj**	he took (sthg) out; he directed (a play)	**ikhrij**
	as@af	he gave (someone) first aid	**is@if**
fishil	**afshal**	he caused (sthg) to fail	**ifshil**
	ankar	he denied	**inkir**
thabat	**athbat**	he proved	**ithbit**
	awşa	he recommended; he left a will	**iwşi**
	akhlaş	he remained faithful	**ikhliş**

Vocabulary (exercise 36)

@aduww (*pl.* **a@dā"**)	enemy
@an ţarīq	by means of
Afrīqya	Africa
jdīd/eh	new
jur(u)ḥ (*pl.* **j(u)rūḥ; j(i)rāḥ**)	wound
lajneh (*pl.* **lijān**)	committee
mā	not
mazrū@āt	lit., things planted: crops

nazaf (I.5)	bled
sukkān (*sing*. **sākin**)	inhabitants; population
ta@yīn	appointment to job
tijāra	trade
ẓahr	back

Exercise 36

tarjim el-jumal et-tālyeh la 'l-lugha 'l-ingilīziyyeh:

1 Aḥmad nazzal akhū @an ẓahr el-ḥiṣān.
2 kthīr min sukkān Afrīqya aslamu @an ṭarīq et-tijāra.
3 eth-thalj atlaf el-mazrū@āt.
4 el-@aduww akhrajna min bilādna / mn iblādna.
5 jurḥu ẓall yinzif ḥatta as@afatu Huda.
6 Ḥāmid fishil fi 'l-imtiḥān, bass shū afshalu?
7 Nu@mān ankar innu shāf Layla mbāriḥ.
8 ithbit inta innu shāfha.
9 awṣat el-lajneh bi ta@yīn mudarris jdīd.
10 @afāf akhlaṣat la zōjha lākin huwweh mā @akhlaṣ ilha.

26 Class V verbs

Verbs of this class are mostly reflexive in meaning (i.e., the action of the verb, performed by the subject, also affects the subject). The reflexive form is, however, not always obvious in the natural English translation. The form is **taCaCCaC** (which according to the short-vowel elision rule becomes **tCaCCaC** or, depending on the sounds preceding it, **itCaCCaC**) and it is usually directly derived from Class II verbs. Truncated verbs, predictably, give us **taCaCCa**/ **tCaCCa/itCaCCa**.

Perfect			*Imperative*
I	II	V	
kasar	**kassar**	**tkassar** it got broken	**tkassar**
@ilim	**@allam**	**t@allam** he learned	**t@allam**
@irif	**@arraf**	**t@arraf** he recognized	**t@ arraf**
	akkad	**t"akkad** he ascertained	**t"akkad**
dhakar	**dhakkar**	**tdhakkar** he remembered	**tdhakkar**
	ghayyar	**tghayyar** he has changed	**tghayyar**
		t@ammad he acted deliberately	**t@ammad**
		tnakkar he disguised himself; he denied any involvement	**tnakkar**
	salla	**tsalla** he entertained himself	**tsalla**
	khalla	**tkhalla** he let down, abandoned	**tkhalla**

As you can see, all of these verbs have identical forms for the perfect and the imperative.

Vocabulary (exercise 37)

aḫla	sweeter; more beautiful
fashal	failure
kumbyūtar	computer
mashrū@ (*pl.* **mashārī@**)	project
min bain	from among
miriḍ (I.1)	he fell ill
sā@tain (*dual of* **sā@a**)	two hours
ṣaḫīḫ/a	true; correct
shurṭa	police collectively
shurṭi/yyeh	policeman/woman
tamāman	exactly; completely
thuq(u)l	weight
yuṣdum	(3rd person m. sing. subjunctive of **ṣadam**: he collided with (I.4))

Exercise 37

tarjim el-jumal et-tālyeh la 'l-lugha 'l-ingilīziyyeh:

1 tkassar esh-shajar min thuql eth-thalj.
2 t@allamtu ingilīzi fi 'l-madraseh?
3 t@arraf Taḥsīn @ala 'l-mujrim min bain khamis mujrimīn.
4 tdhakkartīni? ana Maḥmūd.
5 inti tghayyarti; ṣurti aḥla.
6 sāyiq es-sayyāra t@ammad yuṣdum esh-shurṯi.
7 Huda tnakkarat la Aḥmad ba@id mā miriḍ.
8 t"akkad tamāman inn el-khabar ṣaḥīḥ.
9 el-awlād itsallu bi 'l-kumbyūtar akthar min sā@tain.
10 esh-sharikeh tkhallat @an el-mashrū@ ba@id mā thabat fashalu.

27 Class VI verbs

The form here is **taCāCaC**, which becomes **tCāCaC** by the elision of the first short vowel (**taCāCa/tCāCa** for truncated verbs). The meaning is derived from that of Class III verbs, with a strong suggestion of reciprocity. The Class III forms given in square brackets are unused, but are included for clarity.

Perfect

I	III	VI
qatal	**qātal**	**tqātal** he took part in a brawl or a battle
katab	**kātab**	**tkātab** he corresponded with
badal	**bādal**	**tbādal** he exchanged
fihim	**[fāham]**	**tfāham** he came to mutual understanding with
kisil	**[kāsal]**	**tkāsal** he was too lazy to act
sa"al	**sā"al**	**tsā"al** he wondered
		tfā"al he felt optimistic
		tshā"am he felt pessimistic
riḍi	**rāḍa**	**trāḍa** he made it up with (someone)

Here again the imperative is identical with the perfect.

Vocabulary (exercise 38)

akthar min el-lāzim	too much (lit., more than is necessary)
khilāf (*pl.* **khilāfāt**)	disagreement
kull mā hunāk	all there is to it
lā . . . wa la	neither . . . nor
lāzim	necessary
qabil mā	before
zawāj	marriage

Exercise 38

tarjim et-jumal et-tālyeh la 'l-lugha 'l-ingilīziyyeh:

1 Aḥmad tqātal ma@ maratu.
2 eṯ-ṭullāb tqātalu ma@ esh-shurṭa.
3 tkātabit ma@ha muddit khamsi snīn.
4 tbādalna rasā"il kthīreh.
5 tfāhamna @a 'z-zawāj, lākin ez-zaman nassāha w@ūd-ha.
6 en-nās tsā"alu @an sabab el-khilāf bainna.
7 qal li Aḥmad, 'inta tfā"alit akthar min el-lāzim.'
8 qult lu, 'lā tfā"alit wala tshā"amit; kull ma hunāk inni kunt majnūn.'
9 'rūḥ trāḍa ma@ha qabil mā trūḥ minnak.'
10 'rāḍait-ha akthar min el-lāzim.'

28 Class VII verbs

Most verbs in this class are reflexive (see Class V) and/or passive in meaning (i.e., the action of the verb affects the subject). The pattern is **inCaCaC** (**inCaCa** for truncated verbs); theoretically, the imperative (rare because of the passive nature of the form) should take the form **inCaCiC**, but it often takes the form **iniCCiC** (**iniCCi** for truncated verbs).

Perfect

I	VII
kasar	**inkasar** he / it got broken
qalab	**inqalab** he / it got overturned
	indahash he was surprised
dafa@	**indafa@** he was pushed; he acted recklessly
qibil	**inqabal** he was accepted or admitted
da@a	**inda@a** he was invited
ṭalab	**inṭalab** he was summoned; it was asked for

Exercise 39

tarjim et-jumal et-tālyeh la 'l-lugha 'l-ingilīziyyeh:

1 el-kūb wiqi@ w inkasar.
2 inqalbat es-sayyāra ba@id mā ṣadmat el-bāṣ.
3 Nizār indahash lamma simi@ el-khabar.
4 indaf@at bi 'l-kalām akthar min el-lāzim.
5 Sawsan inqablat fi 'l-jāmi@a *(university).*
6 iḥna 'nda@aina la ḥaflit zafāf *(wedding)* Muna.
7 hādha 'n-nō@ min el-kutub inṭalab kthīr.

29 Class VIII verbs

The pattern here is **iCtaCaC (iCtaCa** for truncated verbs, **iCtaCC** for verbs ending in double letters), and the meaning is derived from that of Class I verbs, made reflexive (again, this is not always obvious in the English translation), with various modifications. The imperative is **iCtaCiC (iCtaCi** for truncated verbs, **iCtaCC** for those ending in double letters).

Perfect		*Imperative*
I	VIII	
fa@al he did	**ifta@al** he contrived	**ifta@il**
	ishtaha he desired	**ishtahi**
	intaha he ended, came to a stop	**intahi**
naẓar he looked	**intaẓar** he waited, expected	**intaẓir**
simi@ he heard	**istama@** he listened (i.e., made himself hear)	**istami@**
naṣar he aided	**intaṣar** he triumphed	**intaṣir**
madd he extended, stretched	**imtadd** he extended himself, stretched	**imtadd**
faraḍ he imposed, gave as a possibility	**iftaraḍ** he supposed, took for granted	**iftariḍ**

Vocabulary (exercise 40)

amlāk (*sing.* **mulk** or **milk**)	possessions; property
azmeh (*pl.* **azamāt**)	crisis
intikhābāt	elections
sing. **intikhāb**	election; choice
jur"a	boldness; audacity
muḥāḍara	lecture
muḥāḍir/a	lecturer
niyyeh	intention
sū"	badness
sū" en-niyyeh	ill will
ṭūl (*pl.* **aṭwāl**)	length
ṭūl ha 'l-muddeh	all this time

Exercise 40

tarjim el-jumal et-tālyeh la 'l-lugha 'l-ingilīziyyeh:

1 el-Amairkān ifta@alu azmeh ma@ Awrubba.
2 ishtahaina nshūfak. wain kunt ṭūl ha 'l-muddeh?
3 intahat a@māl esh-sharikeh.
4 intaẓartik nuṣṣ sā@a, lākin inti mā jīti.
5 en-nās istama@u la 'l-muḥāḍara w indahashu min jur"it el-muḥāḍir.
6 intaṣar Fikri @ala Maḥmūd fi 'l-intikhābāt.
7 imtaddat amlāk @abdalla 'n-Nāṣiri min shāri@ Ṣalāḥ ed-Dīn ḥatta shāri@ el-Mutanabbi.
8 laish iftaraḍit sū" en-niyyeh fi kalāmi?

30 Class IX verbs

This is a minor class of verbs, of which only a handful are still in use. The pattern is **iCCaCC** for both the perfect and the imperative.

iṣfarr it became yellow
ikhḍarr it became green
iswadd it became black
izraqq it became blue
ighbarr it became dusty
iḥmarr it became red

Vocabulary (exercise 41)

ān el-awān	it's high time (for something to be done)
awān	time; season (right time for . . .)
dinya or **dunya**	world
fuj"atan	suddenly

jaww	atmosphere; weather
lā	don't
ōksijīn	oxygen
qilleh	scarcity; paucity
shata (I.6)	it rained
ṭōz	dust, esp. that brought by dust storms in Gulf area
wij(i)h (*pl.* **w(u)jūh**)	face

Exercise 41

tarjim el-jumal et-tālyeh la 'l-lugha 'l-ingilīziyyeh:

1 iṣfarr waraq esh-shajar qabil awānu.
2 ikhḍarri yā dinya w lā tighbarri.
3 izraqq wijh el-walad min qillit el-ōksijīn.
4 fuj"atan ighbarr el-jaww w ṣārat ed-dinya tishti ṯōz.

31 Class X verbs

The form of this class is **istaCCaC** (**istaCCa** for truncated verbs, **istaCaCC** for verbs ending in double letters). The meaning expressed by these verbs is often asking for the quality of the root verb or assigning that quality to something. The imperative takes the form **istaCCiC** (**istaCCi** for truncated verbs, **istaCiCC** for verbs ending in double letters).

Perfect		*Imperative*
I	X	
@imil he made	**ista@mal** he made use of	**ista@mil**
qibil he accepted	**istaqbal** he received (sthg or someone)	**istaqbil**
ghini he got rich	**istaghna** he was no longer in need of (sthg specified)	**istaghni**
raḥam he gave mercy to	**istarḥam** he asked for mercy	**istarḥim**

ghafar he forgave	**istaghfar** he asked for forgiveness	**istaghfir**
riji@ he came back	**istarja@** he took (sthg) back; he remembered	**istarji@**
	istaghall he exploited	**istaghill**
	ista@add he made himself ready; he expressed willingness to	**ista@idd**
	istarkha he relaxed himself; he stretched himself to relax	**istarkhi**

Vocabulary (exercise 42)

@ummāl (*sing.* **@āmil**)	workers
aflas (IV.1)	became bankrupt
maḩkameh (*pl.* **maḩākim**)	court
mawwal (II.1)	financed
nashāţ	activity; freshness (to resume work)
rabb	god; God
shiddeh	force; strictness; intensity

Exercise 42

tarjim el-jumal et-tālyeh la 'l-lugha 'l-ingilīziyyeh:

1 ista@mil esh-shiddeh ma@hum; ana 'sta@malt-ha w najḩat.
2 el-yōm istaqbal el-wazīr khamis sufara Awrubbiyyīn.
3 esh-sharikeh istaghnat el-yōm @an nuşş el-@ummāl.
4 el-mujrim illi qatal maratu istarḩam el-maḩkameh bi sabab bintu 'z-zghīreh.
5 istaghfir rabbak.
6 el-bank istarja@ kull amwālu ba@id mā aflasat esh-sharikeh.
7 Huda 'staghallatak w inta 'staghallaitni.
8 ista@add el-bank ymawwil el-mashrū@.
9 istarja@it nashāţi ba@id mā 'starkhait @a 'ş-şōfa muddit nuşş sā@a.

32 Class XI verbs

The verb patterns so far given are all based on either triliteral or truncated roots (i.e., roots having three or two consonants respectively), but Arabic also uses quadriliteral roots (i.e., those that have four consonants). These, however, are far fewer in number and should pose no problem to the foreign learner of Arabic. They are regular in their behaviour and their pattern is **CaCCaC – CaCCiC** (cf. Class II verbs).

Perfect	*Imperative*
tarjam he translated	**tarjim**
@askar he camped	**@askir**
zakhraf he decorated with arabesques	**zakhrif**
falsaf he philosophized, over-complicated (a subject)	**falsif**
salsal he put in a series	**salsil**
handas he engineered	**handis**
kharbaṭ he confused	**kharbiṭ**
lakhbaṭ he confused	**lakhbiṭ**

Vocabulary (exercise 43)

falsafeh	philosophy
Islāmi/yyeh	Islamic
mafhūm/eh	easy to understand
masjid	mosque
Yūnāni/yyeh	Greek
zakhārif (*sing.* **zukhruf**)	decorative designs; arabesques

Exercise 43

tarjim el-jumal et-tālyeh la 'l-lugha 'l-ingilīziyyeh:

1 el-@arab tarjamu kthīr min kutub el-falsafeh 'l-Yūnāniyyeh.
2 wain @askartu?
3 zakhrafu 'l-masjid ib zakhārif Islāmiyyeh.
4 falsafat el-mawḍū@ akthar min el-lāzim.
5 salsalat el-mawḍū@ ḥatta ṣār mafhūm.
6 mīn handas hādha 'l-mashrū@?
7 kalāmik kharbaṭ kull afkāri.
8 Su@ād lakhbaṭat kull masharī@na.

33 Verb summary

We can now summarize all the above patterns as follows:

Class	*Perfect*	*Imperative*
I.1	CiCiC	iCCaC
I.2	CiCi	iCCa
I.3	CaCaC	iCCaC
I.4	CaCaC	uCCuC
I.5	CaCaC	iCCiC
I.6	CaCa	iCCi
I.7	CaCC	CuCC
I.8	CaCC	CiCC
I.9	CaCC	CaCC
I.10	CāC	CūC
I.11	CāC	CīC
I.12	CāC	CāC
II.1	CaCCaC	CaCCiC
II.2	CaCCa	CaCCi
III.1	CāCaC	CāCiC
III.2	CāCa	cāCi
IV.1	aCCaC	iCCiC
IV.2	aCCa	iCCi

V.1	tCaCCaC	tCaCCaC
V.2	tCaCCa	tCaCCa
VI.1	tCāCaC	tCāCaC
VI.2	tCāCa	tCāCa
VII.1	inCaCaC	inCaCiC / iniCCiC
VII.2	inCaCa	inCaCi / iniCCi
VIII.1	iCtaCaC	iCtaCiC
VIII.2	iCtaCa	iCtaCi
IX	iCCaCC	iCCaCC
X.1	istaCCaC / istaCaCC	istaCCiC / istaCiCC
X.2	istaCCa	istaCCi
XI	CaCCaC	CaCCiC

It is clear from this summary that Classes II–XI are fairly regular in the way their vowels change to make imperatives and, as we shall see, imperfect verbs. The last vowel is always a short **i** except in Classes V, VI and IX, which do not change at all. If the verb begins with an **a**, as do Class IV verbs, that **a**, too, changes into an **i**. It is Class I verbs that are somewhat unpredictable, and you are advised to consult the Mini-dictionary whenever you are in doubt about the conjugation of any verb, so as to learn the correct vowelling.

Chapter 7

In this lesson you will expand your knowledge of verbs by looking at different tenses. The chapter introduces:

- *the imperfect tense, which is used to talk about the present*
- *the subjunctive mood, used for hypothetical situations and in some set phrases*
- *two ways of talking about the future*
- *the verb* **kān**, *literally 'was', which is used with other verbs to form further tenses*

34 The imperfect verb

The imperfect is the Arabic equivalent of the simple present tense or present continuous tense ('am -ing', etc.) in English. It is easy to derive the imperfect from the imperative, for all that is required is the addition of set prefixes and sometimes suffixes to the imperative form. It may be helpful to give a few examples illustrating all possibilities. The prefixes and suffixes will be spaced so as to show the components of the verb. In the case of transitive verbs (i.e., those which can have an object), accusative pronominal suffixes may, of course, be added as well (see Section 13). Remember, too, that the rules governing the behaviour of short vowels and consonants also apply here. Elements in brackets are optional: some people pronounce them, some do not.

Singular

ana	inta	inti
ba shrab	bt ishrab	bt ishrab i
(I drink, am drinking)	*(you drink, are drinking)*	*(you drink, are drinking)*
ba nsa	bt insa	bt ins i
ba drus	bt udrus	bt udrus i
ba ḥuṭṭ	bit ḥuṭṭ	bit ḥuṭṭ i
ba ḥārib	bit ḥārib	bit ḥārb i
ba tkassar	bt itkassar	bt itkassar i

huwweh	hiyyeh
b(y) ishrab	bt ishrab
(he drinks, is drinking)	*(she drinks, is drinking)*
b(y) insa	bt insa
b(y) udrus	bt udrus
bi(y) ḥuṭṭ	bit ḥuṭṭ
bi(y) ḥārib	bit ḥārib
b(y) itkassar	bt itkassar

Plural

iḥna	intu	intin
bn ishrab	bt ishrab u	bt ishrab in
(we drink, are drinking)	*(you drink, are drinking)*	*(you drink, are drinking)*
bn insa	bt ins u	bt ins in
bn udrus	bt udrus u	bt udrus in
bin ḥuṭṭ	bit ḥuṭṭ u	bit ḥuṭṭ in
bin ḥārib	bit ḥārb u	bit ḥārb in
bn itkassar	bt itkassar u	bt itkassar in

hummeh	hinneh
b(y) ishrab u	b(y) ishrab in
(they drink, are drinking)	*(they drink, are drinking)*
b(y) ins u	b(y) ins in
b(y) udrus u	b(y) udrus in
bi(y) ḥuṭṭ u	bi(y) ḥuṭṭ in
bi(y) ḥārb u	bi(y) ḥārb in
b(y) itkassar u	b(y) itkassar in

By looking at these examples, we observe the following:

1 The letter **b** is common to all verbs and persons. It is a curious addition to modern spoken Arabic used only with the imperfect. We shall discuss later when it can be dropped.
2 The prefix for the first person singular is always **ba-**, after which all initial vowels in the stem are dropped; the **a** sound in the prefix is the first person singular marker.
3 All second persons have a **t** in the prefix, which is preceded by an **i** when the verb itself begins with a consonant. The **t** is the second person marker.
4 The second person singular, feminine gender, has a suffix **-i** as well as a prefix; if the verb itself ends in an **i**, one **i** is dropped.
5 The third persons singular, masculine gender, and plural have an optional **y** sound. If the verb starts with a consonant, an **i** is inserted after the **b**. The **i** or **y** or both are the third person marker except for the third person singular, feminine gender, which takes the feminine **t** as its marker.
6 The second and third persons plural, masculine gender, have a suffix **-u** as well as a prefix. This suffix replaces the vowel of the stem if it has one.
7 The second and third persons plural, feminine gender, have a suffix **-in** as well as a prefix; the vowel of the stem, if it exists, is dropped when **-in** is used.
8 The prefix for the first person plural is **bn-** before vowels, **bin-** before consonants. The **n** sound is the first person plural marker.
9 If a suffix that either is or starts with a vowel is used, the short vowel of the last syllable of the stem is either dropped (**bitḫārbin** instead of **bitḫāribin**) or shifted backwards (**btudursin** instead of **btudrusin**). This does not apply when the short vowel in question is an **a** or when the vowel is itself the last letter, as in truncated verbs. Although the operation is optional, the alternative sounds unnatural or formal in spoken Arabic.

Now study the following table:

Detached pronouns	*Attached nominative pronouns: perfect*	*Imperfect without* **b-**
ana	-t	a-
inta	-t	t-
inti	-ti	t- -i
hū/huwweh	—	i(y)- *or* (y)i-
hī/hiyyeh	-at	t-
iḥna/niḥna	-na	n-
intu	-tu	t- -u
intin	-tin	t- -in
hummeh	-u	(y)i/i(y)- -u
hinneh	-in	(y)i/i(y)- -in

Although the pronouns attached to perfect verbs are not always identical, they are clearly related to the imperfect verb prefixes and suffixes.

Exercise 44

Break each of the following into its various components, then translate it into English:

1 bitshufūhin?
2 badarris-ha.
3 badrus-ha.
4 ba@rifhum.
5 bti@irfī?
6 bti@irfīni.
7 bni@irfik.
8 bti@irfik.
9 bi@irfak.
10 bti@rafhum?
11 bi@rafūna?
12 bni@rafhin?
13 byi@rafinna?
14 btit@allami?
15 btit@allamī?
16 btit@allamū?
17 bit@allmu?
18 bit@allmū?
19 btit@allamīha.
20 biy@allmūkum?
21 bnit@allamu.
22 bin@allmu.
23 biy@allimna.
24 bit@allam.
25 bi@allimkum.

Vocabulary (exercise 45)

@ādi/yyeh	ordinary; normal
@arabi/yyeh	an Arab; Arabic
ḥadīth	conversation
ikhtalaf (VIII.1)	he differed
maḥki/yyeh	spoken
mish	not
nafis-hum, nafisna (etc.)	themselves, ourselves (etc.)
rakkaz (II.1)	he concentrated
shwayy	a little
ṭabī@i/yyeh	natural
willa	or

Exercise 45

Translate the following into English:

1 ana bat@allam @arabi.
2 bti@rif inn el-lugha 'l-@arabiyyeh min el-lughāt es-Sāmiyyeh?
3 mīn biy@allmak @arabi?
4 badrus-ha fi kitāb jdīd maktūb bi 'l-lugha 'l-Ingilīziyyeh.
5 btit@allam el-lugha 'l-maḥkiyyeh willa 'l-lugha 'l-maktūbeh?
6 barakkiz @ala 'l-lugha 'l-maḥkiyyeh ḥatta atfāham ma@ en-nās.
7 lākin ana ba@rif inn el-kutub el-@arabiyyeh maktūbeh b-lugha btikhtalif @an el-lugha 'l-maḥkiyyeh.
8 btikhtalif shwayy, lākin el-@arab nafis-hum biyḥissu inn el-lugha 'l-maktūbeh mish ṭabī@iyyeh la 'l-ḥadīth el-@ādi.

Vocabulary (exercise 46)

antaj (IV.1)	he produced
el-@ālam eth-thālith	the Third World
khanzīr (*pl.* **khanāzīr**)	pig
laḥim (*pl.* **luḥūm**)	meat
laḥim khanzīr	pork
sīnama (*pl.* **sīnamāt**)	cinema
(yōm) el-jum@a	Friday

Exercise 46

Study the conjugations of the irregular verbs **aja** *('he came'),* **akal** *('he ate'), and* **akhadh** *('he took'), and then translate the sentences that follow into Arabic.*

ana	bāji	bākul*	bākhudh*
inta	btīji	btākul	btākhudh
inti	btīji	btākli	btākhdhi
huwweh	b(y)īji	b(y)ākul	b(y)ākhudh
hiyyeh	btīji	btākul	btākhudh
iḥna	bnīji	bnākul	bnākhudh
intu	btīju	btāklu	btākhdhu
intin	btījin	btāklin	btākhdhin
hummeh	b(y)īju	b(y)āklu	b(y)ākhdhu
hinneh	b(y)ījin	b(y)āklin	b(y)ākhdhin

* Many speakers in the Eastern parts of the Arab World say **bōkil,** etc., and **bōkhidh,** etc. The form of the 2nd person plural, masculine gender, is frequently used for the feminine as well.

1 The Third World eats more than it produces.
2 She comes to our house every day.
3 What are you eating? (All possibilities.)
4 Where do you take them? (All possibilities.)
5 We come to your house every day. (All possibilities.)
6 Do you eat pork? (All possibilities.)
7 Does she come to school?
8 They come to our house on Friday.
9 Aḥmad takes his son to the cinema every Friday.
10 They take us to their house every Friday.

35 The subjunctive mood

The subjunctive mood is used for hypothetical situations. In English it can be expressed by means of the past tense (the only verb with a distinctive past subjunctive form is 'be': 'If I *were* a king . . . ') or by a special form of the present ('If he *be* man enough . . . '), though this is nowadays little used except in wishes ('Long *live* the Queen!'). In either case, no *real* time is indicated; the italicized verbs deal with a *hypothetical* time. In Arabic, the hypothetical nature of the mood remains, but only the imperfect form of the verb is used, without the initial **b-**, which seems to indicate continuity, frequency or habit. Consider the following examples:

1 **bashrab shāy.** (imperfect)
This sentence can mean: 'I am drinking tea' (an answer to 'What are you doing?') or: 'I usually drink tea' (an answer to 'What do you usually drink?').

2 **tishrab shāy?** (subjunctive)
This sentence can only mean: 'Would you like to drink tea?'

3 **btishrab shāy?** (imperfect)
This sentence can mean: 'Are you drinking tea?' or: 'Do you normally drink tea?'

Sentences 1 and 3 deal with either continuity of action or habit. Sentence 2, however, is an offer; no action is really involved except in the hypothetical situation of acceptance.

The subjunctive form is also used in Arabic when the imperfect is governed by another verb:

Ḥusām nawa yitjawwaz/yitzawwaj. (both forms acceptable)
Ḥusām has decided to marry.
ṣār yibki.
He started to cry.
naṣaḥtu ybaṭṭil yishrab.
I advised him to give up drinking.

In the last sentence, the second verb is governed by the first, and the third by the second.

Certain words or phrases also require the use of the subjunctive form of the imperfect:

lā don't
lā tinsa maw@idna.
Don't forget our appointment.

lāzim should
lāzim tiḥki la ummak @an el-mawḍū@.
You should tell you mother about the matter.

min shān/@ala shān/@a shān in order that
batalfin min shān aḥkī lak @an Suha.
I am calling in order to tell you about Suha.

ḥatta in order that, so as to
nām bakkīr ḥatta tiṣḥa bakkīr.
Go to bed early so as to wake up early.

la (emphatic particle)
w Allah la akhabbir esh-shurṭa.
By God/I assure (you) I will inform the police.

bid(d)- (see Sections 36 and 50 below)

expressions of prayer or request
Allah yi@ṭīk el-@āfyeh.
May God give you good health.
wiḥyātak ti@ṭīni ha 'l-kitāb.
Please (lit., *I am asking you by your life,) give me this book.*

Vocabulary (exercise 47)

@īd mīlād	birthday
algha (IV.2)	he cancelled
Alla yirḥam (person)	may God give mercy to (person)
biddi	I want (see Section 50)
bukra	tomorrow
dhakkar (II.1)	he reminded
faṣ(i)l	chapter
khalla (II.2)	he let; he allowed
qara" (I.3)	he read (final **hamza** of **qara"** and **iqra"** is retained only in emphatic speech)
shugh(u)l	work; job
waq(i)t	time

Exercise 47

tarjim el-jumal et-tālyeh la 'l-lugha 'l-ingilīziyyeh:

1. Maḥmūd, khalli Huda tinzil min faḍlak.
2. qūli la abūki yīji bukra ḥatta niḥki fi 'l-mawḍū@.
3. wiḥyātik ti@malī li finjān qahweh.
4. w Alla la a@mal lak ḥaflit @īd mīlād aḥsan min ḥaflit @īd mīlād-ha.
5. iqra hādha 'l-faṣil ḥatta tifham el-fikra.
6. alghait maw@idi ma@ Sāmi min shān āji ashūfik.
7. biddi adhakkir Sāmi bi 'l-maw@id.
8. lāzim ti@ṭi shughlak kull waqtak.
9. lā tākhudh flūs min @ādil; ana ba@ṭīk.
10. Alla yirḥamna b' raḥimtu.

36 The future tense

Standard Arabic employs two devices to indicate future time: one the independent word **sawfa,** the other the prefix **sa-,** both of which precede the verb. But these are no longer used in spoken Arabic; instead, the word **raḥ** ('went') is gradually losing its basic sense and acquiring the force of 'shall' (cf. 'going to' in English).

raḥ aḥkī lu @an el-mawḍu@ bukra.
I shall talk to him about this matter tomorrow.
aimta raḥ tzūru?
When will you pay him a visit?
mīn raḥ yistaqbilha fi 'l-maṭār?
Who is going to meet her at the airport?
ha 'l-mushkileh raḥ tinḥall?
Will there be a solution to this problem? Will this problem ever be solved?

Notice that the imperfect verb that follows **raḥ** is governed by this verb and, therefore, loses its **b-.**

Another way of expressing futurity is by means of the word **bid(d)-** ('want'), which, like the English word 'will', expresses both desire and future time (see further in Section 50 below):

biddi azūrkum qarīban.
I will visit you shortly.

The use of the active participle (see Section 44 below) also sometimes indicates futurity:

ana msāfir la Barīs ba@d usbū@.
I am leaving for Paris in a week's time.
mistannīki bukra.
I will be waiting for you tomorrow.

In English, as you know, the present sometimes functions as a future tense ('Tomorrow, we first meet him at the airport, then we take him to the hotel'). This is also true of Arabic:

ashūfak bukra.
See you tomorrow.
baktib lak ba@dain.
I shall write to you later.
bitshūfha 'l-laileh?
Are you seeing her tonight?
@umri mā *(not)* **bansa jamīlak.**
I will never forget your kindness. (**@umri:** lit., *my age, my life span,* i e., *ever;* here *never,* since the sentence is negative in meaning. **jamīlak: jamīl** means *beautiful,* i.e., *beautiful deed, a favour.)*
eţ-ţayyāra btiwşal es-sā@a thamānyeh w rubi@.
The plane arrives at 8:15.

Vocabulary (exercise 48)

handaseh	engineering
kull shī	everything
khiliş (I.1)	it was finished; it was over; (supplies were) exhausted
marḩaleh	stage; phase; period
nafţ	oil; petroleum
shī (*pl.* **ashyā"**)	thing
talfan (XI)	he telephoned
ţibb	medicine (science)
wājah (III.1)	he faced

Exercise 48

tarjim el-jumal et-tālyeh la 'l-lugha 'l-ingilīziyyeh:

1 el-@ālam raḩ iywājih marḩaleh şa@beh ba@id mā yikhlaş en-nafţ.
2 biddi adrus ţibb fi Barīţānya.
3 msāfir bukra ma@ akhūy. huwweh biddu yudrus handaseh.
4 batalfin lak min hunāk.
5 ed-dirāseh hunāk raḩ tnassīk kull shī.

37 The verb 'kān'

In discussing the tenses, we have talked about the perfect (roughly equivalent to the English simple past tense or present perfect), the imperfect (roughly equivalent to the simple present or present continuous) and the future. The verb **kān** ('was'), however, can add various refinements to these tenses that enable spoken Arabic to express time relations with greater precision. These are best approached through examples:

qarait *Hamlet*. *I read* Hamlet / *I have read* Hamlet.
(simple past and present perfect tense)
kunt baqra *Hamlet*. *I was reading* Hamlet.
(past continuous)
kunt qarait *Hamlet*. *I had read* Hamlet.
(past perfect)
kunt raḫ aqra *Hamlet*. *I would have read* Hamlet / *I had planned to read* Hamlet.
(future in the past)
baqra *Hamlet*. *I am reading* Hamlet.
(present continuous)
baqra *Hamlet* ba@dain. *I shall read* Hamlet *later*.
(present tense expressing future time)
raḫ aqra *Hamlet*. *I shall read* Hamlet.
(simple future)
raḫ akūn qarait *Hamlet*. *I shall have read* Hamlet.
(future perfect)
raḫ akūn baqra *Hamlet*. *I shall be reading* Hamlet.
(future continuous)

The verb **kān** is used, of course, in its basic sense of 'being', but, as we observed earlier, it is never used in the present tense in the way that 'is' is used in English. The following sentences illustrate the uses of **kān** not covered so far:

@abd el-Qādir hunāk.
@abd el-Qādir is there. (**kān** dropped)
@abd el-Qādir kān hunāk.
He was there. **(kān** retained)

raḥ akūn hunāk.
I will be there. (**akūn** governed by the verb **raḥ**)
jā"iz iykūn hunāk.
He may be there. (**iykūn** governed by the active participle **jā"iz/jāyiz:** *likely* – see Section 44 below)
mumkin akūn insīt?
Could it be that I have forgotten? (**akūn** governed by the active participle **mumkin:** *might be)*
kān lāzim
should have (subject depending on context)
kān lāzim tiḥkī lu.
You should have told him.
kān mumkin
it would have been possible
kān mumkin asā@dak law innak jīt abkar.
It would have possible for me to help you, had you come earlier/I would probably have helped you, had you . . .
la ykūn nisi?
Could it be that he has forgotten?
la tkūn za@lān?
Could it be that you are cross with me?

The last two expressions with **kān** can only be used in questions expressing the hope that things are *not* what they seem to be, or surprise that they are.

Chapter 8

By the end of this chapter you will be able to make more complex sentences in Arabic. It concentrates on linking words and other 'little words' which expand the range of the sentence:

- *conjunctions, such as 'and', 'or' and 'when'*
- *the relative pronoun* **illi** *(who, which, etc.) and the particle* **in(n)** *(that)*
- *question words or particles (who?, what?, where?, etc.)*
- *negative particles and suffixes for saying 'not', 'don't', 'neither . . . nor', etc.*

38 Conjunctions

We have already used several conjunctions in the exercises. Now that many of the basic structures of Arabic have been given, we can say a little more about the two varieties of conjunctions in Arabic, the co-ordinating and the subordinating.

A. Co-ordinating conjunctions

The main co-ordinating conjunctions (i.e., those that link elements of equal grammatical value) are:

w and

In Arabic script this conjunction is written as part of the word. We shall keep it separate here to facilitate recognition, but it should never be stressed (cf. the 'n' in 'spick 'n' span').

It should always be read as if it formed part of the next word. Occasionally it is followed by a vowel, **a** or **i**, to facilitate pronunciation; it may even be preceded by an **i** to achieve the same end. When we have a series of things linked by this conjunction, it is repeated before each new item:

Aḥmad iw Sāmi w Huda zārūni mbāriḥ. (The insertion of an **i** before the conjunction that joins the first two names prevents the occurrence of three consecutive consonants.)

Huda bitrūḥ @a l-bank wi btīji mashi kull yōm. (What would happen if the **i** were inserted before the **w** or omitted?)

el-mōt wa la 'l-madhalleh.
I'd rather die than be humiliated.

lākin but

Aḥmad wa@ad yīji, lākin eẓ-ẓāhir inshaghal.
Aḥmad promised to come, but apparently he got busy.

Ribḥi @anīd, lākin qalbu ṭayyib.
Ribḥi is stubborn, but his heart is good/deep down he is a nice fellow.

bass but, only that, just, enough

Huda ḥilweh bass @anīdeh.
Huda is pretty, but she is rather pigheaded.

bass isma@ni.
Just listen to me.

bass, bass.
Enough, enough.

hāy sayyāra mumtāzeh, bass btiṣrif banzīn kthīr.
This is an excellent car; the only thing is that it guzzles (lit., spends, exhausts, uses) too much petrol.

aw or

lāzim tit@allam Ingilīzi aw Faransi ḥatta tit@arraf @a 'l-adab el-ḥadīth.
You should learn English or French in order to get to know modern literature.

willa or (in cases of alternative choices)

shāy willa qahweh?
Tea or coffee?

imma . . . aw either . . . or

imma btidfa@ kāsh aw btiktib shakk.
You either pay in cash or write a cheque.

lā . . . wa la neither . . . nor

lā ba@irfu wa la biddi at@arraf @alai.
I neither know him, nor do I want to be acquainted with him.

B. Subordinating conjunctions

The main subordinating conjunctions (i.e., those that link two grammatical items of unequal value, subordinating one to the other) are:
idha, in, law, lawla (on which see Section 43, Conditional sentences)

ḥatta in order that, so as to, until, even

el-ḥukūmeh raf@at el-jamārik ḥatta tḥidd min el-istīrād.
The government raised customs duties in order to curb imports.
istannaitak ḥatta 's-sā@a khamseh.
I waited for you until five o'clock.
ḥattā anta ya Brutus?
Et tu Brute?
ḥatta 'nta?
You too?
ḥatta Muḥsin mā biqdar iysā@dak.
Even Muḥsin cannot help you.

lamma when

lamma talfant lak kān Rushdi mawjūd.
When I phoned you, Rushdi was present.

ba@id mā after

ghayyar ra"yu ba@id mā kān qarrar yishtari el-bait.
He changed his mind (lit., opinion) after he had decided to buy the house.

wain mā wherever

wain mā bitrūḥ btisma@ nafs el-kalām.
Wherever you go, you hear the same words/the same story.

kīf mā however

kīf mā fakkart fīha, biyẓall shī nāqiṣ.
However you think about it, something is still missing.

bain mā while

bain mā rāḥ w riji@ katabit risāltain.
(lit. *Between the time he went and came back, I wrote two letters.) I wrote two letters while he was gone.*
el-ḥarāmi saraq shaqqit-hum bain mā kānu fi 's-sīnama.
The burglar burgled their apartment while they were at the cinema.

qabil mā before

itghadda bīhum qabil mā yit@ashshu bīk.
Have them for lunch before they have you for supper. (i.e., Attack while you are in a position of power; don't wait for the enemy to attack.)
tinsāsh tittaṣil qabil mā tsāfir.
Don't forget to call (me) up before you leave (lit., travel).

shū mā whatever

mish rāḥ aṣaddqak shū mā qult.
I will not believe you, whatever you say.
shū mā ḥakait btifhamni ghalaṭ.
Whatever I say, you misunderstand me.

mahma whatever

la tiy"as mahma ṣār.
Don't give up, whatever happens.

It is clear that the particle **mā** plays an important role in many of these expressions. It is merely an intensifier (cf. 'so' in 'whatsoever') and must not be confused with the negative **mā** (on which see Section 41 below).

li"ann/la"inn because

ẓallaina fi 'l-bait li"ann el-jaww bārid el-yōm.
We have stayed at home because the weather is cold today.

min shān/@ala shān/@a shān in order that, so that

jīt @ala shān aḥkī lak @an Ṣābir.
I have come in order to tell you about Ṣābir.
el-mudīr faṣal Kawthar min shān yi@ṭīha dars.
The manager fired Kawthar in order to give her a lesson.

Now some of these conjunctions can be attached to the pronominal suffixes:

lākin: lākinnu, lākinha, lākinkum, etc.
talfant lak fi 'l-utail lākinnak ma kuntish fi ghuruftak.
I phoned you at the hotel, but you weren't in your room.

li"ann/la"inn: li"anhum, la"inkum, etc.
intu bitdāf@u @annu li"ankum mā bti@irfū kifāyeh.
You are defending him because you don't know him (well) enough.

min shān, etc.: **min shānak, @ala shānu, @a shānik,** etc. (here the meaning changes: 'for your, his, her, sake')
kull hādha ḥaṣal @ala shānha.
All of this happened for her sake.
raḥ asāmḥu min shānak.
I will forgive him for your sake.

Vocabulary (section 38 and exercise 49)

@anīd/eh	stubborn
adab (*pl.* ādāb)	literature
banzīn	petrol
bārid/ bārdeh	cold
eẓ-ẓāhir	apparently
dāfa@ (III.1)	he defended
fakkar (II.1)	he thought
faşal (I.5)	he fired (from job)
ghalaṭ	wrong; wrongly
ḥadd (I.8)	he curbed; he put a limit to
ḥadīth/eh	modern
ḥarāmi	thief; burglar
ḥaşal (I.3)	took place
inshaghal (VII.1)	he got busy
istanna (X.2, but	he waited
imperative irregular: **istanna**)	
istīrād	importation
ittaşal (VIII.1)	he telephoned; he contacted
jamārik (*sing.* **jumruk**)	customs duties
kāsh	cash
kifāyeh	enough
madhalleh	humiliation
māshi/māshyeh	walking
mawjūd	present; available
mōt	death
mumtāz/eh	excellent
nāqiş/nāqşa	missing
qarrar (II.1)	he decided
qidir (I.1)	he was able to
ra"y	opinion
rafa@ (I.5)	he raised
risāltain (*dual of* **risāleh**)	two letters
sā@ad (III.1)	he helped
sāmaḥ (III.1)	he forgave
saraq (I.5)	he stole; he burgled
şaddaq (II.1)	he believed what was said or what he saw
şaraf (I.5)	he spent; he used up

t@ashsha (V.2)	he had supper (**@asha**)
tghadda (V.2)	he had lunch (**ghada**)
ṭayyib	(of heart) good; (of food) delicious; (of person) alive
utail (*pl.* **utailāt**)	hotel
yi"is (I.1)	he despaired
@indi, @indak, @ind-hum (etc.)	I, you, they have; at my, your, their house
asrār (*sing.* **sirr**)	secrets
baḥath (I.3)	he discussed
ballagh (II.1)	he conveyed a message; he reported
fāshil/fāshleh	unsuccessful
fi@il (*pl.* **af@āl**)	action; verb
fikra (*pl.* **afkār**)	idea
@ala fikra	by the way
fustān (*pl.* **fasatīn**)	dress
ḥaqīqa (*pl.* **ḥaqā"iq/ḥaqāyiq**)	truth
ḥawl	on; about
iḥtāj (VIII.2 but somewhat irregular)	he needed
khāyif/khāyfeh	afraid
māhir/māhreh	skilful
mittifqīn	in agreement
nuqṭa (*pl.* **nuqāṭ/nuqaṭ**)	point
qalīl/eh	little (in number or quantity)
qalqanīn	worried
sakrān/eh	drunk
sayyi"/sayy"a	bad
ṭabakh (I.4)	he cooked
ṭabbākh/a	cook
ṭabīkh	food; cooking
ṭaḥiyyāt (*sing.* **taḥiyyeh**)	greetings
ṭili@ (I.1)	he went up; he went out; he turned out to be
zāki/zākyeh	tasty; delicious

Exercise 49

tarjim el-jumal et-tālyeh la 'l-lugha 'l-ingilīziyyeh:

1 ana w inta mittifqīn ḥawl hāy en-nuqṭa.
2 ana ba@rif aqra Faransi, lākin mā ba@rif aḥki.
3 el-wu@ūd kthīreh bass el-fi@il qalīl.
4 Sāmi biyḥibbha lākinnu khāyif yiftaḥ el-mawḍū@.
5 ẓallaina qalqanīn @alai li"annu lā talfan wa la katab.
6 lamma tshūfu ballghu taḥiyyāti.
7 Fu"ād fāshil wain mā rāḥ.
8 Salwa ṭabbākha māhreh. kīf mā btuṭbukh biṭla@ ṭabīkh-ha zāki.
9 baḥtāj qarḍ min el-bank min shān aftaḥ supermarket.
10 mīn aḥsan, hādha 'l-fustān willa hādha?
11 imma btīji @indi aw bāji @indak; lāzim nibḥath hādhi 'l-mushkileh el-laileh.
12 ḥatta Salīm wiqif ḍiddi? ba@id kull illi @miltu @ala shānu?
13 lā tbī@ mahma dafa@ū lak.
14 ḥaka kull asrāru bain ma kān sakrān.
15 Othello qatal maratu qabil mā yi@rif el-ḥaqīqa.
16 shū mā qult w shū mā @milt, rāḥ tẓall fikirti @annak sayyi"a.

39 The relative pronoun

English has several relative pronouns including: 'which', referring back to things, 'who(m)/whose', referring back to people, and 'that', referring to either. The numerous relative pronouns of Standard Arabic have luckily all been reduced to a single one, **illi**, which is used in spoken Arabic to refer back to things or people, whether masculine or feminine, singular or plural. The only thing to be remembered here is that the first vowel of the word is dropped if the preceding word ends in a vowel. If the word that follows **illi** begins with a vowel, it, too, loses its initial vowel.

ana ḥakait lu.
I told him.
ana 'lli ḥakait lu.
(It was) I who told him.
iḥna 'lli ḥakainā lu. [Translate.]
hiyyeh 'lli ḥakat lu. [Translate.]
intin illi hakaitin lu. [Translate.]
illi 'nḥakā lak kidhib.
What (or: *That which) you were told is false.*

The word is often used at the beginning of semi-conditional sentences to introduce inferences, generalizations or proverbial sayings:

illi buṣbur binūl.
He who is patient eventually wins.
illi saraq esh-shaqqa lāzim bi@rif aṣḥābha.
He who burgled the apartment must be acquainted with its owners.
illi 'nkatab @a 'l-jabīn lāzim tishūfu 'l-@ain.
That which is written on the forehead must be witnessed by the eye. (proverb indicating belief in predestination)

There is, however, another particle, **in(n),** which is used very much like the English relative pronoun 'that'. In spoken Arabic, **in(n)** is often used at the beginning of an embedded sentence (i.e., a sentence that falls within a longer one) that is introduced by a verb or a verbal noun (about which more in Section 44 below).

smi@tu inn Aḥmad sāfar la 'l-Yābān?
Have you heard that Aḥmad has left for Japan?
(The embedded sentence here is: **Aḥmad sāfar** . . . : *Aḥmad has left* . . ., and it is introduced by **smi@tu inn**.)
akkad li Shukri inn el-mushkileh 'nḥallat.
Shukri asserted to me that the problem had been solved.
intu ḥakaitū li inkum musta@iddīn la musā@adit Ramzi; laish baṭṭaltu?
You told me that you were willing to help Ramzi; why have you reneged?

inti bti@irfi inni baḥibbik.
You know that I love you.

As you can see, **in(n)** can be attached to the pronominal suffixes:

mish mafrūḍ fīk innak tiḥkī lu @an asrārak.
You shouldn't talk to him about your private affairs (lit., secrets).

The **in(n)** sentence can also be introduced by linking or transitional words or phrases, such as **el-ḥaqīqa** (lit., 'the truth'), 'to tell you the truth'; **eş-şaḥīḥ** (lit., 'the correct thing'), 'actually', 'in fact', **el-mushkileh,** 'the problem is', 'the trouble is', and the like. These may often better be translated as subjects followed by 'is that':

el-ḥaqīqa inni mā shuft el-ḥādith lākin smi@it @annu.
To tell you the truth/In fact/The truth is that I didn't see the accident; I only heard about it.
el-mushkileh inn el-mudīr akhadh fikra sayyi"a @anni.
The problem is that the manager has formed (lit., has taken) a bad idea about me.

Vocabulary (section 39 and exercise 50)

@ain (*pl.* **@(u)yūn**)	eye
aşḥāb (*sing.* **şāḥib**)	owners
inḥall (VII.1 but somewhat irregular)	it was solved
jabīn	forehead
kidhib	falsehood; prevarication
mafrūḍ/a	supposed; imposed
mish mafrūḍ	(one) shouldn't/is not supposed to
musā@adeh	help
musta@idd/eh	ready; willing
nāl (I.10)	he got what he desired; he achieved sthg desirable

ṣabar (I.4)	he was patient
ashhur (*sing.* **shah(a)r**)	months
firiḥ (I.1)	he felt happy
ḥaẓẓ	luck
ishtaghal (VIII.1)	he worked
mabrūk!	congratulations!
makhṭūb/eh (*pl.* **makhṭubīn/ makhṭubāt**)	engaged
qabl ishwayy	a little while ago
sa@īd el-ḥaẓẓ	the lucky man

Exercise 50

tarjim el-jumal et-tālyeh la 'l-lugha 'l-ingilīziyyeh:

1 illi talfan qabl ishwayy huwweh Mḥammad.
2 mīn illi kānat ma@ak imbāriḥ fi maṭ@am X?
3 smi@it innik raḥ titzawwaji Shafīq; ṣaḥiḥ?
4 laish mā bti@irfi inna makhṭubin min khamis ashhur?
5 kunt a@rif innik makhṭūbeh, lākin mā kunt a@rif isim sa@īd el-ḥaẓẓ.
6 mīn illi @arrafu @alaiki?
7 @arrafatu @alayy Su@ād illi btishtaghil ma@u fi 'l-bank.
8 eş-ṣaḥiḥ inni friḥit lamma smi@it bi 'l-khabar. mabrūk.

40 Questions

Yes/no questions (questions which invite the answer 'yes' or 'no') are asked by letting one's voice rise at the end of the sentence in exactly the same way as you change the statement 'You saw him' into the question 'You saw him?' in English. So a rising tone changes the following statements into yes/no questions:

el-walad nāyim.
The boy is asleep.
el-walad nāyim?
Is the boy asleep?
el-mudīr mawjūd.
The manager is here.
el-mudīr mawjūd?
Is the manager here? (i.e., Can I talk to him?)
shuftūha.
You saw her.
shuftūha?
Did you see her?

The answer to these questions may be **aywa** ('yes'), **na@am** ('yes'; rather formal), **"ā** ('yes'; familiar), **la** ('no'; may end in a **hamza: la"** or even **la" "a**). The word **abadan** ('never') is also used to express categorical denials:

– **shufit qalami?**
Have you seen my pen?
– **abadan.**
Not at all.
– **ḥakat lak Huda shī?**
Has Huda told you anything?
– **la, abadan.**
No, nothing at all.

Other kinds of questions, however, are formed with the help of question words or particles:

mīn who / whom / what / which

mīn aja?
Who has come?
la (to) **mīn a@ṭait-ha?**
Whom did you give it to?
mīn aḥsan, hāy er-riwāyeh willa hāy?
Which is better, this novel or this one?

aish what

aish ra"yak?
What is your opinion?
@an aish btiḥki?
What are you talking about?
min aish btin@amal ha 'l-akleh?
What is this meal made of? (i.e. *What are the ingredients of this dish?)*

wain where

wain rāyiḥ?
Where are you going?
wain ḥaṭṭait el-kitāb? [Translate.]
min wain jay?
Where are you coming from?
(min wain = mnain: mnain jay?)
mnain lak ha 's-sayyāra?
Where did you get this car from?

mata when

mata rāḥ? *When did he leave?*

aimta where

aimta rāḥ?
aimta rāḥ nshūfak? *When shall we see you?*

laish why

laish bi@it sayyārtak?
Why have you sold your car?
laish mā ḥakait li?
Why didn't you tell me?

kīf how

kīf ḥālak?
(lit., *What is your state?) How are you?*
kīf btulfuẓ ha 'l-kilmeh?
How do you pronounce this word?

kīf bitqūl innu msāfir? ana shuftu 'l-yōm.
How/Why do you say he has gone abroad? I saw him today.
kīf ṣiḥḥtak?
(lit., How is your health?) How are you?

shū what

shū ma@na ha 'l-kilmeh?
What is the meaning of this word?
shū biddu?
What does he want?
shū 's-sīreh?
(lit., What is the biography/story?) What is the matter?
shū 'l-mawḍū@?
What is the matter?
shū 'lli ṣār?
What has happened?/What is the matter?

qaddaish how much/how many

qaddaish @umrak?
How old are you?
qaddaish biddak?
How much/many do you want?/How much are you asking for it?
qaddaish @adad sukkān el-Kuwait?
(lit., How many residents are there in Kuwait?) What is the population of Kuwait?
qaddaish fī @indak iwlād?
How many children do you have?

kam how many/how much

kam fari@ fī la 'l-bank?
How many branches does the bank have?
kam el-ujra?
What's the fare?
hāy el-majalleh b' kam?
What is the price of this magazine/How much do you sell it for?
kam nuskha min hādha el-kitāb biddak?
How many copies of this book do you want?

Vocabulary (exercise 51)

aş@ab min	more difficult than
masraḥiyyeh	play; drama
mukhtārāt	selections; an anthology
nashar (I.4)	he published
nath(i)r	prose
shi@(i)r	poetry
şu@ūbāt (*sing.* **şu@ūbeh**)	difficulties

Exercise 51

tarjim el-jumal et-tālyeh la 'l-lugha 'l-ingilīziyyeh:

1 mīn tarjam a@māl Shakespeare la 'l-lugha 'l-@arabiyyeh?
2 aimta tarjamha? tarjamha shi@ir willa nathir?
3 wain nashar hāy et-tarjameh w aish kānat eş-şu@ūbāt?
4 kīf kānat et-tarjameh fi ra"yak?
5 kam masraḥiyyeh tarjamū lu?
6 kam nuskha btunshuru @ādatan min kutub mithil kutub Shakespeare?
7 qaddaish thaman en-nuskha?
8 shū ra"yak fi tarjamit mukhtārāt min esh-shi@r el-@arabi la 'l-lugha 'l-ingilīziyyeh?
9 biyqūlu inn esh-shi@r 'l-@arabi şa@b. şaḥīḥ?
10 mīn aş@ab, shi@ir Shakespeare willa shi@r el-Mutanabbi?

41 Negative sentences

The negative particles are:

ma/mā (according to context) not
lā (used with imperfect verbs) don't
lā . . . wa la (used with both perfect and imperfect verbs) neither . . . nor

Sometimes **ma** is intensified by the suffix **-sh**, which functions very much like *pas* in French.

mā shuftu.
I haven't seen him.
ma shuftūsh.
(Note short vowel in **ma** and long one in verb.)
laish ma trūḥ bi 'ṭ-ṭayyāra?
Why don't you travel by air?
āsif, mā fī ghuraf fāḍyeh.
Sorry, there are no empty rooms.
@umrak mā tṣaddiq munāfiq.
Never believe a flatterer.
lā tzūru 'l-yōm.
Don't pay him a visit today.
lā tidfa@ akthar min @ishrīn dīnār.
Don't pay more than twenty dinars.
lā tiḍḥak @alayy wa la baḍḥak @alaik.
Let's not fool each other.
shāy willa qahweh? lā shāy wa la qahweh, shukran.
Neither tea nor coffee, thank you.
lā shuftu wa la araitu.
I neither saw him nor set eyes on him. (an emphatic denial)

An interesting combination of negatives is the word **balāsh,** which is used with imperfect verbs to mean 'don't': **balāsh tiḥkī lu,** 'You'd better not tell him'. But the word can also be used adjectivally to mean something like 'dirt cheap':

ishtarait-ha b' balāsh.
I bought it almost for nothing.
akhadht-ha b' balāsh.
I got it for free.
yā balāsh! How cheap!

Sometimes, especially with imperfect verbs, the **-sh** suffix is used without **ma** to indicate negation; in the process the mood of the verb changes into the imperative and the **b-** is also dropped:

tifhamnīsh ghalaṭ.
Don't misunderstand me.
truddish @alai.
Don't answer him back; ignore him.
tiḥkīsh ma@hum.
Don't talk to them.

However, the suffix **-sh** can be used with the imperfect to indicate simple negation without **ma/mā** at the beginning of the expression:

bashufūsh ha 'l-ayyam.
I don't see him these days.
barāsilhāsh.
I don't correspond with her.
bitḥibbūsh.
She does not love him.
biyḥibbhāsh. [Translate.]

There is also the particle **mish/mush,** which is used to negate adjectives:

mish mumkin
impossible
mish ma@qūl
unbelievable
azraq, mish aḥmar
blue, not red
mish @ārif aḥkī lu willa la".
I *don't know whether to tell him or not.*
mish lāzim
unnecessary

This last expression is often used to indicate negative advice:

mish lāzim ti@mal haik.
You shouldn't be doing this.

Vocabulary (exercise 52)

@amal (*pl.* **a@māl**)	work; action
el-muhimm	the important thing is . . .
ḥada or **ḥadd**	somebody
infaṣal (VII.1)	he was fired; he was separated
ittafaq (VIII.1)	he agreed with
miqtani@/miqtin@a	convinced
muntabih or **mintabih**	attentive
tadakhkhul	interference; intervention
tdakhkhal (V.1)	he interfered; he intervened
twassaṭ (V.1)	he acted as mediator; he used his good offices
waja@ (*pl.* **awjā@**)	pain
waja@ rās	headache

Exercise 52

tarjim el-jamal et-tālyeh la 'l-lugha 'l-ingilīzziyyeh:

1 balāsh ti@ṭīni wu@ūd; biddi minnak @amal.
2 ana ma smi@tish bi 'lli ṣār; inti smi@ti?
3 mish ma@qūl; Aḥmad ḥakā li w inta mawjūd.
4 eẓ-ẓāhir inni ma kuntish mintabih.
5 el-muhimm inhum qarraru yinfiṣlu li''anhum mish mumkin yittifqu.
6 mish mumkin ḥadd yitwassaṭ bainhum?
7 mā ba@rif, lākin inta mā titdakhkhalish.
8 ma atdakhkhalish? willa mīn lāzim yitdakhkhal? iḥna mish aṣdiqā''hum?
9 aṣdiqa''hum willa mish aṣdiqa''hum, et-tadakhkhul mā bijīb illa waja@ er-rās.
10 ana mish miqtani@.

42 Negation of preposition with pronoun

We said earlier that prepositions can be followed by attached pronouns. Some of these combinations can be negated by **mā/ma** and / or **-sh**. When this negative suffix is tagged on to some of the pronominal suffixes, certain changes occur that take the following forms (see Section 20 for the positive forms):

bi: biyyīsh, bikīsh, bikīsh, bihūsh, bihāsh, bināsh, bikūsh/ bikummish, bikinnish, bihummish, bihinnish

biyyīsh maraḍ.
(lit., *No sickness in me.) I'm not sick.*
bikummish khair.
(lit., *No good in you.) You're no good.*

fi: suffixes as in **bi**. More often than **bi**, this preposition is used to mean 'there is / are'; when so used, its vowel becomes long: **fī**.

– **fī nakhil fi Libnān?**
Are there any date trees in Lebanon?
– **lā, ma fīsh** (or **ma fishsh**).
No, there aren't any.
– **fī ma@ak maṣāri?**
Have you any money?
– **aywa, fi.**
Yes, I have.

When, however, it is used in its basic prepositional sense it is negated by means of **mish/mush:**

Sa@īd mish fi 'l-maktab.
Sa@īd is not in the office.

@ala: @alayyīsh, @alaikīsh, @alaikīsh, @alaihūsh, @alaihāsh, @alaināsh, @alaikūsh/@alaikummish, @alaikinnish, @alaihummish, @alaihinnish (in all of these, **ai** is short and **ma** is obligatory)

ma @alayyīsh dhanb.
(lit., *On me no guilt.) I'm not guilty/I'm not responsible.*
ma @alaihāsh ḥaki.
(lit., *On her no talk.) She's all right.*
ma @alaināsh dyūn.
(lit., *On us no debts.) We're free of debt.*

ila: ilīsh, ilkīsh, ilkīsh, ilūsh, ilhāsh, ilnāsh, ilkūsh/ilkummish, ilkinnish, ilhummish, ilhinnish (**ma** is obligatory and the **i** of the preposition is dropped)

ma līsh @annik ghina.
I can't do without you.
mā lhummish ḥaqq.
They have no right.
mā lkīsh fi 'ṭ-ṭayyib (*good*) **naṣīb.**
(lit., You don't have a share in good things.) You are unlucky.

ma@: ma@īsh, ma@kāsh/ma@kīsh, ma@kīsh, ma@ūsh, ma@hāsh, ma@nāsh, ma@kūsh/ma@kummish, ma@kinnish, ma@hummish, ma@hinnish (**ma** may be used but more often it is not)

ma@i khabar.
(lit., I have news.) I know.
ma@īsh khabar.
(lit., I don't have news.) I don't know.
ma@hāsh qalam.
She hasn't a pen.
ma@hinnish sayyāra.
They don't have a car.

min: minnīsh (rare), **minkāsh/minkīsh, minkīsh, minnūsh, minhāsh, minnāsh, minkūsh/minkummish, minkinnish, minhummish, minhinnish**

minhāsh fāydeh *(profit, use).*
She is hopeless. (i.e., She is terminally ill.)
ma minnāsh ḥada *(someone)* **bi@rif Faransi.**
None of us knows French.

minkūsh wāḥad bi@rif wain Suha?
Isn't there anyone amongst you who knows where Suha is?

@an: rarely negated by the suffix **-sh**

bala: gives only **balāsh** (on which see Section 41)

@ind: @indīsh, @indkāsh/@indkīsh, @indkīsh, @indūsh, @ind-hāsh, @indnāsh/@innāsh (note omission of **d**), **@indkūsh/@indkummish, @indkinnish, @ind-hummish, @ind-hinnish** (**ma** obligatory)

ma @indūsh khabar.
He doesn't know/hasn't heard the news.
ma @ind-hāsh fikra @an el-mawḍū@.
She has no idea about this matter.

bain: gives us negatives with **-sh** only with the plural pronouns: **bainnāsh, bainkūsh/bainkummish, bainkinnish, bainhummish, bainhinnish.**

bainhummish asrār.
They don't keep secrets from each other.
ma bainnāsh wāḥad *(one)* **bi@rif Almāni.**
Not one of us knows German.

It is to be noted, however, that many of these preposition + pronoun combinations are often negated by means of the phrase **ma fishsh:**

ma fishsh bainna wāḥad bi@rif Almāni.
ma fishsh bainhin asrār.
ma fishsh ma@i flūs.
ma fishsh @alaihum ḥaqq.

Exercise 53

tarjim el-jumal et-tālyeh la 'l-lugha 'l-@arabiyyeh:

1 I don't have any money.
2 She hasn't heard anything about the matter.
3 Are there any Germans (**Almān,** *sing.* **Almāni**) among you?
4 Where did you put the books?
5 She can't do without me.
6 Suha is not in her room.
7 She is not guilty.
8 Are there any date trees in Kew Gardens (**ḥadā"iq Kyū**)?

Chapter 9

This chapter builds on what you have learned about verbs. You will find out:

- *how to talk about what might have happened, what may happen, and what you hope will happen*
- *how you can form many nouns and adjectives from the verbs you know, according to regular patterns*

43 Conditional sentences

English expresses conditions by using words such as 'if', 'even if', 'unless'. In Arabic, the main conditional particles are **in, idha** (sometimes pronounced **iza**), **law** and **lawla** (sometimes pronounced **lōla**). The first two mean 'if' and are often interchangeable. The other two are negative in meaning: **law** denotes the non-occurrence of an event or a state because of the absence of the required conditions, while **lawla** indicates that the conditions or state now in existence would not have come about had not the proper conditions existed first. To begin with **law** and **lawla**, here are some examples:

A. law

law ḥakait li la-kunt sā@adtak.

Had you told me, I would certainly have helped you.

(The use of emphatic **la-** before (usually) perfect verbs is a frequent feature of this type of sentence. This **la-** is used in the main clause, not in the **law** or **lawla** clause.)

law khaṭabt-ha la-wāfaqat.
Had you proposed to her, she would have accepted.

Obviously, these constructions are similar to the impossible condition (also called the 'third conditional', i.e., 'If I had . . ., I would have . . .') in English. But the expression **ḥatta wa law** is similar to 'even if':

iqtiṣād el-balad mish raḥ yitḥassan ḥatta wa law tḍā@afat as@ār el-fōsfāt.
The economy of the country would not improve even if phosphate prices were to double.
mish raḥ aṣaddiq ḥatta wa law ḥalaft *(swore)* **ibsharafak**.
I would not believe what you are saying (lit., I *am not going to believe), even if you swore upon your honour.*

The phrase **law samaḥt,** originally conditional, simply means 'if you don't mind'. It is used in such circumstances as when one wants to worm one's way through a crowd, to interrupt a speaker, to object politely to what is being said, and in a whole variety of similar situations.

Used alone, **wa law** means 'even so', suggesting persistence in one's position even when certain conditions have been met:

– **ifriḍ innu i@tadhar lak?**
Suppose he apologized to you?
– wa law!
Even so! (i. e., *That wouldn't change my position.)*

With a surprised tone, the word means 'that much?', 'to that extent?'

– bakrahu kurh el-@ama.
I hate him as much as I hate blindness. (a cliché expressing intense hatred)
– wa law?
To that extent?

B. **lawla:** were it not for

lawla innak akhadhtu la 'l-mustashfa ra"san la-kān māt.
Had you not taken him to the hospital immediately, he would certainly have died.
lawla 'n-nafṭ la-mā ḥaṣal kull ha 't-taqaddum et-tiknōlōji fi 'l-@ālam.
Were it not for oil, all this technological progress would not have taken place.

Unlike **law, lawla** can be attached to the pronominal suffixes (but note that the form of the first person singular is **lawlāy** and that of the third person singular, feminine gender, is **lawlāki**):

lawlāk la-mutna mn (for **min**) **el-jū@.**
But for you, we would have starved to death.
lawlāki la-mā 'ntaḥar Sāmi.
Were it not for you, Sāmi would not have committed suicide.
(To which verb class does the verb **intaḥar** belong?)

C. **in** *and* **idha**

As for the other two particles, **in** cannot be followed by the imperfect, but **idha** can be followed by both the perfect and the imperfect. As the examples below will show, the use of the perfect or imperfect after **idha** has little effect on the meaning apart from, perhaps, a suggestion of greater improbability in the perfect.

idha bti@rif inglīzi, iqrā li ha 'l-i@lān.
If you know English, read this ad to me.
(The assumption here is that the person addressed may know English.)
idha kunt bti@rif inglīzi, iqrā . . .
(The translation would be the same, but the Arabic sentence may suggest a slight challenge:
I don't know whether you know English or not, but if you say you do, here is the test.)
in shuftu, sallim li @alai.
If you see him, give him my greetings/say hello to him.

(Here the perfect in the Arabic sentence does not suggest unlikelihood, as the past tense in English does. This is why the translation changes the perfect of the original into the present tense.)
idha bitḥibbha, laish ma tukhṭubha?
If you love her, why don't you propose to her?

Both **in** and **idha** can be used in the sense of 'whether':

mā ba@rif in/idha kān fi 'l-bait willa lā.
I don't know whether he is at home or not.

In, but not **idha**, is used in the conventional phrase **in shā" Allāh** (emphatic form) or **in shā 'lla** (in less emphatic speech), which literally means 'if God wills it', 'God willing', but is really nothing more than a mild expression of hope.

– **raḥ trūḥ la 'l-Iskandariyyeh hāy es-saneh?**
Will you be going to Alexandria this year?
– **in shā 'lla.**
I hope so.

The phrase **illā idha** means 'unless', and the clause that follows it comes after the main clause:

lā tghayyru kutub el-lugha 'l-ingilīziyyeh illā idha wajadtu aḥsan minha.
Don't change the English language books unless you find better ones.
raḥ atruk hāy esh-shaqqa illā idha nazzal ṣaḥibha 'l-ujra.
I will leave this apartment unless the owner lowers the rent.

The word **illa** itself means 'except':

kullhum aju illa Mḥammad.
They all came except Moḥammad.

D. No particle

Finally, there is a type of conditional sentence in which no particle is used. It starts with an imperative expressing the condition to be met first, before the state of affairs in the other part of the sentence can exist:

@īsh kthīr bitshūf kthīr.
Live long and you will see much.
khālif tu@raf.
Be different and you will get known.
(A proverbial saying from Standard Arabic in which the verb **tu@raf** is in the passive voice, a form no longer used in spoken Arabic except in such importations from the standard language. The phrase is ironic in that it suggests that the person is deliberately being different in order to get known.)

Vocabulary (section 43 and exercise 54)

@ama	blindness
@āsh (I.11)	he lived
bada(") (I.3)	he started
fōsfāt	phosphates
ḥalaf (I.5)	he swore (a solemn oath)
i@lān	advertisement
i@tadhar (VIII.1)	he apologized
intaḥar (VIII.1)	he committed suicide
iqtiṣād	economy; economics
kirih (I.1)	he hated
khālaf (III.1)	he acted differently; he differed with
khaṭab (I.4)	he proposed
Maṣir	Egypt
mustashfa	hospital
ra"san	immediately
sallam (II.1)	he greeted
samaḥ (I.3)	he allowed; he did not mind
sharaf	honour
taqaddum	progress

tarak (I.4)	he left; he abandoned
tḍā@af (VI.1)	it doubled; it increased twofold
tḥassan (V.1)	he improved
wajad (I.5)	he found (out)
akhīr	last (*adj.*)
en-Nīl	the Nile
fi@lan	indeed
ghāli/ghālyeh	(of prices) expensive; (of persons) dear
intāj	production
jādd	serious
khamseh bi 'l-miyyeh	five percent
ṣādirāt	exports
ṣaḥra	desert
warṭa	predicament

Exercise 54

tarjim el-jumal et-tālyeh la 'l-lugha 'l-ingilīziyyeh:

1 law fī ḥada fi 'l-bait la-radd @a 't-talafōn.
2 lawla 'n-Nīl lā-ṣārat Maṣir ṣaḥra.
3 iqtiṣād el-balad mish raḥ yitḥassan illā idha tḍā@afat eṣ-ṣādirāt.
4 esh-sharikeh raḥ tifṣil nuṣṣ el-@ummāl idha mā tḍā@af el-intāj hāy es-saneh.
5 qarait kull el-kitāb illa 'l-faṣl el-akhīr.
6 in kunt ṣadīqi fi@lan, sā@idni fi hāy el-warṭa.
7 khallīna nibda 'l-mashrū@ idha kunt jādd.
8 biyẓall es-si@ir ghāli ḥatta wa law nazzal lak khamseh bi 'l-miyyeh.

44 Derived forms

We have given verb patterns for Classes I–XI (Sections 22–32) and said that from them one can form dozens of words, all related in meaning. These derived forms, too, fall into patterns, which it will be useful for you to learn. We shall give here three categories: the first is broadly similar to the English gerund (the '-ing' form of the verb, which names an activity such as 'walking', 'drinking', 'reading', etc.); the second names the agent of the action (i.e., the one who performs it: 'the walker', 'drinker', 'reader', etc.); and the third names the person or thing on whom or on which the action falls (roughly equivalent to the past participle in English: '(distance) walked', '(liquid) drunk', '(passage) read', etc.). Remember, however, that in Arabic all of these are nouns and that the participles function also as adjectives, as participles do in English. We shall call the first category the verbal noun (VN) and the other two the active and passive participle (AP and PP) respectively. To illustrate, the verb **daras** (I.4: 'he studied') gives us **dirāseh** (the process of studying: 'study') for the verbal noun, **dāris** (the person doing the studying: 'scholar', 'student') and **madrūs** (that which is studied: anything from a lesson to a project). The verb **darras** (II.1: 'he taught') gives us **tadrīs** (the process or profession of 'teaching'), **mudarris** (the person doing the teaching: 'teacher') and **mudarras** (the person who or the thing that is taught: anything from a lesson being taught to a student receiving instruction).

In the following paragraphs we shall give the derived forms of a selection of verbs already given under verb Classes I–XI, in the order in which they are listed under each class, and all additional meanings created by the derivation. It is to be noted that the patterns for Classes II–XI are fairly regular and that the participles of Class I are regular, too. Only the verbal nouns of Class I are too unpredictable for any useful patterns to emerge. These are better learnt individually.

Class I

Active participle: **CāCiC** (**CāCi** for truncated verbs)
Passive participle: **maCCūC** (**maCCi** for truncated verbs)

I.1	VN	AP	PP
shirib	**shurb/shurub** drinking	**shārib** drinker	**mashrūb** thing drunk; has been drunk
simi@	**samā@** hearing	**sāmi@** hearer	**masmū@** loud enough to be heard
@irif	**ma@rifeh** knowledge	**@ārif** one who knows	**ma@rūf** known; well known

I.2			
nisi	**nisyān**	**nāsi**	**mansi** forgotten
riḍi	**riḍa**	**rāḍi** feels satisfied	**marḍi** (**@annu**)* causes satisfaction
ṣiḥi	**ṣaḥayān**	**ṣāḥi** wakeful, alert	[PP not used]

* Preposition **@an** + pronominal suffix **-u** = **@annu**, meaning (here) 'about, over'

I.3			
fataḥ	**fatḥ/fatiḥ**	**fātiḥ** opener, conqueror	**maftūḥ** open, opened
najaḥ	**najāḥ** success	**nājiḥ** successful	[PP not used]
zara@	**zirā@a**	**zāri@** farmer	**mazrū@** planted, cultivated
ba@ath	**ba@th** sending, resurrection	**bā@ith**	**mab@ūth** sent, emissary
sa"al	**su"āl** question	**sā"il** questioner	**mas"ūl** asked, responsible
mana@	**man@/mani@** prohibition	**māni@** prohibitor	**mamnū@** prohibited

I.4

katab	**kitābeh**	**kātib** writer, author	**maktūb** written; letter
qatal	**qatl/qatil**	**qātil** killer, murderer	**maqtūl** murdered (person)
sakan	**sukna**	**sākin** resident	**maskūn** inhabited; haunted
sakan	**sukūn** quietude	**sākin** quiet	[PP in this sense not used]
nashar	**nashr/nashir**	**nāshir** publisher	**manshūr** published

I.5

kasar	**kasr/kasir**	**kāsir**	**maksūr** broken
sajan	**sijn/sijin**	**sājin** [rarely used]	**masjūn** prisoner
rasam	**rasm/rasim**	**rāsim** [rarely used]	**marsūm** drawn; edict
ghasal	**ghasl/ ghasil**	**ghāsil**	**maghsūl** washed, clean

I.6

masha	**mashi**	**māshi**	**mamshi** (of a track:) beaten
rama	**rami**	**rāmi** thrower, marksman	**marmi** thrown; neglected
saqa	**saqi**	**sāqi** giver of drinks (archaic)	**masqi** irrigated
kawa	**kawi**	**kāwi** caustic	**makwi** cauterized; ironed

I.7

ḥaṭṭ put	**ḥaṭṭ**	**ḥāṭiṭ**	**maḥṭūṭ**
radd answered, returned	**radd**	**rādid**	**mardūd** returned; returns (from a business)
sadd shut	**sadd**	**sādid**	**masdūd**

I.8

madd extended	**madd**	**mādid**	**mamdūd**
ḥabb	**ḥubb**	**ḥābib** desiring	**maḥbūb** desired, beloved
ḥass	**iḥsās** feeling	**ḥāsis** able to feel	**maḥsūs** felt, tangible

I.9

ẓall remained	[VN not used]	**ẓālil**	[PP not used]

I.10

shāf saw	**shōf/shawafān**	**shāyif**	**mashyūf** [rare]
māt died	**mōt**	**mayyit** dead [note double consonants for long vowel]	[PP not used]
rāḥ went	**rawāḥ/rawaḥān**	**rāyiḥ** going to	[PP not used]
qāl said	**qōl/qawalān**	**qāyil**	[PP not used]
qād led	**qiyādeh**	**qāyid, qā''īd** leader	[PP not used]
kān was	**kōn/kawn** being, universe	**kāyin, kā''in**	[PP not used]

I.11

ṣār became	**ṣayrūra** [literary] **ṣayarān** [rare]	**ṣāyir** becoming	[PP not used]
ṭār flew	**ṭayarān** flight, airways	**ṭāyir**	[PP not used]
jāb brought	**jayabān**	**jāyib**	[PP not used]

I.12

nām slept	**nōm**	**nāyim**	[PP not used]

bāt spent the night	**bayāt, bayatān**	**bāyit** spending the night; (of news:) stale	**mabīt** [somewhat irregular:] an instance of spending the night which may require payment of money [may be used instead of VN]
khāf	**khōf** fear	**khāyif** afraid	[PP not used]

The following sentences illustrate certain uses of some of the words given above. We have left several of them untranslated, for you to attempt yourself (see Exercise 55). You can of course consult the translations in the Key if you wish.

1 **shurb el-khamra mamnū@ fi 'l-Islām.**

2 **inta shārib?**

Are you drunk?

3 **qahwitku mashrūbeh.** (in answer to an invitation to drink coffee:)

Consider it drunk, thank you.

4 **Tawfīq el-Ḥakīm kātib Maṣri ma@rūf.**

5 **ana ṣōti masmū@ fi 'l-bank.**

I have some influence (lit., My voice is loud enough to be heard) at the bank.

6 **en-nisyān min @alāmāt el-kabar.**

Forgetfulness is one of the signs of old age.

7 **akhūna kān ḥābib yikhda@ni, bass ana kunt ṣāḥi.**

Our friend there was planning to cheat me, but I was alert.

8 **udkhul, el-bāb maftūḥ.**

9 **kull el-mawaḍī@ maftūḥa la 'n-niqāsh.**

10 **mustaqbal iqtiṣād el-balad bi@tamid @ala 'z-zirā@a.**

11 **el-mab@ūth el-Amrīki jāyib ma@u risāleh min wazīr el-khārijiyyeh.**

The American emissary is bringing/carrying a letter from the Secretary of State.

12 **kitābi manshūr fi Barīṭānya, lākin mamnū@ bai@u fi Amrīka.**

13 **kul w lā tkhāf; kull shi maghsūl ghasil jayyid.**

14 **wiṣil en-niqāsh ila ṭarīq masdūd.**
The discussion reached a dead end/led nowhere.

15 **kānat hadhi ramyeh min ghair rāmi.**
This was sheer luck (lit., a bull's eye without a marksman).

16 **ktābak ẓall mabḥṭūṭ @a 'r-raff kull ha 'l-muddeh.**
Your book remained on the shelf all this time.

17 **mardūd el-kitāb aqall min takālīf nashru.**
Returns (or *Earnings) from the book are less than the costs of publishing it.*

18 **ana ḥāsis inn el-@ilāqāt bain Ḥamdi w Sāmi sayyi"a.**
I feel that relations between Ḥamdi and Sāmi are bad.

19 **inti shāyif haik?**
Do you think so?/Is this your opinion?

20 **ana rāyiḥ azūrha bukra.**
I'll pay her a visit tomorrow.

21 **sharikāt eṭ-ṭayarān btikhsar bi sabab et-tanāfus bain ba@aḍ.**
Airline companies lose because of competition among themselves.

22 **laish khāyif? el-mōt nōm ṭawīl. w shū raḥ tikhsar ghair ta@āstak? imma bit@īsh ib sharaf aw bitmūt ib sharaf.**

Vocabulary (section 44, class I)

@alamāt (*sing.* **@alāmeh**)	signs
aqall	less than
bai@	sale
bain ba@aḍ	among each other
ghair	except
i@tamad (VIII.1)	he depended or relied on
jayyid	well
kabar	old age
khada@ (I.3)	he cheated; he fooled
khamra	alcoholic drink
khāriji/yyeh	external; foreign (affairs)
khisir (I.1)	he lost
mab@ūth	emissary

min ghair	without
niqāsh	discussion
rāmi	a thrower; a marksman
ramyeh	a hit
ta@āseh	unhappiness; misery
takālīf (*sing.* **taklifeh** or **taklufeh**)	costs
tanāfus	competition
ṭarīq masdūd	blind alley; dead end
zirā@a	agriculture

Class II

Verbal noun: **taCCīC** or **tiCCīC**, the first being more formal
Active participle: **m(u)CaCCiC**; retention of **u** more formal
Passive participle: **m(u)CaCCaC**; retention of **u** more formal

II.1

rajja@	**tarjī@** returning	**m(u)rajji@** returner	**m(u)rajja@** sthg returned
harrab	**tahrīb**	**m(u)harrib**	**m(u)harrab** smuggled, contraband
haddad	**tahdīd**	**muhaddid** threatening	**muhaddad** under a threat
ḥarrar	**taḥrīr**	**muḥarrir** liberator, editor	**m(u)ḥarrar** liberated, edited

II.2 Participles here are rarely used, although they can be coined. Even the verbal nouns are not very frequent.

mashsha caused/helped to walk/go	**tamshiyeh**
mawwat killed	**tamwīt**
ṭayyar caused to fly	**taṭyīr**

23 **tahrīb el-mukhaddirāt mushkileh @ālamiyyeh.**
24 **shū bi@malu bi 'l-kutub el-murajja@a** (or **li-mrajja@a**)?
25 **kull el-@alam muhaddad ib** (for **bi**) **khaṭar el-mukhaddirāt.**
26 **mā akthar mā** (*How frequent it is*) **ṣār muḥarrir el-waṭan diktatōr** (*dictator*) **lāzim el-waṭan yitḥarrar minnu.**

Class III

Verbal noun: **m(u)CāCaCa**; final **a**, a feminine ending, may take the **eh** form
Active participle: **m(u)CāCiC**
Passive participle: **m(u)CāCaC**

III.1

wāfaq	**muwāfaqa**	**m(u)wāfiq**	**m(u)wāfaq**
agreed			
ḥārab	**muḥārabeh**	**muḥārib**	**muḥārab**
fought			
@ālaj	**mu@ālajeh**	**mu@ālij**	**mu@ālaj**
treated			
hājar	**muhājara**	**muhājir**	**muhājar** [rare]
emigrated			

III.2
Here the verbal noun lengthens its final **a.**

nāda	**munādā**	**munādi**	**munāda**
called			
māsha	**mumāshā**	**mumāshi**	**mumāsha** [rare]
went along with			
lāqa	**mulāqāt**	**mulāqi**	**mulāqa** [rare]
met	meeting	person who meets	

27 **akhadht muwāfaqa min abūy min shān dirāsit el-mawḍū@; huwweh mwāfiq min ḥaith el-mabda".**
28 **muḥārabit el-iḥtikār wājib waṭani.**
29 **hādha 'l-marīḍ mu@ālaj @ilāj sayyi".**

30 **muhājarit en-nabi Muḥammad min Makkeh ila 'l-Madīneh hiyyeh bidāyit et-taqwīm el-Hijri.**
31 **khallīna nibda bi munādāt el-asma".**
Let us begin by calling the names.

Vocabulary (section 44, class III)

asmā" (*sing.* **isim**)	names
bidāyeh	beginning
iḥtikār	monopoly
marīḍ	sick (person)
min ḥaith el-mabda"	as a matter of principle; to begin with
nabi	prophet
taqwīm	calendar
wājib (*pl.* **wājibāt**)	duty

Class IV

Verbal noun: **iCCāC**, for truncated verbs **iCCā"**
Active participle: **muCCiC**, for truncated verbs **muCCi**
Passive participle: **muCCaC**, for truncated verbs **muCCa**

IV.1

anzal took down	**inzāl**	**munzil**	**munzal**
atlaf damaged	**itlāf**	**mutlif**	**mutlaf**
akhraj took out	**ikhrāj**	**mukhrij**	**mukhraj**
as@af gave first aid to	**is@āf**	**mus@if**	**mus@af**

IV.2

awṣa recommended, left a will	**īṣā"***	**mūṣi***	**mūṣa***
anha put an end to	**inhā"** putting an end to	**munhi** the one who puts an end to	**munha** [rare]

* Note dropping of **w** from derived forms and substitution of long vowels

32 **ista@addat el-madīneh ḥatta twājih khaṭar el-inzāl min el-baḥar.**
33 **yimkin iykūn ghalṭān; kalāmu mish munzal.**
34 **itlāf el-wathā"iq er-rasmiyyeh jarīmeh khaṭīreh.**
35 **ana mukhrij mutakhaṣṣiṣ fi 'l-ikhrāj el-masraḥi.**
36 **el-mukhrajāt lāzim titnāsab ma@ el-mudkhalāt.**
37 **nādaitu sayyārit el-is@āf? ḥāltu khaṭīreh jiddan.**
38 **inhā" khadamāt Aḥmad kān ghalṭa; mā fī ḥada bi@rif tafāṣīl el-@amal mithlu.**

Vocabulary (section 44, class IV)

ghalṭa (*pl.* **ghalṭāt** or **aghlāṭ**)	an error
ghalṭān/eh	(of a person) wrong, mistaken
ikhrāj	film or play directing
inzāl	landing (military sense)
ista@add (like class I.7 verbs but with the prefix of class X.1)	he prepared himself; he was ready; he was willing
jarīmeh (*pl.* **jarā"im**)	crime
khadamāt (*sing.* **khidmeh**)	services
khaṭīr/eh	serious, dangerous
masraḥi/yyeh	theatrical
mudkhalāt	input
mukhrajāt	output
mukhrij	director (of film or play)

munzal	(of words, sayings, writings) divine revelation
mutakhaṣṣiṣ/a	specialized
rasmi/yyeh	official
tafāṣīl	details
tnāsab (VI.1)	he / it was commensurate with or proportionate to
wathā"iq (*sing.* **wathīqa**)	documents

Class V

Verbal noun: **taCaCCuC**, for truncated verbs **taCaCCi**
Active participle: **m(u)taCaCCiC** or **mitCaCCiC,** and for truncated verbs **m(u)taCaCCi** or **mitCaCCi**
Passive participle: none

V.1

t@allam	**ta@allum**	**muta@allim/mit@allim** educated
t@arraf	**ta@arruf**	**muta@arrif/mit@arrif** acquainted with
tdhakkar	**tadhakkur**	**mutadhakkir/mitdhakkir** remembering

V.2

tghadda had lunch	**taghaddi**	**mutaghaddi/mitghaddi**
tsalla had fun	**tasalli**	**mutasalli/mitsalli**

39 **lā budd min ta@allum mabādi" el-kumbyūtar qabil dirāsit @ilm 'l-ihsā".**
40 **et-ta@arruf @ala asbāb el-mushkileh huwweh 'l-khuṭweh 'l-ūla la ḥallha.**
41 **ana mish mitdhakkir mīn jāb li hadha 'l-qamīṣ min Barīs, Shawqi willa Layla.**
42 **– tfaḍḍal tghadda ma@na.**
– shukran, mitghaddi.
43 **eẓ-ẓāhir Aḥmad kān byitsalla ma@ Samīra. tarak-ha bidūn mā yiḥkī lha ma@ es-salāmeh.**

Vocabulary (section 44, class V)

@il(i)m (*pl.* **@ulūm**)	science
ḥall (*pl.* **ḥulūl**)	solution
iḥṣā"	statistics
khaṭweh or **khuṭweh** (*pl.* **khaṭawāt** or **khuṭuwāt**)	step
lā budd min	it is necessary to or that; it is inevitable that . . .
ma@ es-salāmeh	goodbye
mabādi" (*sing.* **mabda"**)	principles; rudiments
t(a)faḍḍal (V.1)	he was good enough to; be good enough to

Class VI

Verbal noun: **taCāCuC**, for truncated verbs **taCāCi**
Active participle: **mutaCāCiC** or **mitCāCiC,** for truncated verbs **mutaCāCi** or **mitCāCi**
Passive participle: **mutaCāCaC,** for truncated verbs **mutaCāCa** (but the PP is rare)

VI.1

tqātal fought with	**taqātul**	**mutaqātil/mitqātil**	**mutaqātal @alai***
tbādal exchanged	**tabādul**	**mutabādil/mitbādil**	**mutabādal**
tfāham came to a mutual understanding	**tafāhum**	**mutafāhim/mitfāhim**	**mutafāham @alai***
tsā"al wondered	**tasā"ul**	**mutasā"il/mitsā"il @annu****	**mutasā"al**

* Preposition **@ala** + pronominal suffix **-u** = **@alai**, meaning (here) 'about', so 'fought about', 'mutual understanding about'.
** Preposition **@an** + pronominal suffix **-u** = **@annu**, meaning (here) 'about', so 'wondered about'.

VI.2

tnāsa	**tanāsi**	**mutanāsi/mitnāsi**	[PP not used]

pretended to forget

tmāda	**tamādi**	**mutamādi/mitmādi**	[PP not used]

went too far; went beyond reason

44 **el-gharīb innu taqātul el-aṣdiqā" ashadd @ādatan min taqātul el-a@dā".**
45 **jara mu"akhkharan tabādul sufarā" mā bain dawlitna w dawlitkum, w ṣār fī bainna @ilāqāt tijāriyyeh mutabādaleh.**
46 **waqqa@at duwal el-manṭiqa mu"akhkharan mudhakkirit tafāhum ḥawl ḥuqūq eṣ-ṣaid fi 'l-khalīj.**
47 **taṣā"ulak fi maḥallu; ana nafsi mish @ārif sabab illi ḥaṣal.**
48 **fahhimni, inta nāsi willa mitnāsi? et-tanāsi mā bifīd.**
49 **et-tamādi fi 'l-ghalaṭ aswa" min el-ghalaṭ nafsu.**

Vocabulary (section 44, class VI)

a@dā" (*sing.* **@aduww**)	enemies
ashadd	more intense; stricter; more powerful
aswa"	worse
dawleh (*pl.* **duwal**)	state
fād (I.11)	he benefited someone or was useful to
fi maḥallu, maḥallha (etc.)	in the right place; (of a suggestion or an objection) well taken
gharīb	stranger
el-gharīb	the stranger; the strange thing about it is; oddly enough
ḥuqūq (*sing.* **ḥaqq**)	rights
jara (I.6)	it took place
khalīj	gulf
(mā) bain	between

manṭiqa (*pl.* **manāṭiq**)	region; district; area
mudhakkira	memorandum
ṣaid	fishing
tijāri/yyeh	commercial, trading

Class VII

Verbal noun: **inCiCāC**, for truncated verbs **inCiCā"**
Active participle: **munCaCiC** or **miniCCiC**, for truncated verbs **munCaCi**
Passive participle: none

VII.1

inkasar got broken	**inkisār**	**munkasir/miniksir**
inqalab got overturned; turned coat	**inqilāb** an overturning; a coup	**munqalib/miniqlib**
indafa@ bolted, rushed; was pushed	**indifā@**	**mundafi@/minidfi@** reckless; incited by others

VII.2

inqaḍa reached an end	**inqiḍā"** termination	**munqaḍi/miniqḍi** is over; is finished
injala cleared up	**injilā"**	**munjali/minijli**

50 **inkisār rijlu mā mana@u min el-istimrār fi ḥubb er-riyāḍa.**
51 **sabab ẓuhūr qaws el-quzaḥ huwweh inkisār eḍ-ḍaww fi 'l-maṭar.**
52 **el-inqilābāt el-@askariyyeh addat ilā @adam el-istiqrār fi kthīr min duwal el-@ālam eth-thālith.**
53 **inta mundafi@ akthar min el-lāzim; khaffif ishwayy.**
54 **inqaḍat muddit es-samāḥ w mā saddad dyūnu.**
55 **injilā" el-mawqif hunāk raḥ yākhudh fatra ṭawīleh. lā titsarra@.**

Vocabulary (section 44, class VII)

@adam	lack of; non-existence
@askari/yyeh	military
adda (II.2)	it led to
ḍaww	light (n.)
inqilāb	overturning; coup d'état
istimrār	continuation
istiqrār	stability
khaffif ishwayy	slow down a little; take it easy
mana@ (I.3)	he prohibited or prevented
mawqif (*pl.* **mawāqif**)	situation; position
muddit es-samāḥ	grace period
qaws quzaḥ	rainbow
rijil (*pl.* **arjul**)	leg
riyāḍa	sports
saddad (II.1)	he paid back
samāḥ	forgiveness
tsarra@ (V.1)	he acted hastily
ẓuhūr	appearance

Class VIII

Verbal noun: **iCtiCāC**, for truncated verbs **iCtiCā"**
Active participle: **muCtaCiC**, for truncated verbs **muCtaCi,** for verbs ending in double letters **muCtaCC**
Passive participle: **muCtaCaC**, for truncated verbs **muCtaCa**

VIII.1

ifta@al contrived (e.g., a problem, a fight)	**ifti@āl**	**mufta@il**	**mufta@al**
istama@ listened	**istimā@**	**mustami@**	[PP not used]
intaṣar triumphed	**intiṣār**	**muntaṣir**	[PP not used]
intaẓar waited, expected	**intiẓār**	**muntaẓir**	**muntaẓar**
imtadd extended, stretched	**imtidād**	**mumtadd** [also **mimtadd**]	[PP not used]
ishtadd got stronger, got worse	**ishtidād**	**mushtadd** [also **mishtadd**]	[PP not used]

VIII.2

ishtaha desired	**ishtihā"**	**mushtahi**	**mushtaha**
intaha came to an end	**intihā"**	**muntahi** has expired	**muntaha minnu*** finished; done away with

* Preposition **min** + pronominal suffix **-u** = **minnu**, meaning (here) 'with'. The word **muntaha** is also used as an intensifier: **muntaha 'l-ḥubb** 'extreme love'; **muntaha 'l-karam** 'great generosity'.

56 **el-@awāṭif el-mufta@aleh btiḥtāj ila juhud kbīr.**
57 **el-mustami@īn mallu min tikrār hāy el-aghāni es-sakhīfeh.**
58 **el-ḥarb el-@ālamiyyeh eth-thāltheh mish raḥ iykūn bīha muntaṣir aw munkasir.**
59 **shū muntaẓar min wāḥad mithlu?**
60 **fī buq@it nafṭ kbīreh @ala imtidād es-sāḥil el-gharbi.**
61 **mutawaqqa@ ishtidād el-bard khilāl el-usbū@ el-qādim.**
62 **ana mushtahi/mishtahi/misht-hi asma@ minnak kilmeh ḥilweh, lākin ma@ el-asaf.**
63 **raḥ azūrkum in shā" Allāh ba@d intihā" el-faṣl ed-dirāsi.**
64 **hādha muntaha 'l-karam minnak.**
This is exceedingly generous of you. (**muntaha** used as an intensifier)

Vocabulary (section 44, class VIII)

@awāṭif (*sing.* **@āṭfeh**)	feelings
aghāni (*sing.* **ughniyeh**)	songs
buq@a (*pl.* **buqa@**)	spot
buq@it nafṭ	oil slick
gharbi/yyeh	western
ishtidād	intensification; increase; worsening
juhūd (*sing.* **juh(u)d**)	efforts

karam	generosity
kbīr/eh	big
khilāl	during
ma@ el-asaf	alas
mall (I.8)	he got bored
munkasir	lit., broken; defeated
mutawaqqa@/a	expected
qādim/qādmeh	coming; next
sāḥil (*pl.* **sawāḥil**)	coast
sakhīf/eh	silly
tikrār	repetition

Class IX

Verbal noun: **iCCiCāC**
Active participle: **muCCaCC, miCCaCC**
Passive participle: none

iḥmarr	**iḥmirār**	**muḥmarr/miḥmarr** turning red; ruddy
ikhḍarr	**ikhḍirār**	**mukhḍarr** covered with green
izraqq	[none]	**mizraqq** becoming livid

65 **wijhu miḥmarr min el-khajal.**
66 **el-arḍ el-mikhḍarra btin@ish en-nafs.**
67 **laish wijhu mizraqq? la ykūn akal shī masmūm?**
Could he have eaten something poisoned?

Class X

Verbal noun: **istiCCāC**, for truncated verbs **istiCCā"**
Active participle: **mustaCCiC**, for truncated verbs **mustaCCi**, for verbs ending in double letters **mustaCiCC**
Passive participle: **mustaCCaC**, for truncated verbs **mustaCCa**, for verbs ending in double letters **mustaCaCC**

X.1
ista@mal **isti@māl** **musta@mil** **musta@mal**
made use of
istaqbal **istiqbāl** **mustaqbil** **mustaqbal** future
received

istaghall	**istighlāl**	**mustaghill**	**mustaghall**
exploited			
ista@add	**isti@dād**	**musta@idd**	[PP not used]
made himself ready; expressed willingness			

X.2

istaghna was able to do without	**istighnā"**	**mustaghni**	**mustaghna @annu**
istawla	**istīlā"**	**mustawli**	**mustawla @alai**
confiscated			

68 **ishtarait khamis kutub musta@maleh.**
69 **Huda btishtaghil muwaẓẓafit istiqbāl.**
70 **shū mustaqbal el-@ilāqāt el-@arabiyyeh el-Awrubbiyyeh fi ra"yak?**
71 **tharawāt el-biḥār mish mustaghalleh abadan; mustaqbal el-@ālam yimkin iykūn marhūn bi 'stighlālha istighlāl jayyid.**
72 **ana mish musta@idd asma@ ha 'l-kalām es-sakhīf; idha kān @indak inta 'sti@dād, khallik; ana rāyiḥ.**
73 **Nesh-sharikeh qarrarat el-istighnā" @an khadamāt 10% min el-@ummāl.**
74 **el-ḥukūmeh qarrarat el-istīlā" @ala amwāl el-muharribīn.**

Class XI

Verbal noun: **CaCCaCa** (the feminine marker **a** also takes the form **eh**)
Active participle: **muCaCCiC**
Passive participle: **muCaCCaC** or **mCaCCaC**

tarjam	**tarjameh**	**mutarjim**	**mutarjam**
translated			
handas	**handaseh**	**muhandis**	**muhandas**
engineered			
kharbaṭ	**kharbaṭa**	**mukharbiṭ**	**mukharbaṭ**
confused			

75 **a@māl Voltaire mish kullha mtarjameh la 'l-lugha 'l-@arabiyyeh.**
76 **ibni muhandis mi@māri.**
77 **shū ha 'l-kharbaṭa? el-faṣl el-awwal maḥṭuṭ ba@d el-faṣl eth-thālith.**

Vocabulary (section 44, classes IX—XI)

an@ash (IV.1)	he refreshed; he resuscitated
arḍ (*pl.* **arāḍi**)	land
khajal	bashfulness; shame
masmūm/eh	poisoned
nafs (*pl.* **nufūs; anfus**)	soul; self
biḥār (*sing.* **baḥ(a)r**)	seas
istiqbāl	reception
muwaẓẓaf/ muwaẓẓafit istiqbāl	receptionist
khallīk	stay
maḥṭūṭ	placed
marhūn/eh	lit., mortgaged; (of a state of affairs) closely dependent upon (certain other conditions)
musta@mal/eh	used; second-hand
tharawāt (*sing.* **tharweh**)	riches; resources
kharbaṭa	confusion
muhandis mi@māri	architect

Exercise 55

Translate into English the sentences left untranslated in the section on derived forms.

Chapter 10

In this chapter you will learn to talk about how, when or where something happens, and to make comparisons. The chapter introduces:

- *adverbs and adverbial expressions (here, there, tomorrow, sadly, quickly, etc.)*
- *the comparative form of adjectives (quicker, more interesting, etc.)*
- *the superlative of adjectives (quickest, most interesting)*

45 Adverbs

Compared to Standard Arabic or English, spoken Arabic is rather poor in adverbs (words describing how, when or where the action of a verb is performed, and also used to describe adjectives or other adverbs). Therefore, it resorts to any means available to fulfil the function of adverbs, including nouns and adjectives. Words like **el-laileh** ('the night'), **eş-şubiḥ** ('the morning') and **eẓ-ẓuhur** ('the noontime') are, course, nouns, but they function as adverbs in the following sentences:

nshūfak el-laileh in shā" Allāh.
We hope to see you tonight.
raḥ aqāblu 'ẓ-ẓuhur.
I shall meet him at noon.
ta@āl la 'l-bank eş-şubiḥ.
Come to the bank tomorrow morning.

Of the same kind are 'adverbs' like **el-@aşir** ('the afternoon'),

eḍ-ḍaḥa ('the forenoon'), **bukra** ('tomorrow'), **nhār el-aḥad** ('on Sunday'; lit., 'the daytime of Sunday'), **yōm es-sabt** ('on Saturday'; lit., 'the day of Saturday'), **el-usbū@ el-jāy** ('next week'; lit., 'the coming week'). Similarly, it is possible in English to say 'See you Saturday', where 'Saturday', a noun, functions as an adverb of time. It is their function that determines whether words, phrases or clauses can be classified as adverbs, not simply their form.

One of the ways of coining adverbial expressions in Arabic is the use of the preposition **bi** with nouns. The preposition loses its vowel if the noun starts with a vowel and may take the form **ib** if that prevents the occurrence of three consecutive consonants. The vowel of the preposition may also be dropped in accordance with the rule of short-vowel elision (Section 14).

imshi b' sur@a.
lit., *Walk with speed,* i.e. *quickly.*
ibtasam ib khubuth.
lit., *He smiled with slyness,* i.e. *slyly.*
@āmalha b' iḥtiqār.
He treated her disdainfully.
iḥki li b' ikhtiṣār.
Tell me briefly.

Sometimes the adverbial function is served by an adjective describing a verbal noun derived from the same root as the verb of the sentence:

verb + VN from the same root (as object) + adj.

ḥaka ḥaki (VN, *talking)* **kthīr** (adj., *much).*
(lit., *He talked a lot of talking.) He talked at length.*
ḍiḥik ḍiḥik (VN, *laughter)* **muz@ij.**
(lit., *He laughed annoying laughter.) He laughed annoyingly.*
shaka shakwa murra.
He complained bitterly.
nām nōm @amīq.
He slept profoundly or *soundly.*

ghannat ghinā" muḥzin.

She sang sadly.

ribiḥ arbāḥ (pl. of VN **ribiḥ,** *profit)* **@ālyeh** *(high).*

He profited handsomely.

There are also, of course, real adverbs that are used only as such:

inzal ***taḥt.*** *Go downstairs.*
iṭala@ ***fōq***. *Go upstairs.*
udkhul ***juwwa***. *Go inside.*
iṭla@ ***barra***. *Go outside.*
ta@āl ***ba@dain***. *Come later.*
ta@āl ***hassa***. *Come now.*
talfin lu ***ḥālan.*** *Call him up immediately.*
khallī yīji ***ra"san.*** *Let him come immediately.*
ḥuṭṭ el-kursi ***hunāk.*** *Put the chair over there.*
jīb Ghāzi ***hōn***. *Bring Ghāzi here.*
Ghāzi w maratu ẓallu @inna sā@tain ***taqrīban.***

Ghāzi and his wife stayed at our house for about two hours.

The word **@inna** consists of the preposition **@ind** and the pronoun **-na**; the **d** of **@ind** is omitted to prevent a cluster of three consonants. The word **sā@tain** is the dual of **sā@a** ('hour'), and **taqrīban** ('approximately') belongs to a sizable group of adverbs ending in **-an.**

a@jabatni el-qiṣṣa ***jiddan.***

The story appealed to me very much/I liked the story very much.

A **qiṣṣa** is a story or novel. The verb **a@jab** is equivalent to the Elizabethan verb 'like': in Shakespearean English, 'It likes me not' meant 'I don't like it.' The adverb **jiddan** may be repeated any number of times, just like 'very' in English.

– **a@jabak el-film?** *Did you like the film?*
– ***jiddan***. *Very much.*

imshi ***shwayy shwayy.*** *Walk slowly.*
imshi ***shwayy.*** *Walk for a short distance.*
i@ṭīni ***shwayy***. *Give me a little.*

Here **shwayy** is probably NOT an adverb. Can you suggest a reason why?

***shwayy shwayy*!** *Easy does it!*

Vocabulary (exercise 56)

@unf	violence
bāhir	brilliant
bātt	irrevocable; final; absolute [usually used with **mani@** (prohibition) and **rafḍ** (refusal)]
ikhlāṣ	sincerity; loyalty; faithfulness
khuṭṭa or khiṭṭa (*pl.* **khuṭaṭ or khiṭaṭ**)	plan
mubāsharatan	immediately
murīḥ/a	comfortable
muskirāt	intoxicants
mutaqaṭṭi@ or **mitqaṭṭi@**	intermittent
riḥleh	trip; journey
taqrīban	nearly; approximately

Exercise 56

tarjim el-jumal et-tālyeh la 'l-lugha 'l-ingilīziyyeh:

1 ba@rifhummish ma@rifteh jayydeh.
2 najḥat el-khuṭṭa najāḥ bāhir.
3 shurb el-muskirāt mamnū@ mani@ bātt fi Ramaḍān.
4 Shākir radd @ala el-mudīr ib @unf.
5 Layla ḥabbat Qays bi ikhlāṣ. *[Qays and Layla are famous Arab lovers like Romeo and Juliet.]*
6 nimt imbāriḥ nōm mitqaṭṭi@.
7 sāfaru ra"san min Bayrūt la Barīs.
8 kānat er-riḥleh murīḥa jiddan.
9 akhdhat khamis sā@āt taqrīban.
10 wiṣlu eṣ-ṣubiḥ w talfanu mubāsharatan.

46 Comparison: comparative degree

Common degree	*Comparative degree*	*Common degree*	*Comparative degree*
sarī@ quick	**asra@** quicker	**marīr** bitter	**amarr** more bitter
k(a)bīr big	**akbar**	**shadīd** intense	**ashadd**
k(a)thīr many, much	**akthar**	**qalīl** scanty	**aqall**
faẓī@ horrible	**afẓa@**	**ḥabīb** beloved	**aḥabb**
@aẓīm great	**a@ẓam**	**j(a)dīd** new	**ajadd**
jamīl beautiful	**ajmal**	**khafīf** light	**akhaff**
bārid cold	**abrad**	**raqīq** delicate	**araqq**
nā@im soft	**an@am**	**@amīm** general	**a@amm**
rā"i@ wonderful	**arwa@**		
dāfi warm	**adfa**	**ladūd** intransigent	**aladd**
ghāli dear	**aghla**	**ḥanūn** kind	**aḥann**
wā@i aware	**aw@a**		

These adjectives, all derived from Class I roots, show the following characteristics:

1 That the patterns **CaCīC, CāCiC** and **CāCi** have a comparative degree of the form **aCCaC** or its truncated version **aCCa**.
2 That the adjectives belonging to the same patterns but whose last two consonants are identical have a comparative degree of the form **aCaCC,** in which the last two consonants are also identical. The same is true when instead of **CaCīC** we have **CaCūC.**

In Standard Arabic, adjectives derived from verb classes II–XI usually form their comparative degree by the use of the words **akthar**, **ashadd** or **aqall** plus the verbal noun which corresponds to the adjective. The word **ashadd** ('more' or 'more intense') is reserved for qualities; **akthar** ('more') is used for both qualities and quantities and is by far the more frequent of the two; **aqall** ('less') is the opposite and is used for both qualities and quantities.

Adjective	*Comparative degree*
mustaqill independent	**akthar istiqlāl(an)**
mitfahhim understanding	**akthar tafahhum(an)**
mitnāqiḍ contradictory	**akthar tanāquḍ(an)**
munfa@il excited	**ashadd infi@āl(an)**
mista@jil in a hurry	**akthar isti@jāl(an)**

But the form sounds too literary, too affected, to be comfortable on everyday occasions, and the suffix **-an** belongs mainly to the written form of the language, although it survives in a few fossilized expressions (like the adverbs mentioned above). Moreover, some verbal nouns sound rather remote from everyday language. This is why most speakers say **mustaqill akthar, mitfahhim akthar, munfa@il akthar**, etc.

47 Comparison: superlative degree

The superlative degree is much simpler. For adjectives from Class I roots, it is expressed by prefixing the definite article to the comparative degree:

Fāyiz dhaki.
Fāyiz is clever.
Nu@mān adhka.
Nu@mān is cleverer.
Khaḍir el-adhka.
Khaḍir is the cleverest.

The last sentence is more frequently given this way:
Khaḍir huwweh 'l-adhka. The pronoun is felt to be more emphatic in a sentence where emphasis is of the essence of the statement.

Huda aḥla min Rīma, lākin Khaḍra hiyyeh 'l-aḥla.
Huda is more beautiful than Rīma, but Khaḍra is the most beautiful.

As for adjectives derived from verb classes II–XI, in spoken Arabic the comparative degree has to do for the superlative degree as well, with some additional phrasing to indicate what is meant:

Aḥmad kān munfa@il akthar min Ramzi, lākin @abdalla kān munfa@il akthar min el-kull.
Aḥmad was more excited than Ramzi, but @abdalla was excited more than anybody else.

Alternatively:

@abdalla kān munfa@il akthar wāḥad.
@abdalla was the most excited (one).

Here the word **wāḥad** ('one') singles @abdalla out as the most excited person from among others who, by implication, were also excited.

Vocabulary (exercise 57)

akbar	bigger; older
akhaff	less heavy
barīd	mail; post office
bi kthīr	by far
dā"iman or **dāyman**	always
khafīf/eh	not heavy
malābis (sing. not used)	clothes
mista@jil/ mista@ijleh	in a hurry
mustaqill/eh	independent
shā@ir (*pl.* **shu@arā"**)	poet
takālīf el-ma@īsheh	cost of living

Exercise 57

Translate the following sentences into Arabic:

1 Who is dearer to you, your father or your mother?
2 There are planes which are faster than sound.
3 My brother is older than I, but I am older than my sister.
4 el-Mutanabbi is the greatest poet in Arabic literature.
5 The cost of living in Egypt is much less than in Europe.
6 In my opinion, Shakespeare is the greatest poet in the world.
7 Is it (use: **el-jaww**) colder in France than in Britain?
8 Clothes are lighter than books. Take your clothes with you and send the books in the mail.
9 You are always in a hurry. Today I am in a greater hurry than you are.
10 Who is more independent, Rāshid or Luṭfi?

Chapter 11

This chapter looks at, among other things, nationalities, numbers and how to say 'I want'. You will learn:

- *how adding* **-i** *to nouns turns them into adjectives, forming words for nationalities and creeds, colours and qualities*
- *how to count up to two million in Arabic*
- *how numbers are used in* **iḍāfa** *constructions to say things like 'two pens' and 'twenty years'*
- *the word* **bid(d)-**, *meaning 'want', which behaves like a verb but doesn't belong to any of the verb classes*

48 The suffix '-i'

The addition of the suffix **-i** to nouns transforms them into adjectives. If the original noun ends in a vowel, that vowel is dropped and the **-i** is added to the last consonant. In emphatic speech the **-i** is long; otherwise it is short.

Names of countries:

el-Urdun Jordan	**Urduni** Jordanian, **el-Urduni**
el-Kuwait	**Kwaiti, Kuwaiti**
el-Maksīk Mexico	**Maksīki**
el-Hind India	**Hindi**
Libnān Lebanon	**Libnāni**
Falasṭīn Palestine	**Falasṯīni**
Maṣir Egypt	**Maṣri**
Maṣr, Miṣr Egypt	**Miṣri**
el-Jazā"ir Algeria	**Jazā"iri**

el-Yūnān Greece	**Yūnāni**
el-Majar Hungary	**Majari**

The feminine form of these masculine adjectives has the suffix **-iyyeh**, so we have:
ṣādirāt Urduniyyeh *Jordanian exports*
muḥādathāt Maṣriyyeh Jazā"iriyyeh *Egyptian-Algerian talks*
el-qaḍiyyeh 'l-Falasṭīniyyeh *the Palestinian problem*
el-lugha 'l-Yūnāniyyeh *the Greek language*
el-ḥudūd el-Maksīkiyyeh *the Mexican borders*

Added to proper nouns or certain other nouns, the suffix denotes a follower of a creed or doctrine (cf. '-ist' in English), while the feminine form also refers to the creed or doctrine itself (cf. '-ism'):

isti@mār colonialism	**isti@māri** colonialist
el-Masīḥ Christ	**el-Masīḥiyyeh** Christianity
Yahūd Jews	**Yahūdi** Jewish
Islām	**Islāmi** Islamic (you cannot have **Muslimi;** why not?)
Aflāṭūn Plato	**Aflāṭūni** Platonic
	Aflāṭūniyyeh Platonism
malik king	**malaki** monarchist
	malakiyyeh monarchism, monarchy
Mārks Marx	**Mārkisi** Marxist
	Mārkisiyyeh Marxism

Added to the names of things with distinctive colours, the suffix gives the name of the colour:

bunn coffee beans	**bunni/binni** brown
sama/samā" sky	**samāwi** sky blue, (in other contexts:) heavenly
burtuqāl oranges	**burtuqāli** orange in colour
lamūn/laymūn lemons	**lamūni/laymūni** lemon yellow
dhahab gold	**dhahabi** golden in colour
faḍḍa/fiḍḍa silver	**faḍḍi/fiḍḍi** silver in colour
zaytūn olives	**zaytūni** olive green

In general, the suffix turns the quality in the noun into an adjective. The following categories may be useful:

Qualities:	**ḥadīdi**	iron-like
	khashabi	wooden
	ḥarīri	silken
	sukkari	sugary; sweet
Directions:	**gharbi**	western
	janūbi	southern
	shamāli	northern
	sharqi	eastern
Fields of study:	**adabi**	literary
	@ilmi	scientific
	fīzyā"i	physicist
	iqtiṣādi	economic, economist
	zirā@i	agricultural
	falsafi	philosophical
	fikri	intellectual

Vocabulary (exercise 58)

@iddeh (in iḍāfa construction: **@iddit)**	several
@uṣi (*sing.* **@aṣa)**	sticks
afẓa@	more horrible
dabbābāt (*sing.* **dabbābeh**)	tanks
fikri/yyeh	intellectual
ḥassan (II.1)	he improved sthg
ḥijāra (*sing.* **ḥajar**)	stones
i@taqad (VIII.1)	he believed, he thought
izdād (VIII.1, irregular)	it increased
jānib (*pl.* **jawānib**)	side
jān(i)bain	two sides; both (sides)
jundi (*pl.* **j(u)nūd**)	soldier
karafatta	cravat
lābis/lābseh	wearing
mīzān (*pl.* **mawāzīn**)	balance
mīzān el-madfū@āt	balance of payments

muḥādathāt	talks; negotiations
sing. **muḥādatheh**	conversation
rabṭa	necktie
sitār/a	curtain
ṣāḥib (*pl.* **aṣḥāb**)	friend
ṣāḥibna	our friend: that fellow over there; the one we are talking about
tbayyan (V.1)	it appeared that
thalath (in **iḍāfa** construction)	three
ustādh	professor

Exercise 58

Translate the following into Arabic:

1 Arab-European economic relations were the subject of lengthy talks among the leaders of the two sides.
2 Professor Nāṣir has published scientific studies in several European journals.
3 Agricultural exports must increase in order that we may improve the balance of payments.
4 Can a Muslim marry a Christian woman?
5 Our friend there is wearing a brown suit, a blue shirt and an orange tie.
6 The north-south talks reached a dead end.
7 The colour of my car is olive green; what is the colour of your car?
8 His wife is Sudanese and speaks three European languages.
9 The iron curtain has turned out to be a silken curtain.
10 I think that intellectual colonialism is more horrible than military colonialism. We can fight military colonialism with sticks and stones, but how can we fight something that is not as tangible as tanks and soldiers?

49 Numerals

Numerals in Arabic have three forms: cardinal (as used for counting), ordinal (indicating order: 'first', 'second', etc.) and **iḍāfa** (see below).

A. Cardinal numbers

1	wāḥid / wāḥad
2	ithnain / tinain
3	thalātheh / talāteh
4	arba@a
5	khamseh
6	sitteh
7	sab@a
8	thamānyeh / tamānyeh
9	tis@a
10	@ashara
11	iḥdāsh
12	iṭnāsh
13	thalaṭṭāsh
14	arb@ṭāsh
15	khamisṭāsh
16	sitṭāsh
17	saba@ṭāsh
18	thamanṭāsh / tamanṭāsh
19	tisi@ṭāsh
20	@ishrīn
21	wāḥad w @ishrīn
22	ithnain w @ishrīn
30	thalathīn / talatīn
40	arba@īn / arb@īn
50	khamsīn
60	sittīn
70	sab@īn
80	thamanīn / tamanīn
90	tis@īn
100	miyyeh
101	miyyeh w wāḥad
200	mitain
300	thalath miyyeh
400	arba@ miyyeh
500	khamis miyyeh
600	sitt miyyeh
700	sabi@ miyyeh
800	thaman miyyeh
900	tisi@ miyyeh
1000	alf
2000	alfain
2619	alfain w sitt miyyeh w tisi@ṭāsh
1,000,000	malyōn
2,000,000	malyōnain

Note: the **ā** in numbers from 12 to 19 sounds like the *a* in *father*.

B. Ordinal numbers

	Masculine	*Feminine*
1st	**el-awwal**	**el-ūla**
2nd	**eth-thāni**	**eth-thānyeh**
3rd	**eth-thālith**	**eth-thāltheh**
4th	**er-rābi@**	**er-rāb@a**
5th	**el-khāmis**	**el-khāmseh**
6th	**es-sādis**	**es-sādseh**
7th	**es-sābi@**	**es-sāb@a**
8th	**eth-thāmin**	**eth-thāmneh**
9th	**et-tāsi@**	**et-tās@a**
10th	**el-@āshir**	**el-@āshreh**
11th	**el-ḥādi @ashar**	
12th	**eth-thāni @ashar,** etc.	

From '11th' onwards, particularly for the feminine gender, the ordinal numbers begin to sound too close to the written language (Standard Arabic) for speakers to feel comfortable with them on everyday occasions, and instead of the ordinal form they use the word **raqim** ('number') followed by the cardinal number they have in mind. So **al-ḥādiyata @ashrata** (Standard Arabic for 'the eleventh') is more naturally given as **raqm iḥdāsh** and **as-sādisata wa 'th-thalāthīn** ('36th') as **raqim sitteh w thalathīn,** and so on.

C. Numbers in **iḍāfa** *constructions*

In English the number that precedes a noun (e.g. 'ten books') is an adjective that occupies its natural position in front of the noun. In Arabic the number that precedes a noun is an indefinite noun that acquires definiteness by the **iḍāfa: @ashir kutub, tisi@ banāt,** and so on. When placed in this kind of construction, some numbers undergo slight changes that are worth noting.

The numbers **wāḥad** and **ithnain,** however, are exceptions. They can be used only as free cardinal numbers, as in normal counting, or as adjectives. As adjectives, they follow the nouns they describe and agree with them in gender:

qalam wāḥad *one pen* (*m.*)
bint wāḥideh/waḥdeh *one girl* (*f.*)
Only the second is used in spoken Arabic. Why?
aqlām ithnain, banāt thintain *two pens, two girls*

Now this last example, strictly speaking, is wrong. The words **aqlām** and **banāt** are plural, i.e., they denote numbers greater than two. Standard Arabic has a dual form to refer to two of anything, but modern spoken Arabic is gradually dropping the dual and adopting the plural for all numbers exceeding one, as in English. The dual survives in naming pairs of things: **qalamain, bintain, malyōnain, bābain, sayyārtain,** etc., but it has almost completely disappeared from verbs, relative pronouns and personal pronouns.

The numbers from 3 to 10 drop their feminine ending when used as adjectives, and the noun they describe is plural:

thalath banāt *three girls*
sitt lā@ibin *six male players*
@ashar/@ashir sayyārāt *ten cars*

The numbers from 11 to 19 add the missing **-ar** of **@ashar** (Standard Arabic for '-teen'), but the noun they describe is singular:

iḥdāshar mara *eleven women*
iṭnāshar zalameh or **rajul** *twelve men*
The word **zalameh** is feminine in form but masculine in gender, and it is more colloquial than **rajul**; cf. 'chap' as opposed to 'man' in English.
saba@ṭashar ṭann *seventeen tons*

The numbers from 20 to 99 do not change, and the nouns they describe are singular:

wāḥad w @ishrīn saneh *21 years*
tis@a w tis@īn walad *99 boys*

The figure 100 takes the form **mīt (mīt dīnār:** '100 dinars') and describes a singular noun, but it returns to its normal form in figures from 101 upwards. The figure 200 is **mitain** (dual of **miyyeh**), 300 **thalath miyyeh,** and so on. Then we have **alf** (1000), **alfain** (2000), **thalath ālāf** (3000) or **thalath-t-ālāf**, the **-t-** being the original feminine marker of the figure **thalātheh** in an **iḍāfa** construction (cf. **mīt**, originally **miyyit**, simplified to **mīt**). The figure 1,617,895 is read as follows: **malyōn w sitt miyyeh w saba@ṭāshar alf w thaman miyyeh w khamseh w tis@īn.**

Exercise 59

Translate the following into Arabic:

1	69 years	6	100 boys
2	2 keys	7	23 books
3	2 rooms	8	7 weeks
4	3 rooms	9	216 pages
5	176 dinars	10	6 million dollars

50 The word 'bid(d)-'

A curious word in spoken Arabic is the word **bid(d)-,** which seems to be derived from the expression in Standard Arabic **bi-wudd-** ('it is my, his, etc., desire that'). It has the force of a verb but does not belong to any of the verb classes recognized as such. It cannot be used without a pronominal suffix attached to it. Like verbs, it can be negated by either the word **ma** or the suffix **-sh**, or by both. Furthermore, the prefix **bi-**, originally a preposition, seems to be the equivalent of the prefix **b-**, which is an indication of the imperfect tense.

biddi I want	**bidna** we want
biddak you (*m.*) want	**bidkum** you (*m.*) want
biddik you (*f.*) want	**bidkin** you (*f.*) want
biddu he wants	**bid-hum** they (*m.*) want
bid-ha she wants	**bid-hin** they (*f.*) want

Each of these forms can be followed by

(a) a noun functioning as object:
biddi sayyāra. *I want a car.*
biddi ghurfeh bi srīrain. *I want a double-bedded room.*
bid-hum flūs. *They want money.*
bid-hin malābis. *They need clothes.*

(b) a verb in the subjunctive mood:
biddi aktib riwāyeh. *I want to write a novel.*
bid-hum iyrūḥu la 'l-Başra. *They want to go to Başra.*

(c) a pronominal object in an **iḍāfa** construction; the pronoun in question is **iyy-** attached to any of the pronominal suffixes:
biddi-yyāk. *I want you.*
bid-hum-iyyāk. *They want you.*
biddi-yyāhin. *I want them.*
bid-hin-iyyāhum. *They want them.*
bidkum-iyyāna. *You want us.*
Each of these phrases can be followed by a verb in the subjunctive mood:
idha bidkum-iyyāna nzūrkum, ta@ālu khudhūna li"anna mā bni@rif wain baitkum.
If you want us to visit you, come and fetch us, because we don't know where your house is.
biddi-yyākum tintibhu la ahammiyyit aḥruf *(letters)* **el-@illeh** *(ailment).*
I want you to pay attention to the importance of the vowel letters.
The sounds of the long vowels in Arabic are the ones naturally used to express pain. Hence the phrase **aḥruf** or **ḥurūf el-@illeh** (lit., 'letters of ailment') for 'vowel letters'.

Since the idea of wanting or desiring naturally refers to the future, the word **bid(d)-** usually combines both ideas, sometimes with the idea of futurity uppermost:

el-ḥukūmeh bid-ha tiftaḥ shāri@ min hōn.
The government is going to build a road starting from here.
wain biddak tiqḍi 'l-@utleh?
Where will you spend the holiday?

Vocabulary (exercise 60)

bāba	father; dad
hayyāni, hayyāha, hayyāna (etc.)	here I am, here she is, here we are (etc.)
jāhiz/jāhzeh	ready
mathalan	for example
ṭab@an	of course
ya@ni	lit., he means, but often used vaguely as space filler: I mean, you know, maybe (etc.)

Exercise 60

Translate the following conversation into English:

A: bāba, Maḥmūd @a 't-talafōn biddū-yyāk.
B: shū biddu?
A: mish @ārfeh. tiḥki ma@u?
B: i@ṭini 't-talafōn. aywa ya Maḥmūd. shū biddak?
C: bāba, biddi aḥkī lak innu Sāmir w abū w ummu bid-hum iyzūrūna 'l-laileh. ya@ni lā tiṭla@ barra.
B: khair? *(What's up?/What is the matter?/What for?)*
C: bid-hum yukhṭubu Suha.
B: Suha? w hiyyeh @ārfeh?
C: @ārfeh? ṭab@an @ārfeh.
B: Suha. Suha. wain ruḥti?
A: na@am, bāba. hayyāni hōn.
B: māma jahzeh?
A: laish?
B: bidna niṭla@ barra.
A: bidku tiṭla@u barra? lāzim ya@ni?
B: laish la"?
A: ya@ni (*I don't know*). ma ḥakāsh Maḥmū shī?
B: shī? aish ya@ni?
A: ya@ni (*I don't know*).
B: @an Sāmir mathalan?
A: ya@ni *(maybe)*.
B: bass inti mish @ārfeh.
A: ya@ni (*I don't know*).
B: @ārfeh willa mish @ārfeh?
A: ya@ni *(maybe)*.

Chapter 12

To complete your course, you will learn to talk about the time and dates, and you will meet some useful words and expressions for everyday conversation. This final lesson covers:

- *the units of time, from a second to a century*
- *the names of the days and months and how to ask or give the time and the date*
- *common greetings and forms of address, formal and informal*
- *names and family relationships*
- *useful phrases, including 'please', 'thank you', 'sorry' and some of the many expressions using the word* **Allah**

At the end of the chapter there are some conversations for further practice. Look up the unfamiliar words in the accompanying vocabulary lists, work out the meaning of the conversations and practice reading them aloud. They are translated in the key.

51 Time and dates

A. Units of time

laḥẓa instant (*pl.* **laḥaẓāt**)
laḥẓa min faḍlak.
One moment, please.
mā btākhdhak laḥẓa.
It *will not take you a moment.*

thānyeh second (*pl.* **thawāni**)
qaṭa@ el-masāfeh b-"aqall min sittīn thānyeh.
He ran the distance in under sixty seconds.

daqīqa minute (*pl.* **daqā"iq/daqāyiq**)
el-masāfeh mn/min el-bait la 'l-bank thalath daqāyiq bi 's-sayyāra.
The distance from my house to the bank is three minutes by car.

sā@a hour, watch, clock (*pl.* **sā@āt**)
bashtaghil bi 's-sā@a.
I work on an hourly basis.
mīn aḫsan, es-sā@āt es-Swīsriyyeh willa 's-sā@āt el-Yābāniyyeh?
Which are better, the Swiss watches or the Japanese watches?

yōm day (*pl.* **ayyām**) Frequently used together with the name of a day to form an adverbial phrase: *on* a particular day.
ashūfak yōm es-sabt in shā" Allāh.
I hope to see you on Saturday.
irja@ li ba@id khamis ayyām.
Come back in five days.

n(a)hār day **nhār** refers more specifically to daytime. The word has no plural and is used adverbially like **yōm**.
Fu"ād bishtaghil bi 'l-lail w biqḍi mu@ẓam sā@āt en-nahār nāyim.
Fu"ād works at night and spends most of his daytime hours sleeping.

usbū@ week (*pl.* **asābī@**) The Arab week begins on Saturday. Friday is the holiday in most Arab countries. Occasionally **jum@a** ('Friday'; *pl.* **juma@**) is used to mean 'week', particularly in the plural.
Ṣābir ṣār lu usbu@ain (*two weeks,* dual) **fi 'l-mustashfa.**
Ṣābir has been in the hospital for two weeks now.

shahar month (*pl.* **ashhur, sh(u)hūr**)
kam shahar ṣār lak fi 's-Su@ūdiyyeh?
How many months have you been in Saudi Arabia now?

saneh year (*pl.* **sanawāt, s(i)nīn**)
ṣār li snīn mā shuftu.
It has been years since I saw him last/I haven't seen him in years.

qar(i)n century (*pl.* **q(u)rūn**)
el-qarn el-@ishrīn qarrab *(is about to)* **yikhlaṣ** *(be over)* **w inta ba@dak @āyish fi 'l-qurūn el-wusṭa.**
The twentieth century is coming to a close and you are still living in the Middle Ages.

B. Days of the week

es-sabt Saturday
el-aḥad Sunday
el-ithnain Monday
eth-thalātha Tuesday
el-arb(i)@a/el-arbi@ā" Wednesday
el-khamīs Thursday
el-jum@a Friday

The names of the days from Sunday to Thursday correspond to the Arabic numbers from one to five; **el-jum@a** denotes the Gathering of Muslims to pray together in mosques at noontime, this being the Muslim holiday, while **es-sabt** (cf. 'Sabbath') seems to mean 'the seventh' despite a possible derivation from **sabata,** 'to rest'.

C. The months

et-taqwīm el-mīlādī: the Christian calendar (**mīlād** means 'birth', i.e., Christ's):

1	**kānūn eth-thāni**	**yanāyir**
2	**sh(u)bāṭ**	**fabrāyir/fibrāyir**
3	**ādhār**	**māris**
4	**nīsān**	**abrīl**
5	**ayyār**	**māyō**
6	**ḥuzayrān**	**yūnya/yūnyō**
7	**tammūz**	**yūlya/yūlyō**
8	**āb**	**aghusṭus**
9	**aylūl**	**sibtambar/sibtambir**
10	**tishrīn el-awwal**	**uktōbar/uktōbir**
11	**tishrīn eth-thāni**	**nuvambar/nuvambir**
12	**kānūn el-awwal**	**dīsambar/dīsambir**

It will not have taken you long to recognize the similarity

between the names in the second column and their counterparts in the European languages. These names are used mainly in North Africa, but other countries use them as well in combination with the names in the first column, i.e., both names are given as alternatives. In the eastern part of the Arab world most people use the names in the first column. But in addition to these, there is also the Muslim or lunar calendar (**et-taqwīm el-qamari** or **el-hijri**), in which the year is shorter by about ten days. This calendar is used mainly in Saudi Arabia (**el-mamlakeh 'l-@arabiyyeh 's-Su@ūdiyyeh**), and the names of the months are as follows:

1	**muḥarram**	7	**rajab**
2	**ṣafar**	8	**sha@bān**
3	**rabī@ el-awwal**	9	**ramaḍān** (month of fasting)
4	**rabī@ eth-thāni**	10	**shawwāl**
5	**jumāda 'l-ūla**	11	**dhu 'l-qa@da**
6	**jumāda 'l-ākhira**	12	**dhu 'l-ḥijja** (month of pilgrimage)

D. Asking the time

You may ask the time in any of the following ways:

qaddaish es-sā@a?
What's the time?
Or, more politely:
qaddaish es-sā@a min faḍlak?
What's the time, please?
qaddaish sā@tak?
What time does your watch show?
kam es-sā@a?
es-sā@a kam? } *What's the time?*

The following are possible answers:

es-sā@a @ashara illa *(minus)* **rubi@.**
(lit., *The hour is ten minus a quarter.) It's 9:45.*
@ashara illa thulth/thilth/tult/tilt
(lit., *ten minus a third) 9:40*

iḥdāsh w thilth
11:20
sitteh w nuṣṣ
(lit., *six and a half*) *6:30*
es-sā@a waḥdeh w thalātheh w @ishrīn daqīqa ṣabāḥan.
(lit., *The hour is one and twenty-three minutes in the morning.*) *It's 1:23 a.m.*
thintain w rubi@ ba@d eẓ-ẓuhur
(lit., *two and a quarter in the afternoon) 2:15 p.m.*

E. Asking the date

The date may be asked in any of the following ways:

qaddaish et-tārīkh el-yōm?
What's the date today?
(In other contexts, **tārīkh** means *history.*)
shū 't-tārīkh b' Alla?
What's the date, please?
qaddaish el-yōm bi 'sh-shahar?
What's the day today in the month? or simply: *What's the date?*

Possible answers are:

thamanṭāsh bi 'sh-shahar
18 of the month
ithnain w @ishrīn tammūz
22 July
sab@a iḥdāsh alf w tisi@ miyyeh w tis@īn
7/11/1990 (i.e., *7th November 1990)*

F. Other questions and answers

aimta msāfir?
When are you leaving?
yōm el-jum@a.
On Friday.

aimta raḥ tirja@ min es-safar?
When will you be back from your trip?
ba@id yōmain.
In two days' time. (lit., *After two days.)*
rāji@ ba@id shahrain.
Coming back (i.e., *I'll be back) in two months' time.*
khilāl usbū@.
Within a week.
mish akthar min shahar.
Not more than a month.
Allāhu a@lam.
(lit., *God knows better.*) *I don't know.*

52 Greetings

The most common greetings are the following:

A: **marḥaba!** Hello!
B: **marḥaba!**
Alternative answers are: **marḥabtain** ('A double **marḥaba!**'), **ahlan!** ('welcome!'), **ahlain!** ('A double welcome!'), **ahlan wa sahlan!** (a fossilized phrase from Standard Arabic used particularly to welcome somebody at home).

A: **as-salāmu @alaykum!** Peace be upon you! (the most formal greeting)
B: **wa @alaykum es-salām!** And upon you, too!
This response is sometimes expanded to: **wa @alaykum es-salām/ wa raḥmatu 'llāhi/ wa barakātuh** (oblique lines indicate where you can stop). The sentence may be translated as follows: 'And peace, God's mercy and His blessings be upon you, too'. This is a particularly Islamic greeting. Clearly, it is an importation from Standard Arabic into the spoken language.

A: **ṣabāḥ el-khair!** Good morning!
B: **ṣabāḥ el-khair!** Good morning!

or better:
ṣabāḥ en-nūr! (lit., 'A morning of light', but really meaning nothing more than a polite response)

A: **masa 'l-khair/masā" el-khair!** Good evening!
B: **masa 'l-khair/masā" el-khair!** Good evening!
or better:
masa 'n-nūr/masā" en-nūr! (as above)
The word **masa** includes any time after the noon hour until late at night. There is a word for afternoon, **@aṣir**, but is not used in greetings as is the English 'Good afternoon'.

A: **b' khāṭrak/b' khāṭrik/b' khāṭirkum,** etc. (lit., 'Keep us in mind.') Goodbye.
B: **ma@ es-salāmeḥ.** (lit., 'May you go in safety.') Goodbye.
The English word 'bye' and the phrase 'bye-bye' are now used by practically everybody. You may even hear **ya 'lla bye** ('And now goodbye') spoken by people who otherwise know very little English.

53 Forms of address

Young people who are close friends address each other by their first names. Older people tend to use the name of the addressed person's son together with the word **abu** ('father of') or **umm** ('mother of').

marḥaba, Maḥmūd.
Hello, Maḥmūd.
marḥaba, abu Sāmir.
Hello, Sāmir's father.

Here 'Maḥmūd' and 'abu Sāmir' are the same person. The second is more respectful but no less intimate.

masa 'l-khair, Huda.
Good evening, Huda.
masa 'l-khair, umm Mas@ūd.
Good evening, Mas@ūd's mother.

Huda is Mas@ūd's mother. Again the second sentence is more respectful. Among older women, the use of first names is rare unless deliberately disrespectful. Nowadays, it is becoming more and more acceptable to use the daughter's name in similar situations if there is no son. If there is one, however, it is the son's name that is used even if he is the youngest child.

Sayyid means 'master' (or 'Mr'), but its use in front of family names is more formal than in front of first names. So to call Jamāl el-Manşūr **sayyid Jamāl** is formal, but to say **sayyid el-Manşūr** is much more formal. If Jamāl is being talked about formally, **sayyid** takes on the definite article: **es-sayyid Jamāl,** or **es-sayyid Jamāl el-Manşūr,** or **es-sayyid el-Manşūr.** The absence of the definite article indicates that the person is being addressed, its presence that he is being talked about.

The word **ustādh/ustāz** (lit., 'professor') is frequently used instead of **sayyid** in formal speech, particularly if the person addressed or talked about has a modern, Europeanized look, but the feminine **ustādheh** is rarely used except to refer to an actual female university professor. Physicians and university professors are usually addressed with the title **daktōr** (short **a** and long **ō**: 'doctor', 'Dr'); lawyers and Europeanized gentlemen with **ustādh;** engineers with **muhandis.** An unmarried young girl is an **āniseh**; a **sitt** is usually a married lady, but the word is often used indiscriminately to mean something like 'lady'. The word **madām** (French in origin and pronunciation) is used to mean 'wife', particularly when prefixed with the definite article: **el-madām.**

When you refer to an important person (a very relative term indeed!), you may also use the word **baik** (**baih** in Egyptian Arabic, where it is very frequent):

ahlan, Ḥāmid baik.
  Welcome, Ḥāmid baik.
Ḥāmid baik raḥ ysharrifna bi zyāra.
  Ḥāmid baik will honour us with a visit.

The word **yā** is used when calling or addressing someone (like the archaic 'O' in English):

yā akhkh!
O, brother! (calling somebody whose name you don't know)
yā sayyid!
Hey, mister!
yā Ḥāmid!
O, Ḥāmid! (Here **yā** is often dropped.)
yā rait.
I wish. (used either in response to possible good news or to introduce a specific wish on the part of the speaker)
yā salām!
(lit., O, *peace!) How good! Wonderful!*

The word **sīdi** ('Sir') is used by an inferior addressing a superior. Nowadays, it is also frequently used by equals in formal conversation. **Sitti** is the feminine form, but it is less frequently used. In other contexts these two words refer to the grandfather and grandmother respectively, with the final pronoun changed to suit the situation **(sīdu, sitt-ha,** etc.).

54 Names and family relations

In Arabic, one ordinarily has a single given name followed by any number of ancestors' names until the family name is reached. A name like **Ḥasan Maḥmūd Yāsīn @abdalla 'l-@umari** consists of the following elements:
Ḥasan, the first (given) name of the person in question;
Maḥmūd, Ḥasan's father's first name;
Yāsīn, Ḥasan's grandfather's first name;
@abdalla, Ḥasan's great-grandfather's first name; and
el-@umari, the family name.
So Ḥasan's name may be given variously as
Ḥasan Maḥmūd
Ḥasan Maḥmūd Yāsīn
Ḥasan Maḥmūd Yāsīn @abdalla
Ḥasan Maḥmūd el-@umari
Ḥasan el-@umari.

Increasingly now, official documentation requires four-part names including the family name. More importantly, perhaps, marriage does not change a woman's name to that of her husband's family name. It is only recently that some women have started to use their husbands' family names, but this practice is still rather limited.

Compound first names of the type **@abd el-Qādir, @abd el-Laṭīf,** etc., where **@abd** is the first element, must never be reduced to 'Abdul' or 'Abdel' (**@abd el-**), as we find in some European books about the Middle East. The first element means 'slave' and the second is usually either the name of God (as in **@abd Allah: @abdalla**) or an attribute of God. To say 'Abdul' or 'Abdel' is like saying 'Slave of' and stopping.

Family relations include:

ab father **(abū** in **iḍāfa** constructions: **abūy,** 'my father', **abūki,** etc.)
akhkh brother (**akhū** in **iḍāfa** constructions)
umm mother
ukht sister
bint daughter (also 'girl' in general)
ibin son
@amm paternal uncle
@ammeh paternal aunt
khāl maternal uncle
khāleh maternal aunt
jadd/jidd, sīd grandfather
jaddeh/jiddeh, sitt grandmother

55 The word 'Allah'

This word is, of course, the Arabic equivalent of the English word 'God'. However, it occurs frequently in spoken Arabic in idiomatic uses that have little to do with God.

Allah-Allah! (first **h** fully pronounced)
A strong expression of admiration, appreciation or, depending on the context, disapproving surprise.

ya 'lla. Hurry up.

in shā" Allāh lit., if God wills
In emphatic pronunciation, both **ā**s are long, the **hamza** of **shā"** is pronounced, and only a short **a** at the beginning of **Allāh**, with no break with the previous word. The less emphatic pronunciation gives us **in shā 'lla,** with only one long **ā** and no **hamza.** The phrase is really nothing more than a mild expression of hope.

wa 'lla lit., I swear by God
This is the unemphatic form of the oath **wa 'llāhi.** This unemphatic form is really nothing more than a transitional word (see Section 56) in situations like the following:

wa 'lla w kīf ḥālak?
And how are you? (a resumption of questioning about the addressee's wellbeing; an expression of real interest)
wa 'lla w lamma shuftu tẓāhar innu mā shāfni.
And when I saw him, he pretended not to have seen me.

b' Alla by God
A mild expression of surprise and a polite way of introducing a request:

– **talfant ilha mbāriḥ.** *I phoned her yesterday.*
– **b' Alla?** *Really?*
b' Alla ti@ṭīni hadhāk el-kitāb. *Please give me that book.*

Alla ykhallīk. lit., May God preserve you.
Frequently used to introduce a request or simply as a response to a compliment:

Alla ykhallīk lā tkhayyib amali. *Please don't disappoint me.*
– **inta rajul ṣāḥib mabādi".** *You are a man of principles.*
– **Alla ykhallīk.** *Thank you; you're too kind.*

al-ḥamdu li 'llāh lit., praise be to God
al- is the definite article of Standard Arabic, used here because the whole phrase is an importation from Standard Arabic. The **-u** in **al-ḥamdu** is not a pronoun but the nominative ending of the noun, something nouns in spoken Arabic have dropped. The phrase is one of the standard responses to a question about how one is doing:

– **kīf ḥālak?** *How are you?*
– **al-ḥamdu li 'llāh.** *Very well, thank you.*

56 Familiar phrases and transitional words

Transitional words and phrases are used to introduce or fill out sentences when speaking and could often be dropped without tangibly affecting the meaning. Some English examples are: 'actually', 'to be honest', 'you know'.

baini w bainak between me and you / you and me; confidentially (In Arabic the first person takes precedence.)
eṣ-ṣaḥiḥ to tell you the truth; actually
biddak eṣ-ṣaḥiḥ if you want the truth; actually
el-wāqi@ really, actually
el-ḥaqīqa really, actually
el-mazbūṭ to be honest with you, to be exact
laish tib@id-ha? why go that far afield? i.e., there is an example nearer home
bidūn mubālagha I am not exaggerating when I say . . .
wa la tshidd īdak not as good as it / he / she, etc. seems to be
ṣaddiqni Believe me when I say . . .
kūn wāthiq I assure you . . .
ba"akkid lak I assure you . . .
wiḥyātak, wiḥyātik, etc. I swear by your life (an intensifier in requests and statements; sometimes rephrased **wiḥyāti @annak:** 'I swear by my life instead of yours')
wiḥyātak ti@ṭi ha 'l-kitāb la Ḥamzeh.
Please give this book to Ḥamzeh.

wiḥyātik mā babāligh.
I assure you I am not exaggerating.
wiḥyāti @annik, ha 'l-qiṣṣa mā ilha asās.
I assure you this story is baseless.

mish ma@qūl impossible, unbelievable (said either in situations requiring an expression of disbelief or as an expression of pleasant surprise on meeting somebody not seen for a long time)
mīn, Huda? mish ma@qūl.
Who? Huda? I can't believe my eyes.

@āsh min shāfak. (lit., He who has lived to see you has not lived in vain.) It has been a long time since I saw you. (The word **min** here is a corruption of **man**, 'who', from Standard Arabic.)
wain ha 'l-ghaibeh? Where have you been all this time? **(ghaibeh:** absence)
Allah yi@ṭīk el-@āfyeh. May God give you good health. (used frequently when one is about to leave or as an expression of sympathy with someone who has been working hard)
shukran thank you (may be addressed to anybody, regardless of gender or number)
shukran jazīlan thank you very much
ashkurak, ashkurik, ashkurkum, etc. thank you (Person addressed specified by the pronominal suffix. You cannot say **ashkurak jazīlan** but **ashkurak jiddan.**)
A response to **shukran**, if one is needed, is
@afwan/el-@afw. It's quite all right. Don't mention it. (The phrase **ahlan wa sahlan** may also be used.)
āsif I (male) am sorry
āsfeh I (female) am sorry
āsfīn we (plural or impersonal pronoun) are sorry
ba@id idhnak, idhnik, etc. with your permission
tismaḥ, tismaḥi, etc. Do you mind? / May I?

Conversations

1

A:	ḥaḍirtak min el-Urdun/Sūriyya/el-@irāq/ es-Su@ūdiyyeh?
B:	na@am, w inta?
A:	ana min Barīṭānya.
B:	w jāy la 'l-Urdun/Sūriyya/'l-@irāq/ 's-Su@ūdiyyeh la 's-siyāḥa willa la 'l-@amal?
A:	la 's-siyāḥa w el-@amal.
B:	shū btishtaghil?
A:	ana mumaththil dār nashir. biddi azūr ba@ḍ el-madāris w el-jāmi@āt min shān ashūf ḥājāt-ha.
B:	shū nō@ el-kutub illi btunshurūha?
A:	bnunshur kutub @ilmiyyeh fi mukhtalaf et-takhaṣṣuṣāt, w kutub fi ta@līm el-lugha 'l-ingilīziyyeh.
B:	kutubkum ghālyeh?
A:	fī kutub ghālyeh w fī kutub irkhīṣa. lākin inta bti@raf innu as@ār el-kutub btirtafi@ b' istimrār.
B:	ṣaḥīḥ.
A:	bti@taqid innu fī sūq la 'l-kutub bi 'l-lugha 'l-ingilīziyyeh fi baladkum?
B:	yimkin fī bi 'n-nisbeh la 'l-kutub el-@ilmiyyeh w kutub ta@līm el-lughāt bi sharṭ tkūn as@ārha ma@qūleh. mu@ẓam ṭullābna fuqara.
A:	iḥna bni@ṭi khaṣim kwayyis.
B:	batmannā lak en-najāḥ.
A:	shukran.

2

A: marḥaba yā akhkh.
B: marḥaba.
A: mumkin tiḥkī li wain Funduq el-Madīneh, min faḍlak?
B: Funduq el-Madīneh b@īd min hōn.
A: kīf mumkin awṣal lu?
B: lāzim tākhudh taksi.
A: suwwāq et-taksi bi@rafu wainu?
B: aktharhum bi@rafu. is"al es-sā"iq qabil mā tiṭla@ ma@u.
A: shukran.
B: ahlan wa sahlan.

3

A: ṣabāḥ el-khair.
B: ṣabāḥ en-nūr.
A: biddi ghurfeh, min faḍlak.
B: ḥaḍirtak ḥājiz?
A: lā mish ḥājiz.
B: ṭayyib, fī ghurfeh fi 'ṭ-ṭābiq el-@āshir.
A: kwayyis.
B: aish el-isim, min faḍlak?
A: John Smith.
B: min ayy balad ḥaḍirtak?
A: min Barīṭānya.
B: qaddaish nāwi tẓall fi 'l-funduq?
A: ḥawāli usbū@.
B: ahlan wa sahlan, sayyid Smith. bnitmannā lak iqāmeh ṭayybeh.

A: **shukran.**

B: **tfaḍḍal waqqi@ hōn, min faḍlak. shukran. w hādha muftāḥ el-ghurfeh. ghurfeh raqim alf w sitteh w @ishrīn. esh-shunaṭ raḥ tijīk ḥālan.**

A: **shukran.**

4

A: **alo.**

B: **alo.**

A: **bait Aḥmad el-@umarī, rajā"an?**

B: **aywa. mīn biḥki?**

A: **ana John Smith. mumkin aḥki ma@ Aḥmad, rajā"an?**

B: **laḥẓa, min faḍlak.**

C: **John?**

A: **marḥaba, Aḥmad.**

C: **ahlain, John. mnain btiḥki?**

A: **min el-funduq.**

C: **ayy funduq?**

A: **Funduq el-Madīneh.**

C: **ṭayyib, raḥ akūn @indak ba@id rubi@ sā@a. intaẓirni @ind muwaẓẓaf el-istiqbāl.**

A: **māshi. bass el-laileh mish rāḥ aqdar azūrkum fi 'l-bait.**

C: **ṭayyib, bniḥki fi 'l-mawḍū@ ba@id rubi@ sā@a.**

A: **bass lā tit"akhkhar.**

C: **amrak!**

5

A: as-salāmu @alaykum.

B: @alaykum es-salām.

A: fī @indkum shukulāṭa kwayyseh?

B: fī @inna shukulāṭa maḥalliyyeh w fī shukulāṭa mustawradeh.

A: biddi bakait shukulāṭa hadiyyeh.

B: tākhudh ṣinā@a maḥalliyyeh willa Faransiyyeh? el-Faransiyyeh aghla ṭab@an.

A: mish muhimm. qaddaish el-bakait?

B: sitt danānīr.

A: liff li bakait, rajā"an.

B: amrak.

A: bass ana ma@i istarlīnī.

B: biykūn aḥsan.

A: laish aḥsan?

B: el-@umleh 'ṣ-ṣa@beh la 'z-zaman eṣ-ṣa@b.

A: shū btuqṣud?

B: law ruḥt ana la maḥall fi Landan w @araḍt @alai @umleh min @umlitna ḥatta ashtri bakait shukulāṭa, biybī@ni?

A: ma aẓunnish.

B: hādha huwweh 'z-zaman eṣ-ṣa@b.

A: fhimt @alaik.

6

A: Su@ād, baqaddim lik ṣadīqī John Smith.

B: ahlan wa sahlan, sayyid Smith.

C: John, min faḍlik; ana w Aḥmad aṣdiqā" min sinīn.

B: ḩakā li @annak kthīr.

C: mish kull shī in shā 'lla?

B: kifāyeh!

C: idhan lā ti@ţi Aḩmad wa la qiţ@a min ha 'l-bakait!

B: laish ghallabit ḩālak?

C: mā fī ghalabeh, abadan.

B: ajīb ilkum shī tishrabu?

A: John mish sharrīb qahweh w shāy yā Su@ād.

C: la truddīsh @alai; ana mughram bi 'l-qahweh 't-turkiyyeh.

B: @ala fikra, inta btiḩki @arabi kwayyis. wain t@allamt el-lugha 'l-@arabiyyeh?

C: @ala idain el-ustādh Aḩmad. nassāni 'l-ingilīzi.

B: ẓannait innak inta nassaitu 'l-@arabi li-annu lamma riji@ min Barīţānya iḍţarraina nshaghghil lu mutarjim.

C: mish mutarjim, mutarjimeh: el-ustādheh Su@ād el-@umarī, M. Phil., Ph.D., ilā ākhirihi, ilā ākhirihi!

7

A: ahlan wa sahlan.

B: ahlan bīk.

A: bitḩibbu tishrabu shī qabl el-akil?

B: aywa. shu fī @indkum?

A: kull shī mawjūd. bitḩibbu ajīb ilkum nabīdh aḩmar?

B: ana biddi @aşīr burtuqāl.

A: w ana kamān @aşīr.

B: shū bitḥibb tākul? bitfaḍḍil akil sharqi willa gharbi?

C: sharqi ṭab@an. bass biddi ajarrib akil ghair el-akl el-Hindi aw eṣ-ṣīni.

B: tākul mansaf?

C: aish huwweh 'l-mansaf?

B: akleh waṭaniyyeh Urduniyyeh.

C: min aish btin@amal?

B: ruzz, w laḥim kharūf, w laban maṭbūkh.

C: māshi. khallīna njarribha.

B: willa nkhallī yjīb lak *steak*?

C: lā, lā. biddi ajarrib el . . . aish huwweh?

B: el-mansaf.

C: aywa. el-mansaf.

B: māshi.

8

A: marḥaba.

B: ahlan wa sahlan.

A: ana ismi John Smith. @indi maw@id ma@ el-@amīd.

B: tfaḍḍal. el-@amīd bistannāk.

A: shukran.

C: ahlan wa sahlan, Mr Smith.

A: ahlan bīk.

C: tfaḍḍal.

A: shukran.

C: tishrab qahweh willa shāy?

A: wa la shī, shukran. ḥabbait amurr @alaik min shān a@riḍ @alaik ba@ḍ el-muntajāt et-ta@līmiyyeh illi btintijha sharikitna.

C: kutub?

A: mish bass kutub. iḥna bnintij barāmij ta@līmiyyeh musajjaleh @ala ashriṭit video. jarrabat-ha kthīr min el-madāris fi duwal el-khalīj w najḥat najāḥ kbīr.

C: aish lughit hāy el-barāmij?

A: hiyyeh aṣlan bi 'l-lugha 'l-ingilīziyyeh, lākin fī minha nusakh bi 'l-lugha 'l-@arabiyyeh. in@amlat ed-dablajeh fi Maṣir bi 'l-lugha 'l-@arabiyyeh 'l-maktūbeh – aish bitsammūha el-fuṣḥa?

C: na@am. kwayyis jiddan. khallīna nshūfha.

9

A: ṣabāḥ el-khair.

B: ṣabāḥ el-khair.

A: biddi tikit la Athīna, min faḍlak.

B: aimta nāwi tsāfir?

A: yōm el-arbi@ā".

B: yōm el-arbi@ā" mā fī makān, ma@ el-asaf. fī yōm el-jum@a idha bit-ḥibb.

A: yōm el-arbi@ā" mish mumkin abadan?

B: idha bit-ḥibb, binḥuṭṭak @ala qā"imit el-iḥtiyāṭ.

A: w idha mā ṣār maḥall?

B: bitsāfir yōm el-jum@a. bass lāzim t"akkid el-ḥajiz qabil yōmain.

A: mā fī māni@. lākin arjūk lā tinsa yōm el-arbi@ā".

B: ittaşil bīna şabāḥ yōm el-arbi@ā".

A: ţayyib.

B: aish el-isim, rajā"an?

A: John Smith.

B: tikit dhahāb w @awdeh?

A: la, bass dhahāb.

B: māṣhi.

A: qaddaish et-tikit la Athīna?

B: miyyeh w @ishrīn dīnār. Hāy ḥajaznā lak @ala yōm el-jum@a, es-sā@a thalātheh w nuşş ba@d eẓ-ẓuhur. kūn fi 'l-maţār qabil maw@id eţ-ţayyāra bsā@tain.

A: ţayyib. raḥ attaşil sabāḥ yōm el-arbi@ā" @ala amal iykūn fī maḥall.

B: in shā 'lla.

A: shukran.

B: ahlan wa sahlan.

10

A: Aḥmad, eẓ-ẓāhir ma fishsh ţayyāra la Athīna yōm el-arbi@ā".

B: biykūn aḥsan.

A: aḥsan?

B: bi 't-ta"kīd. ma shufnakīsh kifāyeh w mā akhadhnakīsh @ala ayy maḥall. shū ra"yak nruḥ la 'l-Batra?

A: b@īdeh?

B: mumkin nrūḥ w nirja@ fi yōm wāḥad. w idha bit-ḥibb, binbāt hunāk laileh.

A: fikra kwayyseh.

B: idhan ta@āl bukra 'ṣ-ṣubiḥ. aw el-afḍal iḥna nmurr @alaik es-sā@a sab@a.

A: ajīb shī ma@i?

B: jīb ma@ak kāmirtak. fī hunāk manāẓīr btistaḥiqq et-taṣwīr.

A: fī hunāk maṭ@am kwayyis?

B: aywa, w Su@ād raḥ ti@mal sandawīshāt khafīfeh.

A: ṭayyib.

B: @ala fikra, bit-ḥibb rukūb el-khail?

A: aywa. laish?

B: li-annu fī masāfit ḥawāli arba@ kīlōmitrāt bain el-madkhal w bain el-madīneh 'l-wardiyyeh.

A: rukūb el-khail min hiwāyāti 'l-qadīmeh.

B: mumtāz. w raḥ nrakkbak @ala jamal kamān.

A: jamal?

B: aywa. rukūb el-jimāl hunāk juzu" min el-mut@a. raḥ tkūn aḥla min T. E. Lawrence nafsu.

A: idhan bashūfkum bukra 's-sā@a sab@a @ala bāb el-funduq.

B: in shā" Allah.

11

A: Ḥāmid? mish ma@qūl.

B: ahlan, Bahjat. kīf ḥālak?

A: el-hamdu li 'llāh. kif ḥālak inta?

B: māshi 'l-ḥāl.

A: wain ha 'l-ghaibeh yā rajul?

B: kunt badrus fi Amairka.

A:	**fi ayy wilāyeh?**
B:	**fi California.**
A:	**w shū darast?**
B:	**darasit kīmya.**
A:	**w shū 'sh-shahādeh illi ḥaṣalt @alaiha?**
B:	**ḥaṣalt @ala 'l-mājistair.**
A:	**mabrūk. w shū nāwi tishtaghil?**
B:	**w Alla mish @ārif. shufit i@lān fi 'l-jarīdeh min sharikit adwiyeh. fikrak byākhdhu kimyā"iyyīn?**
A:	**laish la?**
B:	**maṣāni@ el-adwiyeh yimkin bitfaḍḍil nās mutakhaṣṣiṣīn fi 'ṣ-ṣaydaleh.**
A:	**jarrib. w idha rafaḍūk, dawwir @an shaghleh thānyeh.**
B:	**raḥ ajarrib ṭab@an.**
A:	**batmannā lak en-najāḥ.**
B:	**shukran. khallīna nshūfak.**
A:	**bi 't-ta"kīd.**
B:	**ma@ es-salāmeh.**
A:	**ma@ es-salāmeh.**

Vocabulary (conversations)

(1)	
ba@ḍ	some
bi 'n-nisbeh	with regard to
bi sharṭ	on condition that
dār nashir	publishing house
el-@ irāq	Iraq
es-Su@ūdiyyeh	Saudi Arabia
ḥaḍra	presence; in **iḍāfa** constructions often used as a title of respect: **ḥaḍirtak** (sir), **ḥaḍirtik** (madam), **ḥaḍrit el-mudīr** (the honourable manager) (etc.)
ḥājāt (*sing.* **ḥājeh**)	needs
irtafa@ (VIII.1)	it rose up
khaṣim	discount
kwayyis	good
mukhtalaf	various; different
mumaththil	representative; actor
r(a)khīṣ / a	cheap
Sūrya or Sūriyya	Syria
ta@līm	teaching
takhaṣṣuṣāt (*sing.* **takhaṣṣuṣ**)	specializations
tmanna (V.2)	he wished; he expressed the hope that
(2)	
taksi	taxi
(3)	
ḥājiz/ḥājzeh	has had sthg reserved
iqāmeh	residence (in a country); stay
min ayy balad?	from which country?
muftāḥ or **miftāḥ** (*pl.* **mafātīḥ**)	key
nāwi/nāwyeh	intending
ṭābiq	floor of a building

ţayyib/ţayybeh	all right; well; pleasant; good
(4)	
amrak	lit., your command; yes, sir!
t"akhkhar (V.1)	he was late
(5)	
@araḑ (I.5)	offered
@inna (= **@ind + na**)	we have
@umleh or **@imleh**	currency
@umleh şa@beh	hard currency
bā@ (I.11)	he sold
bakait (*pl.* **bakaitāt**)	a box (of chocolates, cigarettes, etc.)
fhimt @alaik	I see what you mean
hadiyyeh (*pl.* **hadāya**)	a present
istarlīni	sterling
laff (I.8)	he wrapped
maḩall (*pl.* **maḩallāt**)	place; shop
maḩalli/yyeh	local; locally made
mustawrad/eh	imported
qaşad (I.4)	he meant
şinā@a	industry; manufacture
shukulāţa	chocolates
ẓann (I.7)	he thought; he supposed
ma aẓunnish	I don't think so
(6)	
@ala idain	at the hands of
ghalabeh	trouble
ghallab (II. 1)	he troubled someone; he took the trouble (usually to bring a present or to do something beyond the call of duty)
iḑţarr (VIII.1, but irregular)	he had to
ilā ākhirihi	and so on and so forth; etc.
mughram/eh	fond of
qaddam (II.1)	he introduced somebody to; he presented
shaghghal (II.1)	he employed

sharrīb	drinker (either a heavy one or a connoisseur)
(7)	
@aşīr	juice
faḍḍal (II.1)	he preferred
Hindi	Indian
jarrab (II.1)	he tried
kharūf	sheep
laḥim kharūf	lamb; mutton (distinction between the two may be made by the adj. **zghīr** or **kbīr**)
laban	yoghurt
mansaf	a Jordanian national dish
māshi	all right
nabīdh	wine
ruzz	rice
Şīni	Chinese
(8)	
@amīd	dean of college
@araḍ (I.5)	he showed; exposed; exhibited
aşlan	originally
ashriṭa (*sing.* **sharīṭ**)	tapes
barāmij (*sing.* **barnāmij**)	programmes
dablajeh	dubbing; doublage
fuşḥa	lit., most eloquent, i.e., Standard Arabic
muntajāt (sing. not used)	products
musajjal/eh	recorded; taped
samma (II.2)	he named
ta@līmi/yyeh	educational
(9)	
@awdeh	coming back
amal (*pl.* **āmāl**)	hope
@ala amal	in the hope
arjūk = rajā"an	I implore you; please

Athīna	Athens
dhahāb	going
iḥtiyāṭ	reserve
qā"imit el-iḥtiyāṭ	waiting list
mā fī mani@	I don't mind
makān	place; vacancy (in an aeroplane, a theatre, etc.)
qā"imeh (*pl.* **qawā"im**)	list
tikit (*pl.* **tiktāt**)	ticket
tikit dhahāb w @awdeh	return ticket

(10)

hiwāyāt (*sing.* **hiwāyeh**)	hobbies
istaḥaqq (X.1, but somewhat irregular)	he deserved
juzu" (*pl.* **ajzā"**)	part
kāmira	camera
kāmirtak	your camera
kīlōmitrāt (*sing.* **kīlōmitir**)	kilometres
khail	horses collectively
madkhal	entrance
manāẓir (*sing.* **manẓar**)	scenes; scenery
qadīm/eh	old
rakkab (II.1)	he caused someone to ride
rukūb	riding
sand(a)wīshāt (*sing.* **sand(a)wīsheh**)	sandwiches
taṣwīr	taking snapshots of
wardi/yyeh	rosy
el-Madīneh 'l-Wardiyyeh	the Rose-Red City, i.e., Petra (**el-Batra**)

(11)

adwiyeh (*sing.* **dawa**)	medical products
al-ḥamdu li 'llāh	lit., praise be to God; very well, thank you
bi 't-ta"kīd	certainly
dawwar (II.1)	he looked for
fi ayy. . . ?	in which. . .?
fikrak . . . ?	do you think (as stated)?
ghaibeh	absence
ghair	not, un-
ghair mutawaqqa@	unexpected
kīmya	chemistry
kīmyā"iyyīn (*sing.* **kīmyā"i**)	chemists
laish lā?	why not?
liqā"	meeting
mājistair	an MA degree
māshi 'l-ḥāl	very well, thank you
maṣāni@ (*sing.* **maṣna@**)	factories
mish ma@qūl!	unbelievable; can't believe my eyes!
rafaḍ (I.4)	he refused; he rejected
ṣaydaleh	pharmacy (as a science)
ṣaydaliyyeh	drugstore
shaghleh	job
shahādeh	certificate; degree
wain ha 'l-ghaibeh yā rajul?	where have you been all this time, old chap?
wilāyeh	state (in a federation)

Key to exercises and conversations

CHAPTER 2

Exercise 1: 1 es-sadd 2 el-faṣīḥ 3 en-naẓar 4 el-@alam 5 el-malik 6 el-kāmil 7 el-fāhim 8 ed-damm 9 el-alam 10 el-bait

Exercise 2: Possible combinations include: 1 kitāb Shawqi 2 qalam Nuha 3 khaṭar el-ḥarb 4 ghurfit el-ab 5 ṣōt el-walad 6 ujrit es-sayyāra 7 ṭūl el-haram 8 thaman el-kīlu 9 amṭār esh-shita. 10 shaqqit Aḥmad

Exercise 3: 1 The bank manager is asleep. 2 Samīra's car is from Germany. 3 Aḥmad's shirt is white. 4 The colour of Ṣubḥi's car is red. 5 Maḥmūd's book is from France. 6 Nāyif's mother is short. 7 My son's chair is broken. 8 The Egyptian's apartment is small. 9 The solution is difficult. 10 The price of the book is five dollars.

Exercise 4: 1 shaqqit mudīr el-bank wās@a. 2 ibnu fi Almānya. 3 ibni mudīr el-bank. 4 ibni mudīr bank. 5 zaman el-ḥarb zaman ṣa@b. 6 yōm el-jaish @uṭleh. 7 isim ṣāḥib el funduq (or el-utail) Ḥāmid. 8 tārīkh Maṣir ṭawīl. 9 el-ab fi Faransa. 10 ghurfit Huda wās@a.

CHAPTER 3

Exercise 5: 1 Huda's red car *(fragment)* 2 The German red car *(frag.)* 3 The red car is German. *(sentence)* 4 The beautiful bank manager's daughter is conceited. *(sen.)* 5 The conceited Huda *(frag.)* 6 Huda is conceited. *(sen.)* 7 Huda, the conceited daughter of the bank manager, is pretty. *(sen.)* 8 The bank manager is the father of conceited Huda. *(sen.)* 9 The red car is the bank manager's car. *(sen.)* 10 The red German cars *(frag.)*

Exercise 6: 1 nāymeh 2 baiḍa 3 qaṣīr zghīr 5 ṣa@beh 6 maqfūleh 7 maqfūleh 8 makrūha 9 maghrūr 10 ṭawīleh

Exercise 7: 1 They (*m.*) visited us. 2 We visited them (*m.*). 3 They (*f.*) visited us. 4 I visited him. 5 She visited us. 6 I visited you (*m. sing.*). 7 I visited them (*m.*). 8 They (*m.*) visited me. 9 You (*f. sing.*) visited them (*m.*). 10 You (*f. pl.*) visited them (*f.*). 11 I visited you (*m. sing.*). 12 You (*f. sing.*) visited me. 13 They (*m.*) visited you (*f. sing.*). 14 We visited you (*m. pl.*). 15 They (*f.*) visited me. 16 You (*m. pl.*) visited them (*m.*). 17 They (*f.*) visited you (*m. pl.*). 18 I visited you (*f. sing.*). 19 You (*f. pl.*) visited us. 20 You (*f. pl.*) visited me. 21 We visited you (*f. pl.*). 22 We visited them (*f.*). 23 They (*m.*) visited her. 24 You (*f. sing.*) visited him. 25 You (*m. pl.*) visited them (*m.*). 26 You (*f. sing.*) visited her. 27 She visited them (*m.*). 28 She visited you (*f. pl.*). 29 She visited them (*f.*). 30 She visited you (*m. sing.*). 31 I visited her. 32 She visited her. 33 We visited you (*f. sing.*).

Exercise 8: 1 imbāriḥ shufna Maḥmūd fi 'l-funduq. 2 el-yōm shuft Huda fi 'l-bank. 3 Huda shāfatni hunāk. 4 akhdhat khamis dūlārāt minni (*or* minni khamis dūlārāt). 5 akhadht khamis dūlārāt minha (*or* minha khamis dūlārāt). 6 mnain hiyyeh? 7 Maḥmūd zārni mbāriḥ. 8 zurna Ghānim fi 'l-utail. 9 akhadht kitāb Maḥmūd minnu. 10 kitābu aḥsan min kitāb Ghānim.

Exercise 9: 1 Salma took my car from me. 2 Yesterday I saw five American tourists in Petra. 3 Is your car from Germany? 4 Who took it from you? 5 Have you seen my book? 6 Your book is on the shelf. 7 Who took Ghānim's book? 8 Ḥāmid bought five books. 9 His books are on the shelf. 10 Salma's books are in her car.

Exercise 10: 1 minnu 2 shuft-ha 3 hinneh 4 akhadhu 5 shuftūhum? 6 zurt-ha? 7 zāratu 8 hiyyeh 9 @ammha 10 abū (abu + u)

CHAPTER 4

Exercise 11: 1 madrasit Huda b@īdeh. 2 madrasti qarībeh. 3 bank-kum b@īd. 4 bait-hin qarīb. 5 ḥadīqit-hum ḥilweh. 6 ghurfit Salma wās@a. 7 funduqi (or utaili) funduq (*or* utail)

khamsi njūm. 8 ktābha ṣa@b. 9 ḥāltu ṣa@beh. 10 malikit *(or* malkit) Barīṭānya Elizabeth eth-thānyeh *(or* hiyyeh Elizabeth . . .).

Exercise 12

qult/qulit	ruḥt/ruḥit	@udt/@udit
qult/qulit	ruḥt/ruḥit	@udt/@udit
qulti	ruḥti	@udti
qāl	rāḥ	@ād
qālat	rāḥat	@ādat
qulna	ruḥna	@udna
qultu	ruḥtu	@udtu
qultin	ruḥtin	@udtin
qālu	rāḥu	@ādu
qālin	rāḥin	@ādin

Exercise 13

maktabti	maktabi	makātbi
maktabtak	maktabak	makātbak
maktabtik	maktabik	makātbik
maktabtu	maktabu	makātbu
maktabit-ha	maktabha	makātibha
maktabitna	maktabna	makātibna
maktabitkum	maktabkum	makātibkum
maktabitkin	maktabkin	makātibkin
maktabit-hum	maktabhum	makātibhum
maktabit-hin	maktabhin	makātibhin

ḥṣāni	ismi	waḍ@i
ḥṣānak	ismak	waḍ@ak
ḥṣānik	ismik	waḍ@ik
ḥṣānu	ismu	waḍ@u
ḥṣānha	isimha	waḍi@ha
ḥṣānna	isimna	waḍi@na
ḥṣānkum	isimkum	waḍi@kum
ḥṣānkin	isimkin	waḍi@kin
ḥṣānhum	isimhum	waḍi@hum
ḥṣānhin	isimhin	waḍi@hin

Exercise 14: 1 The children are asleep. 2 The female peasants of our country are pretty. 3 The students in our school are doing well (lit., are successful). 4 Your street is full of shops. 5 The government has released the political prisoners. 6 Qadri has lost the key to the house. 7 Put the letters in the box.

8 (The really) happy (people) are the mad (people). 9 Five cups of coffee, please. 10 Home(-made) food is better than restaurant food.

Exercise 15: 1 el-mu@allimāt / li-m@allmāt en-nājḥāt ạkthar min el-muhandisāt en-nājḥāt. 2 el-fallaḥīn el-Masriyyīn fuqara. 3 zu@amā" el-@ālam hummeh muhandisīn el-mustaqbal. 4 el-fuqara ghuraba fi waṭanhum (*or* balad-hum). 5 el-ābā" (el-"ābā") salāṭīn fi byūt-hum. 6 iḥna su@ada. 7 akhṭār el-ḥarb zālat. 8 zōj khālti muhandis. 9 as@ār el-kutub @ālyeh jiddan. 10 el-mustaqbal ṣandūq bidūn miftāḥ.

Exercise 16: 1 maqfūleh 2 sa@īdīn / su@ada 3 sa@īdāt 4 @arīḍa 5 waṭaniyyeh 6 waṭaniyyīn 7 majanīn 8 ṣinā@iyyeh 9 nādreh 10 Faransiyyīn 11 shurafa 12 fuqara 13 faqīrāt

Exercise 17: Possible answers: 1 el-abwāb maqfūleh. 2 el-azwāj su@ada. 3 ez-zawjāt sa@īdāt. 4 el-khuṭūṭ @arīḍa. 5 el-a@yād el-waṭaniyyeh kthīreh. 6 ez-zu@amā" el-waṭaniyyīn masjunīn. 7 ba@ḍ (*some*) es-siyāsiyyīn majānīn. 8 el-aqmār eṣ-ṣinā@iyyeh mufīdeh (*useful*). 9 el-anwā@ en-nādreh ghālyeh (*precious, highly priced*). 10 el wusaṭā" el-Faransiyyīn nājḥīn. 11 el-wuzara shurafa. 12 el-umara fuqara. 13 el-mu@allimāt faqīrāt.

Exercise 18: 1 This is my daughter. 2 That is her car. 3 These girls are from her school. 4 That boy is her brother. 5 Deposit this sum in the bank. 6 This hotel is one of the high-class (*or* top-notch) hotels. 7 Put those books on the shelf. 8 Put this book near (i.e., next to) that one. 9 This door is locked; maybe that one is open. 10 This car is better than that one.

Exercise 19: 1 hādha 'l-fīl / ha 'l-fīl 2 hadhulāk el-afyāl / ha 'l-afyāl 3 hādhi 'l-qabīleh 4 hadhīk el-qabīleh 5 hādhi 'l-jawāhir 6 hadhulāk el mafatīḥ 7 hadhāk el-bāb 8 hāy el-aqlām 9 hāy el-akhṭār 10 hadhāk el-bank

Exercise 20: 1 Su@ād told me about you. 2 The Arabic language is one of the Semitic languages. 3 Nizār wrote a cheque without sufficient funds. 4 I usually go to bed without taking supper. 5 There are beautiful pictures in the book. 6 There is someone at the door. 7 This is Aḥmad bringing Ṣubḥi with him. 8 Is there anybody else with them? 9 There is an annoying (*or* jarring) noise in your car / Your car makes a jarring noise. 10 The noise of my car tells about me (i.e., indicates who is coming).

Exercise 21: 1 tarjim hāy el-jumleh la 'l-lugha 'l-@arabiyyeh. 2 ḥuṭṭ li-flūs (li *for* el) fi 'ṣ-ṣandūq. 3 Ṣubḥi fī ma@u flūs? 4 ḥuṭṭ el-kitāb @ala 'ṭ-ṭāwleh. 5 ḥakā lak @anni? 6 ḥakat lu @annak? 7 khudh li-flūs min Huda w ḥuṭṭha fi 'l-bank. 8 mīn kān ma@ Huda? 9 iḥkī lu @an el-mushkileh fi madrasit Huda. 10 id-han ghuruftak b' lōn abyaḍ.

CHAPTER 5

Exercise 22:

ana smi@tu / smi@t-ha	ihna smi@nā / smi@nāha
inta smi@tu / smi@t-ha	intu smi@tū / smi@tūha
huwweh sim@u / simi@ha	intin smi@tinnu / smi@tinha
hiyyeh sim@atu / sim@at-ha	hummeh sim@ū / sim@ūha
inti smi@tī / smi@tīha	hinneh sim@innu / sim@inha

Exercise 23: 1 Listen to this (bit of) news: Aḥmad has won 10,000 dinars. 2 Drink your tea. 3 Huda has returned from Germany. 4 I now know (lit., knew) who has won first prize. 5 Samīr, play with Sawsan in the other (lit., second) room. 6 Have they returned from Paris? 7 The price of the dollar has gone down. 8 Get off the car, boy. 9 Who has drunk my cup? 10 Aḥmad got wind of (lit., knew) the story and went down (i.e., went away) angry.

Exercise 24: 1 ummak nisyatni. 2 Aḥmad ṣiḥi mn (*for* min) en-nōm qabil sā@a. 3 Huda riḍyat @an zōjha w rij@at lu. 4 shaqqit Ḥāmid fiḍyat lamma sāfar la Amairka. 5 si@r edh-dhahab @ili (*or better:* irtafa@). 6 iṣḥi yā Huda; iṣḥa yā Munīr. 7 insa kull el-mawḍū@. ana nsītu. 8 riḍi mudīr el-bank @an @amalak?

Exercise 25: 1 Huda opened the door without permission. 2 My son has passed the final examination. 3 We have succeeded in this difficult test [not necessarily a school exam]. 4 Swim one hour every day / an hour a day. 5 They planted vegetables in their garden. 6 My brother sent me a letter from Italy. 7 Her father has forbidden her to visit us. 8 Sawsan asked about you. 9 They pushed mv car for me when it stalled. 10 *Cherchez la femme* (Look for the woman).

Exercise 26: 1 uktub maktūb (*or* risāleh) la akhūk. 2 udrus li ha 'l-mushkileh. 3 Huda saknat fi shaqqit khālit-ha. 4 Maḥmūd nashar kitābu (*or* iktābu) fi Bayrūt. 5 harbat el-bint min el-madraseh lamma ḍarbat-ha 'l-mudīreh. 6 fī hōn khabar @an mara qatlat zōjha (*or* jōzha). 7 Layla, urkuḍi; Ḥāzim @a 'l-bāb. 8 el-wazīr amar bi ijrā" taḥqīq.

Exercise 27: 1 Mother broke the coffee cup. 2 This door is locked; break it. 3 They incarcerated me unjustly. 4 Ghāda has drawn a picture like Picasso's pictures. 5 The rain has washed the street. 6 The army has attacked the city. 7 The soldiers burned the municipal building. 8 Wash your heart with love.

Exercise 28: 1 Yesterday I walked for a period of five hours. 2 The government fulfilled its promise. 3 He threw the jacket on the sofa and went into the room. 4 The criminal's wife informed on him. 5 Give me a glass of water, please (lit., Make me drink water). 6 Ḥāzim's mother cried joyfully (lit., out of joy) when she heard that her son had won first prize. 7 Salma, iron the white shirt for me, please. 8 The king patronized the ceremony.

Exercise 29: 1 I put the book on the bookshelf. 2 (It was) Salma (who) answered the phone; ask her who it was (lit., who spoke). 3 Shafīq and his wife paid me a visit yesterday (lit., passed on me). 4 Our soldiers have repulsed the attack. 5 You thought the problem (was) easy. 6 Ṣāliḥ has annexed his son's company to his (company).

Exercise 30: 1 Fadwa extended her hand to him but he ignored her. 2 Shut the door, please. 3 They loved each other for five years but fate stood against them. 4 Approval of the release of political prisoners has been finalized. 5 Urge your son to study (lit., on the study). 6 They felt that they made a mistake.

Exercise 31: 1 Where were you? We were at Huda's friend's house. 2 Huda fasted the entire month of Ramaḍān. 3 My grandfather died five years ago (lit., before five years). 4 Have your neighbours returned from Turkey? 5 The girls have gone to school. 6 Go and cash this cheque from the bank. 7 Did you see the accident that took place in front of the bank door? 8 Who told you about it? 9 Ḥusām told me. Did anybody die? 10 A woman who was standing in the street died.

Exercise 32: 1 After graduation Luṭfi became the deputy manager of the company. 2 What happened? 3 Follow the path of your father (i.e., follow in his footsteps). 4 Aḥmad flew joyfully (i.e., was filled with joy) when he heard the news.

5 Bring me five books from the library with you. 6 The government inclined towards raising the interest rates lately. 7 Repeat what you have (just) said in order that we may hear. 8 What has my father brought me from France?

Exercise 33: 1 Salwa went to bed after midnight. 2 When did you go to bed yesterday (i.e., last night)? 3 We spent the night at Sāmi's and went to bed after midnight. 4 I spent the night at the hotel and went to bed early. 5 Nadia was afraid of the dog and screamed. 6 Why were you afraid? This is a harmless dog.

CHAPTER 6

Exercise 34: 1 The school headmistress gave us a severe lecture (lit., made us hear harsh words). 2 Ḥusām, play us some nice music (lit., make us hear pretty music). 3 Maḥmūd returned the suit because the coat was small. 4 They turned us back from the airport because we didn't have a visa. 5 The teacher gave me a pass (lit., made me succeed) because I studied hard (lit., much). 6 Who taught you English at school? 7 Whoever smuggled the cigarettes (must have) smuggled the drugs. 8 The snow broke the trees. 9 Time (i.e., Life) has made me walk on a road full of thorns. 10 The embassy processed (lit., made to walk) my application for a visa quickly. 11 Yesterday (i.e., Last night) we saw a film that made us cry. 12 Your words have made me forget what I have come to tell you about. 13 Show her (lit., Make her see) the pictures in the album. 14 They starved us to death (lit., caused us to die out of hunger). 15 What made you a manager (*or* a head of the department) except your father the minister? 16 Fly your kite (out) in the garden. 17 The manager of the company has threatened to dismiss half of the employees for no clear reason. 18 Who liberated Algeria from France? 19 Shawqi has edited a book on Russo-American relations. 20 Dr Ghāzi freed her from fear when he explained to her the meaning of her dreams.

Exercise 35: 1 wa@adūna yīju 's-sā@a thamānyeh. 2 Huda, nādi Salma min ghurfit-ha. 3 wāfaq mudir el-bank yi@ṭini qarḍ. 4 abūy (abu + *poss. pron.* -i) ḥārab el-Atrāk fi 'l-ḥarb el-@ālamiyyeh 'l-ūla. 5 el-ḥukūmeh @ālajat el-mushkileh b' sur@a. 6 Na@īm māsha mudīr esh-sharikeh ḥatta @ayyanu musā@id mudīr. 7 @rifnāhum ba@id mā khālaṭnāhum. 8 ālāf en-nās hājaru min Libnān bi sabab el-ḥarb.

Exercise 36: 1 Aḥmad took his brother off the back of the horse. 2 Many of the inhabitants of Africa converted to Islam through trading (relations). 3 Snow damaged the crops. 4 The enemy drove us out of our country (**bilād/ blād:** plural in form, here singular in meaning). 5 His wound continued to bleed until Huda gave him first aid. 6 Ḥāmid failed in the exam, but why? (lit., what caused him to fail?) 7 Nu@man denied that he had seen Layla yesterday. 8 Prove (yourself) that he saw her. 9 The committee recommended that a new teacher be appointed. 10 @afāf was faithful to her husband but he was not faithful to her.

Exercise 37: 1 The trees collapsed (lit., got broken) under the weight of the snow. 2 Did you learn English at school? 3 Taḥsīn recognized the culprit *(or* criminal) from among five (other) criminals. 4 Do you remember me? (lit., did you remember me?) I'm Maḥmūd. 5 You've changed; you've become prettier. 6 The car driver deliberately collided with the policeman (lit., made a deliberate effort to . . .). 7 Huda turned her back on Aḥmad when he fell ill. 8 Make sure *(or possibly:* I assure you) that this news is true. 9 The children entertained themselves with the computer for more than two hours. 10 The company abandoned the project after its failure became a certainty.

Exercise 38: 1 Aḥmad has had a row with his wife. 2 The students have had a scuffle with the police. 3 I corresponded with her for a period of five years. 4 We exchanged many letters *(or* wrote many letters to each other). 5 We came to a mutual understanding regarding marriage (i.e., we agreed to get married), but time *(or* life) made her forget her promises. [**ez-zaman** here is a vague name for circumstances beyond one's control.] 6 People wondered about the reasons for (this) disagreement between us. 7 Aḥmad said to me, 'You were too optimistic.' 8 I said to him, 'I was neither optimistic nor pessimistic (i.e., it was not a question of optimism or pessimism); all that there is to it is that I was mad.' 9 'Go and make it up with her before she slips away from you.' 10 'I made it up with her too often (lit., I tried to win her favour back more than is necessary).'

Exercise 39: 1 The cup fell and got broken. 2 The car was overturned after it had collided with the bus. 3 Nizār was amazed when he heard the news. 4 She talked imprudently (lit., she went too far in what she said). 5 Sawsan has been admitted to the university. 6 We have been invited to Muna's wedding ceremony. 7 This kind of book is in high demand (lit., is asked for much).

Exercise 40: 1 The Americans have contrived a crisis with Europe (i.e., they have caused one unnecessarily). 2 We have been anxious (lit., we have desired) to see you. Where have you been all this time? 3 The company's work is over. 4 I waited half an hour for you, but you didn't come. 5 People (i.e., The audience) listened to the lecture and were amazed by the audacity of the lecturer. 6 Fikri was victorious over Maḥmūd in the elections. 7 @abdalla 'n-Nāṣiri's property extended from Ṣalāḥ ed-Dīn Street to el-Mutanabbi Street. 8 Why did you assume ill will in my words (i.e., that my words hide something evil)?

Exercise 41: 1 Tree leaves have turned yellow earlier than usual (lit., before it was time for them [to do so]). 2 Turn green, O world, not dusty. 3 The boy's face turned livid (lit., blue) for lack of oxygen (lit., because there was little oxygen). 4 Suddenly it turned dusty and dust started to fall (lit., rain).

Exercise 42: 1 Use force with them; I used it and it worked (lit., succeeded). 2 Today the minister received five European ambassadors. 3 Today the company laid off half the workers. 4 The criminal who had killed his wife asked the court for clemency today on account of his small daughter. 5 Ask for (i.e., Pray for) forgiveness from God/ Pray God to forgive you. 6 The bank got (was able to get) back all its money after the company had gone bankrupt. 7 Huda used you and you used me. 8 The bank has expressed its willingness to finance the project. 9 Having relaxed on the sofa for half an hour I regained my readiness to resume work (lit., regained my activity, felt fresh again).

Exercise 43: 1 The Arabs translated many of the books of the Greek philosophers. 2 Where did you camp? 3 They decorated the mosque with Islamic arabesques. 4 You have complicated (lit., philosophized) the subject too much. 5 She arranged the subject (lit., put it in interlinking chains) in such a way as to make it understandable. 6 Who designed (lit., engineered, architectured) this project? 7 Your words have confused all my thoughts. 8 Su@ād has upset all our plans (lit., projects).

CHAPTER 7

Exercise 44: (Remember: **ba-**: first person sing.; **bi/b(y)i/bi(y)**: all 3rd persons except 3rd person sing., feminine gender; **bit/bti**: all 2nd persons plus 3rd person singular, feminine gender; **bni/bin**: 1st person pl.; nom. suf. **-i** plus acc. suf. **-u** = **-ī**; nom. suf. **-u** plus acc. suf. **-u** = **-ū**.)
1 **bit shūfū hin:** Do you (*m. pl.*) see them (*f.*)? 2 **ba darris ha:** I teach her. 3 **ba drus ha:** I am studying it (*f.*). 4 **ba @rif hum:** I know them (*m.*). 5 **bti @rif i u:** Do you (*f. sing.*) know him? 6 **bti @irf i ni:** You (*f. sing.*) know me. 7 **bni @irf ik:** We know you (*f. sing.*). 8 **bti @irf ik:** She knows you (*f. sing.*). 9 **bi @irf ak:** He knows you (*m. sing.*). 10 **bti @raf hum:** Do you (*m. sing.*) know them (*m.*)? 11 **bi @raf u na**: Do they (*m.*) know us? 12 **bni @raf hin:** Do we know them (*f.*)? 13 **byi @raf in na:** Do they (*f.*) know us? 14 **bti t@allam i:** Are you (*f. sing.*) learning? (i.e., Do you go to school?) 15 **bti t@allam i u:** Are you (*f. sing.*) learning it (*m.*)? 16 **bti t@allam u u:** Are you (*m. pl.*) learning it (*m.*)? 17 **bi t@all(i)m u:** Are you (*m. sing.*) teaching him/it? 18 **bi t@all(i)m u u:** Are you (*m. pl.*) teaching him/it? 19 **bti t@allam i ha:** Are you (*f. sing.*) learning it (*f.*)? 20 **biy @all(i)m u kum:** Do they (*m.*) teach you (*m. pl.*)? 21 **bni t@allam u:** We learn it (*m.*). 22 **bin @all(i)m u:** We teach him/it. 23 **biy @allim na:** He teaches us. 24 **bi t@allam:** He is learning. 25 **bi @allim kum:** He teaches you/is teaching you (*m. pl.*).

Exercise 45: 1 I am learning Arabic. 2 Do you know that Arabic is one of the Semitic languages? 3 Who is teaching you Arabic? 4 I am studying it in a new book written in English. 5 Are you learning the spoken or the written language? 6 I am concentrating on the spoken language in order to communicate with the people. 7 But I know that Arabic books are written in a language that differs from the spoken language. 8 It differs a little, but the Arabs themselves feel that the written language is not natural for ordinary conversation.

Exercise 46: 1 el-@ālam eth-thālith byākul akthar min ma [*pronounce* mimma] byintij. 2 btīji la baitna kull yōm. 3 shū btākul/btākli/btāklu/btāklin? 4 wain btākhudhhum/btākhudhhin/btākhdhīhum/btākhdhīhin/btākhdhūhum/btākhdhūhin/btākhdhinhum/btākhdhinhin? 5 bnīji la baitak/baitjik/baitkum/baitkin kull yōm. 6 btākul/btākli/btāklu/btāklin laḥim khanzīr? 7 (hiyyeh) btīji la 'l-madraseh?

8 bīju / bījin la baitna yōm el-jum@a. 9 Aḥmad byākhudh ibnu la 's-sīnama kull yōm jum@a. 10 byākhdhūna / byākhdhinna la bait-hum / bait-hin kull yōm jum@a.

Exercise 47: 1 Maḥmūd, let Huda come down, please (i.e., tell her to . . .). 2 Tell your father to come tomorrow in order that we may talk about the matter. 3 Make me a cup of coffee, please. 4 I swear (i.e., I promise) to give you (lit., make you) a birthday party that is better than hers (lit., her birthday party). 5 Read this chapter in order to understand the idea. 6 I have cancelled my appointment with Sāmi in order to see you (lit., to come to see you). 7 I want to remind Sāmi of (our) appointment. 8 You should give your work all your time. 9 Don't take money from @ādil; I will give you (some). 10 May God have mercy on us (lit., May He grace us with His Grace).

Exercise 48: 1 The world will face a difficult period when (lit., after) oil is exhausted. 2 I want to *(or* shall) study medicine in Britain. 3 I am leaving tomorrow with my brother. He wants *(or* is going) to study engineering. 4 I shall phone you from there. 5 Studying there will make you forget everything.

CHAPTER 8

Exercise 49: 1 You and I are in agreement on this point. 2 I can read French (lit., I know how to), but I can't speak it. 3 Promises galore but little action (lit., Promises are plenty but action is little). 4 Sāmi loves her but he is afraid to broach the subject. 5 We remained worried about him because he neither telephoned nor wrote to us. 6 When you see him, give him my greetings. 7 Fu"ād is a loser wherever he goes. 8 Salwa is a good cook. However she cooks, her cooking turns out to be delicious. 9 I need a loan from the bank in order to open a supermarket. 10 Which one is better, this dress or this one? 11 Either you come to my house or I come to yours; we must discuss this problem tonight. 12 Even Salīm stood against me? After all I have done for him (lit., for his sake)? 13 Don't sell, whatever they may pay you (lit., paid you). 14 He divulged (lit., spoke) all his secrets while he was drunk. 15 Othello murdered his wife before he discovered (lit., knew) the truth. 16 Whatever you might say or do, my idea of you will always remain bad.

Exercise 50: 1 The person who (lit., He who) telephoned a little while ago is Mḥammad [*the common pronunciation of* Muḥammad]. 2 Who was the lady (lit., she) who was with you in Restaurant X yesterday? 3 I heard that you are going to marry Shafīq. Is that true (lit., correct)? 4 Why, you don't know that we've been engaged for five months now (lit., from five months)? 5 I knew that you were engaged, but I didn't know the name of the lucky man. 6 Who was it that introduced him to you? 7 Su@ād, who works with him at the bank, introduced him to me. 8 To tell you the truth, I was happy to hear (lit., when I heard) the news. Congratulations.

Exercise 51: 1 Who translated the works of Shakespeare into Arabic? 2 When did he translate them? Did he translate them in verse or in prose? 3 Where did he publish the translation and what were the difficulties? 4 How was the translation in your opinion? 5 How many plays did he translate (lit., plays by him, i.e., Shakespeare)? 6 How many copies do you normally publish of books like Shakespeare's books? 7 What is the price of (each) copy? 8 What do you think (lit., What is your opinion) of translating selections of Arabic poetry into English? 9 They say that Arabic poetry is difficult. Is this true (lit., correct)? 10 Which is more difficult, the poetry of Shakespeare or the poetry of el-Mutanabbi?

Exercise 52: 1 Don't give me promises; I want action from you. 2 I haven't been told (lit., haven't heard) about what happened; have you? 3 It can't be true (lit., doesn't stand to reason); Aḥmad told me in your presence (lit., while you were present). 4 Apparently I wasn't paying attention. 5 The important thing is that they have decided to separate because they cannot live in harmony (lit., agree). 6 Can't someone mediate between them? 7 I don't know; but don't you interfere. 8 I not interfere? Who is to interfere then? Aren't we their friends? 9 Friends or no friends, interference will only cause us (lit., bring) headache. 10 I'm not convinced.

Exercise 53: 1 ma@īsh flūs / maṣāri. 2 ma@hāsh khabar bi 'l-mawḍū@. 3 fī bainkum Almān? 4 wain ḥaṭṭait el-kutub? 5 mā lhāsh @anni ghina. 6 Suha mish fi ghurfit-ha. 7 ma fishsh @alaiha ḥaqq. 8 fī nakhil fi ḥadā"iq Kyū?

CHAPTER 9

Exercise 54: 1 Were there anybody in the house, he would have answered the telephone. 2 But for the Nile, Egypt would have become a desert. 3 The economy of the country will not improve unless exports double (lit., doubled). 4 The company is going to fire half the workers unless production doubles (lit., doubled) this year. 5 I've read the entire book except the last chapter. 6 If you are (lit., were) my friend indeed, help me out of this predicament. 7 Let's start the project if you are (lit., were) serious. 8 The price remains too high even if he gives you a 5% discount (lit., even if he lowered 5% for you).

Exercise 55: 1 Drinking alcoholic beverages is prohibited in Islam. 4 Tawfīq el-Ḥakim is a well-known Egyptian writer. 8 Come in; the door is open. 9 All subjects are open for discussion. 10 The future of this (lit., the) country's economy depends on agriculture. 12 My book is published in Britain, but its sale in America is prohibited. 13 Eat and don't be afraid; everything has been washed well. 22 Why are you afraid? Death is long sleep. And what are you going to lose except your wretchedness? You either live with honour or die with honour. 23 Drug smuggling is an international problem. 24 What do they do with returned books? 25 The entire world is threatened with the danger of drugs. 26 How often it is that the liberator of (his) homeland has become a dictator from whom the country must be liberated. 27 I've obtained my father's approval to study this matter; he accepts (this) in principle (or he has indicated his initial acceptance). 28 Fighting against monopoly is a national duty. 29 This patient has been treated badly. 30 The Prophet Muḥammad's emigration from Mecca to Medina is (*or* marks) the beginning of the Hijri calendar. 32 The city prepared itself to face the danger of landing from the sea. 33 He may be wrong; his words are not divine revelation. 34 Damaging official documents is a serious crime. 35 I am a director specializing in theatrical productions. 36 The output must be commensurate with the input. 37 Have you called for the ambulance (car)? His condition is very serious. 38 Terminating Aḥmad's services was a mistake: nobody knows the details of (our) work like him. 39 It is necessary to learn the rudiments of the computer before studying statistics. 40 Getting to know the causes of the problem is the first step (towards) solving it.

41 I don't remember who brought me this shirt from Paris, Shawqi or Huda. 42 Come and (lit., Be good enough to: the general term for inviting somebody) have lunch with us. Thank you, I've already had lunch. 43 Apparently Aḥmad was playing around with Samīra; he's left her without saying goodbye to her. 44 What is strange is that fighting (lit., mutual fighting) among friends is usually more intense than fighting among enemies. 45 An exchange of ambassadors took place lately between our country (lit., state) and yours, and mutual trade relations have developed (lit., have come into existence). 46 Recently, the states of the region signed an understanding (memorandum) on fishing rights in the Gulf. 47 Your question (lit., wondering) is well taken; I don't know the reason for what happened myself. 48 Tell me (lit., Make me understand), are you forgetting or pretending to forget? Pretending to forget is useless. 49 Persistence (lit., Going too far) in wrong doing is worse than the error itself. 50 The breaking of his leg did not prevent him from continuing to love sports. 51 The reason why rainbows (lit., the rainbow) appear is the refraction of light in raindrops (lit., the rain). 52 Military coups have led to instability in many of the Third World states. 53 You are too impetuous (lit., speeding or racing recklessly); slow down a little. 54 The grace period is over and he hasn't paid back his debts. 55 The situation there will take a long time to clear up. Don't act hastily. 56 Contrived feelings need a lot of effort (i.e., to act them out). 57 The listeners have been bored with the repetition of these silly songs. 58 There will not be a victor and a loser in the Third World War. 59 What is to be expected (i.e., can you expect) from someone like him? 60 There is a large oil slick alongside the entire west coast. 61 It is expected that the cold weather will even be colder (lit., more intense) during the next week. 62 I'm dying to hear a nice word from you, but alas. 63 I hope to visit you after the semester is over. 65 His face is red from bashfulness. 66 Green land refreshes the soul. 67 Why is his face turning blue (*or* livid)? Could he have eaten something poisoned? 68 I bought five second-hand books. 69 Huda works as a receptionist. 70 What is the future of Arab-European relations in your view? 71 The riches of the sea have not been exploited at all; the future of the world may be dependent on exploiting these riches well. 72 I'm not prepared to listen to this absurd nonsense (lit., talk); if you are prepared (to do so), stay. I'm leaving. 73 The company has decided to

lay off (lit., to do without the services of) 10% of the workers. 74 The government has decided to confiscate the smugglers' possessions. 75 Not all of Voltaire's works have been translated into Arabic. 76 My son is an architect. 77 What's this confusion? The first chapter is placed after the third.

CHAPTER 10

Exercise 56: 1 I don't know them well. 2 The plan worked out (succeeded) brilliantly. 3 Drinking intoxicants is strictly prohibited in Ramaḍān. 4 Shākir responded to the manager violently. 5 Layla loved Qays sincerely. 6 Last night I slept intermittently. 7 They travelled from Beirut to Paris directly. 8 The journey was very comfortable. 9 It took approximately five hours. 10 They arrived in the morning and telephoned immediately.

Exercise 57: 1 mīn a@azz @alaik (/aḥabb ilak/aghla @alaik), abūk willa ummak? 2 fī ṭayyarāt asra@ min eṣ-ṣōt. 3 akhūy akbar minni, lākin ana akbar min ukhti. 4 el-Mutanabbi a@ẓam shā@ir fi 'l-adab el-@arabi. 5 takālīf el-ma@īsheh fi Maṣir aqall min Awrubba bi kthīr. 6 fi ra"yi, Shakespeare a@ẓam shā@ir fi 'l-@ālam. 7 el-jaww abrad fi Faransa min el-jaww fi Barīṭānya? 8 el-malābis akhaff min el-kutub. khudh malābsak ma@ak w ib@ath el-kutub bi 'l-barīd. 9 inta dāyman mista@jil. el-yōm ana mista@jil akthar minnak. 10 mīn akthar istiqlālan/ mustaqill akthar: Rāshid willa Luṭfi?

CHAPTER 11

Exercise 58: 1 kānat el-@ilāqāt el-@arabiyyeh 'l-Awrubbiyyeh mawḍū@ mubāḥathāt/munāqashāt ṭawīleh bain zu@amā" el-jānibain. 2 el-ustādh Nāṣir nashar dirāsāt @ilmiyyeh fi @iddit majallāt Awrubbiyyeh. 3 eṣ-ṣādirāt ez-zirā@iyyeh lāzim tizdād ḥatta nḥassin mīzān el-madfū@āt. 4 el-Muslim byiqdar/ biqdar el-Muslim yitzawwaj/yitjawwaz Masīḥiyyeh? 5 ṣaḥibna lābis badleh binniyyeh w qamīṣ azraq w rabṭa/ karafatta burtuqāliyyeh. 6 muḥādathāt/mubāḥathāt esh-shamāl w el-janūb wiṣlat ila ṭarīq masdūd. 7 lōn sayyārti zaytūni; shū lōn sayyārtak? 8 maratu/zōjtu Sūdāniyyeh w ibtiḥki thalath lughāt Awrubbiyyeh. 9 es-sitār el-ḥadīdi tbayyan innu sitār ḥarīri. 10 ba@taqid inn el-isti@mār el-fikri afẓa@ min el-isti@mār el-@askari. iḥana bniqdar inḥārib el-isti@mār el-@askari bi 'l-@uSi w el-hijāra, lākin kif nḥārib shī mish maḥsūs mithl ed-dabbābāt w el-junūd?

Exercise 59: 1 tis@a w sittīn saneh. 2 muftāḥain. 3 ghuruftain / ghurfitain. 4 thalath ghuraf. 5 miyyeh w sitteh w sab@īn dīnār. 6 mīt walad. 7 thalātheh w @ishrīn kitāb. 8 sabi@ asabī@. 9 mitain w sitṭāshar ṣafḥa. 10 sitt malāyīn dūlār.

Exercise 60:

A: Dad, Mahmūd is on the telephone; he wants to talk to you (lit., he wants you).
B: What does he want?
A: I don't know. Will you talk to him?
B: Give me the telephone. Yes, Maḥmūd, what do you want?
C: I want to tell you, dad, that Samīr, his father and his mother will be calling on us tonight. Which means that you shouldn't go out (tonight).
B: What's up?
C: They want to ask for Suha's hand.
B: Suha? Does she know?
C: Know? Of course she knows.
B: Suha. Suha. Where have you gone?
A: Yes, dad. Here I am.
B: Is your mother ready?
A: Why?
B: We're going out.
A: Going out? I mean, do you have to?
B: Why not?
A: I don't know. Didn't Maḥmūd say anything?
B: Anything? What do you mean?
A: I don't know.
B: About Samīr, for example?
A: Maybe.
B: But you don't know.
A: I don't know.
B: Do you know or don't you?
A: Maybe.

CONVERSATIONS

1

A: Are you from Jordan/Syria/Iraq/Saudi Arabia, sir?
B: Yes, and you?
A: I'm from Britain.
B: And you're coming to Jordan/Syria/Iraq/Saudi Arabia on a tour or to do business?
A: On a tour and to do business.
B: What do you do (i.e., what kind of business)?
A: I'm a representative of a publishing house. I want to visit some (of your) schools and universities in order to see (about) their needs.
B: What kind of books do you publish?
A: We publish scientific books in all (lit., various) specializations and books on teaching English.
B: Are your books expensive?
A: There are expensive books and cheap ones, but you know that book prices are rising continually.
B: True.
A: Do you think that there is a market for books in English in your country?
B: There may be with regard to scientific books and books on teaching languages, provided that their prices are reasonable. Most of our students are poor.
A: We give a good discount.
B: I wish you success.
A: Thank you.

2

A: Hello, sir (lit., brother).
B: Hello.
A: Could you tell me where Funduq el-Madīneh is, please?
B: Funduq el-Madīneh is a long way from here.
A: How can I reach it?
B: You should take a taxi.
A: Do taxi drivers know where it is?
B: Most of them do (lit., know it). Ask the driver before you go (lit., go up [into the car]) with him.
A: Thank you.
B: You're welcome.

3

A: Good morning.
B: Good morning.
A: I'd like to have a room, please.
B: Do you have one reserved?
A: No, I haven't reserved.
B: All right, there is a room on the tenth floor.
A: Good.
B: What's the name, please?
A: John Smith.
B: From which country, sir?
A: From Britain.
B: And how long are you going (lit., do you intend) to stay in the hotel?
A: About a week.
B: You're welcome, Mr Smith. We wish you a pleasant stay (here).
A: Thank you.
B: Sign here, please [**tfaḍḍal**: be good enough to; **min faḍlak** intensifies the politeness of the request]. Thank you. Here is the key to your room (lit., And this is the key of the room). Room no. 1026. The suitcases will be up immediately.
A: Thank you.

4

A: Hello [form used on the phone].
B: Hello [people, especially women, are reluctant to identify themselves on the phone to a stranger who has not identified himself first].
A: Is this Aḥmad el-@umarī's residence, please?
B: Yes. Who is speaking?
A: This is (lit., I am) John Smith. May I speak to Aḥmad, please?
B: One moment, please.

C: John?
A: Hello, Aḥmad.
C: Hello, John. Where are you talking from [**mnain = min wain:** from where]?
A: From the hotel.
C: Which hotel?

A: Funduq el-Madīneh.
C: All right, I'll be with you in (lit., after) a quarter of an hour. Wait for me near the reception desk.
A: OK. But I shan't be able to visit you at home tonight.
C: All right. We'll talk about this in a quarter of an hour.
A: But don't be late.
C: No, sir (lit., Your command) [used jocularly among friends to indicate compliance].

5

A: Hello.
B: Hello, sir.
A: Do you have good chocolates?
B: We have locally made and imported chocolates.
A: I want a box of chocolates (to take) as a gift.
B: Would you prefer (lit., take) a locally made or a French (brand)? The French is naturally more expensive.
A: It doesn't matter (lit., Not important). How much is the box?
B: Six dinars.
A: (Gift) wrap a box for me, please.
B: Yes, sir (lit., Your command) [addressed by an inferior to a superior or by a businessman to a customer to indicate compliance].
A: But I have only sterling.
B: That would be even better.
A: Why better?
B: Hard currency for hard times.
A: What do you mean?
B: If I went to a shop (lit., place) in London and offered our currency to buy a box of chocolates, would it sell me (one)?
A: I don't think so.
B: This is (what I mean by) 'hard times'.
A: I see what you mean.

6

A: Su@ād, let me introduce (lit., I am introducing) to you my friend John Smith.
B: Pleased to meet you (lit., You are welcome), Mr Smith.

C: John, please. Aḥmad and I (lit., I and Aḥmad) [first person pronoun takes precedence in Arabic] have been friends for years.
B: He told me a great deal about you.
C: Not everything, I hope?
B: Enough!
C: If so, don't give him a single bar (lit., a piece) from this box!
B: You shouldn't have taken all this trouble [a standard phrase when one is presented with a gift].
C: No trouble at all.
B: Shall I bring you something to drink?
A: Su@ād, John is not a drinker of coffee or tea.
C: Don't listen to him. I love Turkish coffee.
B: By the way, you speak Arabic quite well. Where did you learn it?
C: (I learnt it) at the hands of Professor Aḥmad. He made me forget (my) English.
B: I thought you made him forget (his) Arabic, for when he came back from Britain, we had to employ an interpreter.
C: Not an interpreter: an interpretress – Professor Su@ād el-@umarī, M.Phil., Ph.D., etc., etc.

7

A: Welcome.
B: Thank you (lit., Welcome to you, too).
A: Would you like to drink something before eating?
B: Yes. What do you have?
A: Everything (lit., Everything exists, i.e., is available). Would you like me to bring you (some) red wine?
B: I'd like to have (lit., I want) orange juice.
C: Juice for me, too (lit., Me, too, juice).

B: What would you like to eat? Do you prefer eastern or western food?
C: Eastern, of course, but I'd like to try something other than Indian or Chinese food.
B: Would you like to have (lit., eat) **mansaf**?
C: What's a **mansaf**?
B: A Jordanian national dish.
C: What is it made of?

B: Rice, lamb chops and cooked yoghurt.
C: All right. Let's try it.
B: Or shall we let him (i.e., the waiter) bring you a steak?
C: No, no. I'd like to try . . . what's it called?
B: **Mansaf**.
C: Yes. **Mansaf**.
B: All right.

8

A: Hello.
B: Welcome.
A: My name is John Smith. I have an appointment with the dean.
B: Go in, please [**tfaḍḍal** is the general term to invite somebody to do something, usually accompanied with the appropriate gesture. Literally, it means 'be good enough to']. The dean is waiting for you.
A: Thank you.

C: Welcome, Mr Smith.
A: Thank you (lit., Welcome to you, too).
C: Have a seat, please.
A: Thank you.
C: Would you like to drink coffee or tea?
A: Nothing, thank you. I wanted (lit., loved) to see you (lit., pass by you) in order to show you some of the products our company produces.
C: Books?
A: Not only books. We produce educational programmes recorded on video tapes. Many schools in the Gulf states have tried them, and they have been quite successful.
C: What is the language of these programmes?
A: Originally they were made in English, but there are Arabic versions of them. The dubbing was done in Egypt in the written (form) of Arabic – What do you call it? **el-fuṣḥa**?
C: Yes. Very good, let's see them.

9

A: Good morning.
B: Good morning.
A: I'd like a ticket to Athens, please.
B: When will you be leaving?
A: On Wednesday.
B: I'm afraid (lit., With sorrow), there are no vacancies on Wednesday. There are vacancies on Friday if that is all right with you (lit., if you like/love).
A: Is Wednesday out of the question (lit., quite impossible)?
B: If you wish, we can put you on the waiting list.
A: And if no vacancies are available?
B: You take the Friday flight (lit., You leave on Friday). Anyway, you should confirm the reservation two days in advance (of departure day).
A: All right (lit., No objection). But please, don't forget (about) Wednesday.
B: Call us on Wednesday morning.
A: OK.
B: What's your name, please?
A: John Smith.
B: A return (lit., A going and returning) ticket?
A: No, one-way (lit., going) only.
B: OK.
A: How much is the ticket to Athens?
B: A hundred and twenty dinars. Here, reservation has been made for you (lit., we have reserved for you) [Modern Arabic avoids the passive voice] for Friday at 3:30 p.m. Be at the airport two hours before departure time (lit., the aeroplane's time).
A: OK. I shall call on Wednesday morning in the hope of finding a place.
B: I hope there will be (one).
A: Thank you.
B: You're welcome.

10

A: Aḥmad, it seems that there isn't a plane to Athens on Wednesday.
B: Which is better.
A: Better?
B: Certainly. We haven't seen enough of you and we haven't taken you anywhere. How about (lit., What is your opinion of) going to Petra with us?
A: Is it far (from here)?
B: We can go and come back in one day. And if you wish, we can spend one night there.
A: A good idea.
B: Then come tomorrow morning, or, better still, we shall collect (lit., pass by) you at seven o'clock.
A: Should I bring anything with me?
B: Bring your camera with you. There are scenes there that deserve to be photographed.
A: Is there a good restaurant there?
B: Yes, and Su@ād will prepare some light sandwiches.
A: Good.
B: By the way, do you like horse riding?
A: Yes. Why?
B: Because there is a distance of about four kilometres between the entrance and the Rose-Red City.
A: Horse riding was one of my old hobbies.
B: Very good. And we shall make you ride a camel as well.
A: A camel?
B: Yes. Riding a camel there is part of the fun. You will look more impressive (lit., beautiful) than T. E. Lawrence himself!
A: See you tomorrow morning at seven o'clock, then. I'll be at the door of the hotel.
B: See you (lit., God willing).

11

A: Ḥāmid? I can't believe my eyes.
B: Hello, Bahjat. How are you?
A: Very well (lit., Praise be to God), and you?
B: Very well.
A: Where have you been all this time, old chap?
B: I was studying in the United States (lit., America).

A: In which state?
B: In California.
A: And what did you study?
B: I studied chemistry.
A: And what degree have you obtained?
B: The Master's degree.
A: Congratulations. And what are you going to do (lit., What are you going to work, i.e., What kind of job are you going to look for)?
B: I really don't know. I saw an ad in the paper from a pharmaceutical company. Do you think they will take chemists?
A: Why not?
B: Pharmaceutical factories may prefer people specializing in pharmacy.
A: Try, and if they turn you down, look for another job.
B: I shall try, of course.
A: I wish you all success.
B: Thank you. See you soon (lit., Let's see you).
A: Certainly.
B: Goodbye.
A: Goodbye.

Mini-dictionary

The following Mini-dictionary broadly follows English alphabetical order. Since in this course we have disregarded the Arabic alphabet altogether, no attempt has been made to differentiate between **d/ḍ, h/ḥ, s/ṣ, t/ṭ** and **z/ẓ** within the word, but words with identical initial dotted letters have been put together after the undotted ones for the reader's convenience. The combinations **dh**, **gh**, **kh**, **sh** and **th** are also separated out where they begin a word. Thus the order used is:

" @ a b d ḍ dh e f g gh h ḥ i j k kh l m n o q r s ṣ sh t ṭ th u v w y z ẓ

Capitalization, which has no counterpart in the Arabic alphabet, has been used in accordance with English usage.

The dictionary uses the following abbreviations:

adj.	adjective	part.	particle
adv.	adverb	pl.	plural
AP	active participle	PP	passive participle
conj.	conjunction	prep.	preposition
def. art.	definite article	pron.	pronoun
dem.	demonstrative	rel.	relative
det.	determined	sing.	singular
f.	feminine	sthg	something
imp.	imperative	sub.	subordinating
imperf.	imperfect	usu.	usually
interr.	interrogative	v.*	verb
m.	masculine	var.	variant
n.	noun	VN	verbal noun

* Roman and Arabic numerals after v. indicate verb class.

Words marked † belong more to Standard Arabic than to the spoken language. Where not otherwise stated, adjective and noun forms given in brackets are in the order: m. pl., f., f. pl.

@a (prep., var. of **@ala**) on
@abbar (v.II.1) expressed
@ād (v.I.11) repeated
@ād (v.I.10) returned
@adad (nm, pl. **a@dād**) number
@adam (nm) lack of, non-existence
@ādatan (adv.) usually, normally
@ādi (adj/m, **@ādiyyīn, @ādiyyeh, @adiyyāt**) normal, ordinary
@aduww (nm, **a@dā", @aduwweh, @aduwwāt**) enemy

@afwan (adv.) sorry; you're welcome (in answer to 'thank you')
@āfyeh (nf) good health, bodily strength
@ain (nf, pl. **@(u)yūn**) eye
@āj (nm) ivory
@ajūz (nm/f, pl. **@ajā"iz/ @ajāyiz**) old person
@ala (prep.) on
@ala shān (var. **@a shān**) in order that, so that
@ālaj (v.III.1) treated medically or chemically
@alam (nm, pl. **a@lām**) flag
@ālam (nm, pl. **@awālim**) world
@alāmāt (nf, sing. **@alāmeh**) signs
@ālami (adj/m, f. **@ālamiyyeh**) worldwide, international
@āli (adj/m, **@ālyīn, @ālyeh, @ālyāt**) high
@allam (v.II.1) taught
@ama (nm) blindness
@āmal (v.III.1) treated
@amal (nm, pl. **a@māl**) work
@amāra (nf, pl. **@amārāt**) building
@amīd (nm, pl. **@umada/ @umadā"**) dean (of college)
@amīm (adj/m) prevalent, touching everybody
@amīq (adj/m, f. **@amīqa**) deep
@amm (nm, pl. **a@mām**) paternal uncle
@ammān (nf) Amman
@ammeh (nf, pl. **@ammāt**) paternal aunt
@an (prep.) about
@anīd (adj/m, **@anidīn, @anīdeh, @anidāt**) stubborn
@arab (nm) Arabs
@arabi (adj/m, pl. **@arab**) an Arab; the Arabic language
@arabiyyeh (adj/f, pl. **@arabiyyāt**) Arab, Arabic
@araḍ (v.I.5) exhibited, offered
@arīḍ (adj/m, f. **@arīḍa**) wide, broad
@ārif (AP/nm, **@ārfīn, @ārfeh, @ārfāt**) knowing, not ignorant
@arraf (v.II.2) caused to know, defined
@āsh (v.I.11) lived
@asha (nm) supper
@ashara (nf) ten
@asharāt (nf, sing. **@ashara**) tens, dozens
@āshir (AP/nm, f. **@āshreh**) tenth
@aṣir (nm, var. **@aṣr**, pl. **@uṣūr**) age, era, epoch
@aṣir (nm) afternoon
@aṣīr (nm) juice
@askar (nm) troops, the military collectively
@askar (v.XI) camped, stationed (troops)
@askari(adj/m, f. **@askariyyeh**) military
@awāṭif (nf, sing. **@at(i)feh**) feelings
@awdeh (nf) return (trip)
@āyish (AP/nm, **@āyshīn, @āysheh, @āyshāt**) living
@ayyan (v.II.1) appointed
@aẓīm (adj/m, **@uẓama, @aẓīmeh, @aẓimāt**) great
@īd (nm, pl. **a@yād**) feast, national festival
@iddeh (nf) the quality of being multiple or several
@ilāj (VN/m) treatment
@ilāqa (nf, pl. **@ilāqāt**) relationship
@ili (v.I.2) went up, rose up
@ilim (v.I.1) knew, learned
@ilim (nm, var. **@ilm**, pl. **@ulūm**) science
@illeh (nf) ailment
aḥruf el-@illeh vowel letters
@ilmi (adj/m, f. **@ilmiyyeh**) scientific

@imil (v.I.1) made, did
@ind (prep.) at, with, near
@inna (= **@ind** + **na**) we have
@inwān (nm, pl. **@anāwīn**) address, title (of a book)
@irāq (nm, always with def. art.) Iraq
@irif (v.I.1) knew
@ishrīn (nm / f) twenty
@ishrīnāt (nf, sing. **@ishrīn**) twenties
@ulamā" (nm, sing. **@ālim**) scientists
@ulūm (nf, sing. **@ilm/@ilim**) sciences
@umleh (nf, var. **@imleh**, pl. **@umlāt**) currency
@umleh ṣa@beh hard currency
@ummāl (nm, sing. **@āmil**) workers, labourers
@umr (nm, var. **@umur**) age, life span
@umri, @umrak (etc.) never
@unf (nm) violence
@uṣi (nf, sing. **@aṣa**) sticks
@uṭleh (nf, pl. **@uṭal**) holiday

a@amm (adj / m / f) more general than
a@azz (adj / m / f) dearer
a@dā" (nm, sing. **@aduww**) enemies
a@jab (v.IV.1) caused admiration or liking
a@lam (adj / m / f) of greater knowledge
a@māl (nf, sing. **@amal**) works, business
a@ṭa (v.IV.2) gave
a@ẓam (adj / m / f) greater than
ab (nm, pl. **ābā"**) father
Āb (nm) August
ab@ad (v.IV.1) went too far
ābā" (nm, sing. **ab**) fathers, forefathers
abadan (adv.) never, not at all
abkar (adj / m / f) earlier
abrad (adj / m / f) colder than
Abrīl (nm) April
abu (nm, pl. **ābā"**) father in **iḍāfa** construction
abyaḍ (adj / m, **bīḍ, baiḍa, bīḍ**) white
adab (nm, pl. **ādāb**) literature
adabi (adj / m, f. **adabiyyeh**) literary
adda (v.IV.2) led to
adfa (adj / m / f) warmer than
Ādhar (nm) March
adhka (adj / m / f) more intelligent than
adwiyeh (nf, sing. **dawa**) medicines
afḍal (adj / m / f) better than
afkār (nf, sing. **fikra**) ideas
aflas (v.IV.1) became bankrupt
Aflāṭūn (nm) Plato
Aflāṭūni (adj / m) Platonic
Aflāṭūniyyeh (nf) Platonism
afraj (v.IV.1) released
Afrīqya (nf) Africa
afshal (v.IV.1) thwarted, caused the failure of
afẓa@ (adj / m / f) more horrible than
aghāni (nf, sing. **ughniyeh**) songs
aghla (adj / m / f) dearer, more expensive
Aghusṭus (nm) August
ahabb (adj / m / f) dearer, more lovable than
āḥād (nf, sing. **wāḥad/wāḥid**) ones; units of a figure
Aḥad (nm, usu. attached to def. art.) Sunday
ahammiyyeh (nf) importance
aḥann (adj / m / f) more loving or caring than
aḥla (adj / m / f) sweeter, more beautiful than
ahlain (adv., dual of **ahlan**) a double welcome

aḥlām (nf, sing. **ḥil(i)m/ḥul(u)m**) dreams
ahlan (adv.) welcome
ahlan wa sahlan (adv.) welcome
aḥmar (adj/m, **ḥumur, ḥamra, ḥumur**) red
aḥruf (nf, sing. **ḥarf**) letters of the alphabet
aḥsan (adj/m/f) better
aimta (interr. part.) when
aish (interr. part.) what
aja (v. irreg.) came
ajadd (adj/m/f) newer than
ajmal (adj/m/f) more beautiful than
akal (v. irreg.) ate
akbar (adj/m/f) bigger than
akhadh (v. irreg.) took
akhaff (adj/m/f) lighter than
akhbār (nf, sing. **khabar**) news
akhīr (adj/m, **akhīrīn, akhīreh, akhīrāt**) last
akhkh (nm, pl. **ikhwān/ikhweh**) brother
akhlaṣ (v.IV.1) remained faithful
akhraj (v.IV.1) got sthg out, directed (film or play)
akhu (nm, pl. **akhweh/ikhweh**) brother
akkad (v.II.1) asserted, stressed
akl (nm, var. **akil**) food
akleh (nf, pl. **aklāt**) kind of food, dish
akthar (adj/m/f) more than
ālāf (nf, sing. **al(i)f**) thousands
alam (nm, pl. **ālām**) pain
albōm (nm, pl. **albōmāt**) album
alf (nm, pl. **ālāf**) thousand
alfain (nm, dual of **alf**) two thousand
algha (v.IV.2) cancelled
alīf (adj/m) tame, domesticated
Allah (nm, var. **Alla**) God
Almāni (adj/m, **Almān, Almāniyyeh, Almāniyyāt**) German
Almāniyyeh (adj/f, pl. **Almāniyyāt**) German
Almānya (nf) Germany
Amairka (nf) America
Amairkān (nm, sing. **Amairkāni**) Americans
amal (nm, pl. **āmāl**) hope
amar (v.I.4) ordered
amarr (adj/m/f) more bitter than
amīr (nm, **umara/umarā", amīra, amīrāt)** prince
amlāk (nf, sing. **mil(i)k/mul(u)k**) possessions, wealth
amma (conj.) as for, whereas
amrak (= **amr + -ak**) lit., your command; yes sir!
Amrīka (nf) America
Amrīki (adj/m, **Amrīkiyyīn, Amrīkiyyeh, Amrīkiyyāt**) American
amtār (nf, sing. **mit(i)r**, m.) metres
amṭār (nf, sing. **maṭar**) rain
amwāl (nf, sing. **māl**) possessions, wealth
an@am (adj/m/f) softer than
an@ash (v.IV.1) refreshed
ana (pron.) I
anha (v.IV.2) ended, finished
āniseh (nf, pl. **ānisāt)** Miss
ankar (v.IV.1) denied
antaj (v.IV.1) produced
anzal (v.IV.1) got sthg down
aqall (adj/m/f) less than
aqdām (nf, sing. **qadam**) feet
aqlām (nf, sing. **qalam**) pens, pencils
araqq (adj/m/f) softer, more delicate than
arba@ (nm/f) in **iḍāfa** construction: four
arba@a (nf) four
arba@īn (nf, var. **arb@īn**) forty
arba@ṭāsh (nf) fourteen
arbāḥ (nf, sing. **rib(i)ḥ**) profits

Arbi@a (nf, var. **Arbi@ā"/Arb@a**, usu. attached to def. art.) Wednesday
arḍ (nf, pl. **arāḍi**) land
arjūk (= **raja** (implored) + **-ak**) I implore you, i.e., please
arqām (nf, sing. **raqm/raqim**) numbers, figures
arwa@ (adj/m/f) more wonderful than
aṣ@ab (adj/m/f) more difficult
as@af (v.IV.1) provided with medical aid
as@ār (nf, sing. **si@ir**) prices
asābī@ (nf, sing. **usbū@**) weeks
asaf (nm) sorrow (that sthg is or has been done)
asās (nm, pl. **usus**) basis, foundation
asbāb (nf, sing. **sabab**) reason, cause
aṣdiqā" (nm, sing. **ṣadīq**) friends
āsfeh (AP/nf) I (fem.) am sorry
āsfīn (AP/nm) we (masc.) are sorry
aṣḥāb (nm, sing. **ṣāḥib**) friends
ashadd (adj/m/f) greater than, more so than
ashhur (nf, sing. **shah(a)r**) months
āsif (AP/nm, **āsfīn, āsfeh, āsfāt**) sorry
aslam (v.IV.1) converted to Islam
aṣlan (adv.) originally, to begin with
asra@ (v.IV.1) moved fast, acted quickly
asrār (nf, sing. **sirr**) secrets
aswa" (adj/m/f) worse than
athbat (v.IV.1) proved
Athīna (nf) Athens
atlaf (v.IV.1) damaged, destroyed
Atrāk (nm, sing. **Turki**, f. **Turkiyyeh**, pl. **Turkiyyāt**) Turks
aw (conj.) or
aw@a (adj/m/f) more aware than
awān (nm) right time for sthg to happen
Awrubba (nf) Europe
Awrubbi (adj/m, **Awrubbiyyīn, Awrubbiyyeh, Awrubbiyyāt**) European
awṣa (v.IV.2) recommended, left a will
awwal (adj/m, **awā"il, ūla, awā"il**) first
aydi (nf, var. **ayādi**, sing. **īd**) hands
Aylūl (nm) September
aywa (adv.) yes
ayy (pron.) any
Ayyār (nm) May
azmeh (nf, pl. **azamāt**) crisis
azraq (adj/m, **zur(u)q, zarqa, zur(u)q**) blue

b@īd (adj/m, **b@idīn, b@īdeh, b@idāt**) far away
bā@ (v.I.11) sold
ba@aḍ (pron.) each other
ba@ath (v.I.3) sent
ba@ḍ (pron.) some
ba@d (prep. var. **ba@id**) after
ba@dain (adv.) later
ba@id (prep.) after
ba@id mā (conj.) after
bā@ith (AP/nm, **bā@thin, bā@theh, bā@thāt**) sending, sender
bāb (nm, pl. **abwāb**) door
bāba (nm) father
bābain (nm, dual of **bāb**) two doors
bada (v.I.3, **bada": ibda"**, hamzas omitted for ease of pronunciation) began
bādal (v.III.1) exchanged, bartered
badal (v.I.5) exchanged

badleh (nf; pl. **badlāt**) suit
baḥar (nm, pl. **b(u)ḥūr**) sea
baḥath (v.I.3) looked for, discussed
bāhir (AP/nm) brilliant
bai@ (VN/m) sale
baiḍa (adj/f, pl. **bīḍ**) white
baik (nm) title of respect to addressee
bain (prep.) between
bain mā (conj.) while
bait (nm, pl. **byūt**) house
bajāma (nf, pl. **bajamāt**) pyjamas
baka (v.I.6) cried, shed tears
bakait (nm, pl. **bakaitāt**) box (of chocolates, cigarettes, etc.)
bakka (v.II.2) caused someone to cry
bakkīr (adv.) early
bala (prep.) without
balad (nm, pl. **b(i)lād**) country
baladiyyeh (nf, pl. **baladiyyāt**) municipality
bālagh (v.III.1) exaggerated
balāsh (adj/m/f) dirt-cheap, free of charge
ballagh (v.II.1) informed, told
banāt (nf, sing. **bint**) girls, daughters
bank (nm, pl. **b(u)nūk**) bank
banzīn (nm) petrol
barāmij (nf, sing. **barnāmij/ barnāmaj**) programmes
bard (nm) cold weather
barīd (nm) mail
dā"irit el-barīd post office
bārid (adj/m, **bārdin, bārdeh, bārdāt**) cold
Barīs (nf) Paris
Barīṭāni (adj/m, **Barīṭāniyyīn, Barīṭāniyyeh, Barīṭāniyyāt**) British
barra (adv.) outside
bāṣ (nm, pl. **baṣāt**) bus
bass (conj.) but
bāt (v.I.11) spent the night
baṭal (nm, pl. **abṭāl**) hero, champion
Batra (nf) Petra in Jordan
bātt (adj/m) final, irrevocable, in phrase **mani@ bātt,** irrevocable prohibition
baṭṭal (v.II.1) gave up, left his job
bayāt (VN/m) spending the night
bayatān (VN/m) spending the night
bāyit (AP/nm, **bāytin, bāyteh, bāytāt)** person spending the night
bi (prep., var. **ib, b'**) with, by
bīḍ (adj/m/f, sing. **abyaḍ/baiḍa**) white
bidāyeh (nf, pl. **bidāyāt**) beginning
bid(d)- (v.) I, you, etc., want to
bidūn (prep.) without
biḥār (nf, sing. **baḥar**) seas
bint (nf, pl. **banāt**) girl, daughter
bintain (nf, dual of **bint**) two girls or daughters
blād (nf, var. **bilād**, sing. **balad**) countries
blāstik (nm) plastic
blūzeh (nf, pl. **balāyiz**) blouse
budd in phrase **lā budd** it is necessary that, it must be that, it should be
bukra (adv.) tomorrow
bunn (nm) coffee
bunni (adj/m, f. **bunniyyeh**) brown
buq@a (nf, pl. **buqa@**) spot
buq@it nafṭ oil slick
burtuqāl (nm, f. **burtuqāleh,** an orange, pl. **burtuqālāt**, oranges) oranges collectively
burtuqāli (adj/m, f. **burtuqāliyyeh**) orange in colour

da@a (v.I.6) invited

dabbābāt (nf, sing. **dabbābeh**) (military) tank
dablajeh (nf) dubbing (of tapes)
dafa@ (v.I. 3) paid
dāfa@ (v.III.1) defended
dāfi (adj / m, f. **dāfyeh**) warm
daftar (nm, pl. **dafātir**) copybook
dahan (v.I3) painted (wall, furniture, etc., but not canvas, paper)
dain (nm, pl. **duyūn/dyūn**) debt
dakhal (v.I.4) entered
daktōr (nm, **dakātra, daktōra, daktōrāt**) doctor, Dr, professor, physician
dall (v.I.8) indicated
damm (nm, pl. **dimā"**) blood
daqīqa (nf, pl. **daqāyiq/daqā"iq**) minute
dār (nf, pl. **dūr**) home
daras (v.I.4) studied
darb (nf, pl. **durūb/drūb**) road
dāris (AP / nm, pl. **dārisīn/ dārsīn**) having studied, scholar
darras (v.II.1) taught
dars (nm, pl. **durūs/drūs**) lesson
dawleh (nf, pl. **duwal**) government, state; in **iḍāfa** construction, title of prime minister
dawwar (v.II.1) looked for, searched for
dāyman (adv., var. **dā"iman**) always
diktātōr (nm, pl. **diktātōriyyīn**) dictator
dīn (nm, pl. **adyān**) religion
dīnār (nm, pl. **danānīr**) currency unit in some Arab countries
dinya (nf) world
dirāseh (nf, pl. **dirāsāt**) study
dirāsi (adj / m) of study
Dīsambar (nm, var. **Dīsambir**) December
dukhkhān (nm) tobacco, cigarettes
dukkān (nm, pl. **dakākīn**) shop
dūlār (nm, pl. **dūlārāt**) dollar

ḍamm (v.I.7) annexed, embraced
ḍarab (v.I.4) hit
ḍarar (nm) damage, harm
ḍaww (nm, pl. **aḍwā"**) light
ḍayya@ (v.II.1) lost
ḍidd (adv.) against
ḍiḥik (v.I.1) laughed
ḍiḥik (VN / m) laughter

dhahab (nm) gold
dhahāb (nm) departure, going, leaving
dhaki (adj / m, **adhkiyā", dhakiyyeh, dhakiyyāt**) bright, intelligent
dhakkar (v.II.1) reminded
dhalīl (adj / m, **dhalilīn, dhalīleh, dhalilāt**) humble, humiliated
dhanb (nm, pl. **dh(u)nūb**) sin, guilt
dharra (nf, pl. **dharrāt**) atom
dhirā@ (nm, var. **dhrā@,** pl. **adhru@**) arm (in human body)
Dhu 'l-ḥijja (nm) 12th month of the Muslim lunar year
Dhu 'l-qa@da (nm) 11th month of the Muslim lunar year

fa (particle denoting reason or contrast often used in clauses beginning with **amma**)
fā"ideh (nf, pl. **fawā"id**) use, interest
fa@al (v.I.3) did
Fabrāyir (nm, var. **Fibrāyir**) February
fād (v.I.11) benefited someone
faḍḍa (nf, var. **fiḍḍa**) silver
faḍḍal (v.II.1) preferred
faḍḍi (adj / m, var. **fiḍḍi**, f. **faḍḍiyyeh/fiḍḍiyyeh**) silver in colour

fāḍi (adj / m, **fāḍyīn, fāḍyeh, fāḍyāt**) empty, free
faḍl (nm) goodness
min faḍlak please
fahham (v.II.1) made someone understand
fāhim (AP / nm, **fāhmīn, fāhmeh, fāhmāt**) understanding
fāḥim (AP / nm) pitch-black
fakhāmeh (nf) excellency
fakhāmit er-ra"īs honorary title of presidents and prime ministers
fakkar (v.II.1) thought
Falasṭīn (nf) Palestine
Falasṭīni (adj / m, **Falasṭīniyyīn, Falasṭīniyyeh, Falasṭīniyyāt**) Palestinian
fallāḥ (nm, **fallāḥīn, fallāḥa, fallāḥāt**) peasant
falsaf (v.XI) philosophized
falsafeh (nf, pl. **falsafāt**) philosophy
falsafi (adj / m, f. **falsafiyyeh**) philosophical
faqīr (nm, **fuqara, faqīreh, faqīrāt**) poor
faraḍ (v.I.5) supposed, imposed (e.g. tax)
faraḥ (nm, pl. **afrāḥ**) happiness, joy
Faransa (nf) France
Faransi (adj / m, **Faransiyyīn, Faransiyyeh, Faransiyyāt**) French (person or language)
fari@ (nm, pl. **f(u)rū@**) branch
fārqa (AP / nf) making a difference
mish fārqa it makes no difference
faṣal (v.I. 5) fired, separated
fashal (nm) failure
fāshil (AP / nm, **fāshlīn, fāshleh, fāshlāt**) losing, unsuccessful
fāṣīḥ (adj / m, f. **fāṣīḥa**) eloquent, speaking good Arabic
fasīḥ (adj / m, f. **fasīḥa**) spacious
faṣil (nm, var. **faṣl**, pl. **f(u)ṣūl**) chapter
fassar (v.II.1) explained, expounded
fataḥ (v.I.3) opened, conquered
fatiḥ (VN / m, var. **fatḥ**) opening, conquest
fātiḥ (AP / nm, **fātḥīn, fātḥa, fātḥāt**) opener, conqueror
fatra (nf, pl. **fatarāt**) period
fayy (nf) shade
faẓī@ (adj / m, f. **faẓī@a**) horrible
fi (prep.) in
fī (prep.) there is
fi@il (nm, pl. **af@āl**) action, deed
fi@lan (adv.) actually
fiḍi (v.I.2) became empty, became free of engagements
fihim (v.I.1) understood
fikir (nm) thought
fikrak do you think?
fikra (nf, pl. **afkār**) idea
fikri (adj / m, f. **fikriyyeh**) intellectual
fīl (nm, pl. **afyāl**) elephant
filim (nm, var. **film**, pl. **aflām**) film
finjān (nm, pl. **fanājīn**) small coffee cup
firiḥ (v.I.3) was happy, rejoiced
fishil (v.I.1) failed
fishsh (**fi + sh**) there isn't
fīzyā"i (adj / m, **fīzyā"iyyīn, fīzyā"iyyeh, fīzyā"iyyāt**) physical, physicist
flūs (nf) money; (sing.) **fils** 1000th of a dinar in several Arab countries
fōq (prep. & adv.) up, above
fōsfāt (nf) phosphates
fuj"atan (adv., var. **faj"atan**) suddenly
funduq (nm, pl. **fanādiq**) hotel
fuṣḥa (adj / f) eloquent; designates the purest form of Arabic

fustān (nm, pl. **fasātīn**) dress

gōl (nm, pl. **agwāl**) goal (in soccer)

ghafar (v.1.5) forgave
ghaibeh (nf) absence
ghair (adj / m / f) other (than)
ghalabeh (nf) trouble
ghalaţ (nm, pl. **aghlāţ**) error, wrong
ghāli(adj / m, **ghālyīn, ghālyeh, ghālyāt**) dear, expensive
ghalţa (nf, pl. **ghalţāt**) error, mistake
ghalţān (adj / m, **ghalţanīn, ghalţāneh, ghalţānāt**) in error, wrong
ghani (adj / m, **aghniyā", ghaniyyeh, ghaniyyāt**) rich
ghanna (v.II.2) sang
gharb (nm) west
gharbi (adj / m, **gharbiyyīn, gharbiyyeh, gharbiyyāt**) western
gharīb (adj / m, **ghuraba, gharībeh, gharibāt**) strange, stranger
ghasal (v.I.5) washed
ghasil (VN / m, var. **ghasl**) washing
ghayyar (v.II.1) changed
ghiliţ (v.I.1) made a mistake
ghina (nm) ability to do without, wealth
ghinā" (VN / m) singing
ghini (v.I.2) became rich
ghurfeh (nf, pl. **ghuraf**) room

ha (dem. pron.) this
hadd (v.I.8) pulled down (a building)
haddad (v.II.1) threatened
hādha (dem. pron., var. **hāda**) this (m.)
hadhāk (dem. pron., var. **hadāk**) that (m.)
hādhi (dem. pron., var. **hādi**) this (f.)
hadhīk (dem. pron., var. **hadīk**) that (f.)
hadhōl (dem. pron., var. **hadōl**) these (m. / f.)
hadhulāk (dem. pron., var. **hadulāk**) those (m. / f.)
hadiyyeh (nf, pl. **hadāya**) a present
haik (adv.) thus, like this
hajam (v.I.5) attacked
hajar (v.I.4) deserted
hājar (v.III.1) emigraìed
hamm (nm, pl. **h(u)mūm**) worry, irritating problem
hamza (nf, pl. **hamzāt**) the glottal stop (represented by " in this book)
handas (v.XI) engineered, was the architect of
handaseh (nf) engineering, architecture
harab (v.I.4) ran away
haram (nm, pl. **ahrām**) pyramid
harrab (v.II.1) smuggled
hassa (adv.) now
hawa (nm) air
hāwi (AP / nm, **huwāt, hāwyeh, hāwyāt**) amateur
hāy (dem. pron.) this (f.)
hayyāni, hayyātak, hayyātu, etc. (adv.) here I am, here you are, here he is, etc.
hī *see* **hiyyeh**
Hijri (adj / m, f. **Hijriyyeh**) of the Hijri or Muslim lunar calendar
Hind (nf, always with def. art.) India
Hindi (adj / m, **H(u)nūd, Hindiyyeh, Hindiyyāt**) Indian
hinneh (pron.) they (f.)
hiwāyeh (nf, pl. **hiwāyāt**) hobby
hiyyeh (pron.) she

hōn (adv.) here
hū *see* **huwweh**
hujūm (VN / m) attack
hummeh (pron.) they (m.)
hunāk (dem. pron.) there
huwweh (pron.) he

ḥabb (v.I.8) loved
ḥabbeh (nf, pl. **ḥ(u)būb**) grain, any single fruit
ḥabīb (nm, **aḥbāb/aḥibba/ḥabāyib**) lover, sweetheart
ḥābib (AP / nm, **ḥābbīn, ḥābbeh, ḥābbāt**) desiring, wanting
ḥada (nm) someone, anybody
ḥadd (nm, pl. **ḥ(u)dūd**) boundary
ḥadd (v.I.8) curbed
ḥadīdi (adj / m, f. **ḥadīdiyyeh**) iron, unyielding
ḥadīqa (nf, pl. **ḥadā"iq/ḥadāyiq**) garden
ḥadīth (nm) conversation
ḥadīth (adj / m, f. **ḥadītheh**) modern
ḥādith (nm, pl. **ḥawādith)** accident, event
ḥaḍra (nf) presence; in **iḍāfa** construction: a title of respect given to addressee
ḥafleh (nf, pl. **ḥaflāt**) party, celebration
ḥaith (adv.) in phrase **min ḥaith el-mabda"** as a matter of principle, to begin with
ḥājāt (nf, sing. **ḥājeh**) needs
ḥājiz (AP / nm) having sthg reserved (e.g. hotel room)
ḥaka (v.I.6) spoke, told
ḥaki (VN / m) speech, conversation, words
ḥāl (nm, pl. **ḥālāt** state, condition
ḥalaf (v.I.5) swore
ḥālan (adv.) immediately
ḥalaq (v.I.5) shaved, had a haircut
ḥāleh (nf, pl. **ḥālāt**) state, condition, case
ḥall (nm, pl. **ḥulūl**) solution
ḥallaq (v.II.1) soared
ḥamd (VN / m) praise
al-ḥamdu li 'llāh praise be to God (an expression of satisfaction)
ḥamra (adj / f, pl. **ḥumur,** m. **aḥmar,** pl. **ḥumur**) red
ḥanūn (adj / m, f. **ḥanūneh**) kind-hearted, loving, caring
ḥaqīqa (nf, pl. **ḥaqā"iq/ḥaqāyiq**) truth
ḥaqq (nm, pl. **ḥ(u)qūq**) right (in something), truth
ḥārab (v.III.1) fought against
ḥarāmi (nm, pl. **ḥaramiyyeh**) burglar
ḥaraq (v.I.5) burned
ḥarb (nf, pl. **ḥurūb**) war
ḥarīri (adj / m, f. **ḥarīriyyeh**) silken
ḥarrar (@.II.1) liberated, edited
ḥasab (prep.) according to
ḥaṣal (v.I.1) happened, took place, obtained (a degree)
ḥāsis (AP / nm, **ḥāssīn, ḥāsseh, ḥāssāt**) (having the) feeling
ḥass (v.I.8) felt
ḥassan (v.II.1) improved
ḥāsūb (nm, pl. **ḥawāsīb**) computer
ḥathth (v.I.8) urged
ḥāṭiṭ (AP / nm, **ḥāṭṭīn, ḥāṭṭa, ḥāṭṭāt**) having put, having placed
ḥaṭṭ (v.I.7) put
ḥatta (adv.) even, until
ḥawāli (prep.) about
ḥawl (prep) about
ḥaẓẓ (nm, pl. **ḥ(u)ẓūẓ**) luck, fortune
ḥijāra (nf, sing. **ḥajar**) stones
ḥilw (adj / m, **ḥilwīn, ḥilweh, ḥilwāt**) sweet, beautiful

ḥiṣān (nm. var. **ḥṣān,** pl. **khail**) horse, stallion
ḥubb (nm) love
ḥudūd (nf, sing. **ḥadd**) boundaries, limits
ḥukūmeh (nf, pl. **ḥukūmāt**) government
Ḥuzayrān (nm) June

i@lān (nm, pl. **i@lānāt**) advertisement, announcement
i@tadhar (v.VIII.1) apologized
i@tamad (v.VIII.1) depended
i@taqad (v.VIII.1) believed
ibdā@ (VN / m) creativity, creation
ibin (nm, pl. **abnā"**) son
ibtasam (v.VIII.1) smiled
īd (nf, var. **yad**, pl. **ayādi**, dual **idain**) hand
@ala idain at the hands of
iḍāfa (nf, pl. **iḍāfāt**) addition, annexation, genitive / possessive relationship
idha (conj.) if
idhan (adv.) therefore
idhin (nm) permission
ba@id idhnak with your permission
iḍṭarr (v.VIII.1, but irreg.) he had to
ifrāj (VN / m) release
ifta@al (v.VIII.1) contrived
iftaraḍ (v.VIII.1) supposed, took for granted
ifti@āl (VN / m) contrivance
ighbarr (v.IX) became dusty
iḥdāsh (nf) eleven
iḥdāshar (nm / f) eleven in **iḍāfa** construction
iḥmarr (v.IX) turned red
iḥmirār (VN / m) reddening, blushing
iḥna (pron, var. **niḥna**) we
iḥṣā" (VN / m) taking stock, statistics
iḥsās (VN / m, pl. **aḥāsīs**) feeling
iḥtāj (v.VIII.1, irreg. imp. **iḥtāj**) needed
iḥtikār (VN / m) monopoly
iḥtiqār (VN / m) contempt
iḥtiyāt (nm) reserve
qa"imit iḥtiyāṭ waiting list
ijrā" (VN / m) carrying out; (pl.) **ijrā"āt** necessary measures
ikhḍarr (v.IX) turned green
ikhḍirār (VN / m) the process of becoming green
ikhlāṣ (VN / m) faithfulness
ikhrāj (VN / m) getting sthg out, direction (of film, play)
ikhtalaf (v.VIII.1) disagreed
ikhtiṣār (VN / m) abbreviation, conciseness, brevity
ila (prep.) to, for
illa (conj.) except, minus, less
khamseh illa rubi@ five minus a quarter, i.e., a quarter to five
illa idha (conj.) unless
illi (rel. pron.) who, which, that
imbāriḥ (adv., var. **mbāriḫ**) yesterday
imma (conj.) either
imtadd (v.VIII.1, irreg. imp. **imtadd**) stretched, extended
imtidād (VN / m) extent, length
imtiḥān (nm, pl. **imtiḥānāt)** examinations
in (conj.) if
in@amal (v.VII.1) was made, was done
inda@a (v.VII.2) was invited
indafa@ (v.VII.1) was pushed, acted recklessly
indahash (v.VII.1) was amazed
indifā@ (VN / m) momentum, reckless behaviour
infaṣal (v.VII.1) separated, was fired
Ingilīzi (adj / m, var. **Inglīzi, Inglīz, Inglīziyyeh, Inglīziyyāt)** English

inhā" (VN / m) putting an end to, termination
inḥall (v.VII.1, but somewhat irreg.) (of a problem) was solved, (of an assembly) was dissolved
injilā" (VN / m) clearing up (of situation)
inkasar (v.VII.1) got broken
inkisār (VN / m) act or process of getting broken, defeat
inn (rel. pron.) that
inqabal (v.VII.1) was accepted / admitted
inqaḍa (v.VII.2) was over, (of a specified period) lapsed
inqalab (v.VII.I) was overturned, turned his back on
inqiḍā" (VN / m) termination, reaching the end, lapse of (specified time)
inqilāb (VN / m, pl. **inqilābāt**) act / process of being overturned, coup
inshaghal (v.VII.1) got busy
inta (pron.) you (m. sing.)
intabah (v.VIII.1) was attentive
intaha (v.VIII.2) reached the end
intaḥar (v.VIII.1) committed suicide
intāj (VN / m) production
inṭalab (v.VII.1) was asked for
intaṣar (v.VIII.1) was victorious
intaẓar (v.VIII.1) waited, expected
inti (pron.) you (f. sing.)
intihā" (VN / m) coming to a close, termination
intikhābāt (nf, sing. **intikhāb**) elections
intin (pron.) you (f. pl.)
intiṣār (VN / m, pl. **intiṣārāt**) victory
intiẓār (VN / m) waiting
intu (pron.) you (m. pl.)
inzāl (VN / m) landing of troops, getting sthg down
iqāmeh (nf) stay, sojourn, residence
iqtiṣād (VN / m) economizing, economy
iqtiṣādi (adj / m, pl. **iqtiṣādiyyīn**) economic, economical, economist(s)
iqtiṣādiyyeh (adj / f) economical; (nf) female economist; (pl.) **iqtiṣādiyyāt** economists, economies
irtafa@ (v.VIII.1) went up
is@āf (VN / m) provision of medical aid
īṣā" (VN / m) leaving a will, giving a recommendation
iṣbā@ (nm, pl. **aṣābi@**) finger
iṣfarr (v.IX) turned yellow
ishtadd (v.VIII.1) got stronger / more intense
ishtaghal (v.VIII.1) worked
ishtaha (v.VIII.2) desired
ishtara (v.VIII.2) bought
ishtidād (VN / m) increase in strength / intensity
ishtihā" (VN / m) desiring
isim (nm, pl. **asmā"**) name
Iskandariyyeh (nf, var. **al-Iskandariyyeh)** Alexandria
Islām (VN / m) Islam
Islāmi (adj / m, f. **Islāmiyyeh**) Islamic
ista@add (v.X.1) was ready / willing, prepared himself
ista@mal (v.X.1) used
istaghall (v.X.1) exploited
istaghfar (v.X.1) asked for forgiveness
istaghna (v.X.2) was able to do without, fired (employees)
istaḥaqq (v.X.1, but somewhat irreg.) he deserved
istama@ (v.VIII.1) listened
istanna (v.X.2, irreg. imp. **istanna)** waited
istaqbal (v.X.1) received
istarḥam (v.X.1) asked for mercy

istarja@ (v.X.1) got back, remembered
istarkha (v.X.2) relaxed (physically)
istarlīni (adj / m) sterling
istawla (v.X.2) confiscated
isti@dād (VN / m) readiness, willingness
isti@jāl (VN / m) haste, urgency
isti@māl (VN / m) using, use
isti@mār (VN / m) colonization, colonialism
isti@māri (adj / m, pl. **isti@māriyyīn**, f. **isti@māriyyeh)** colonialist
istighlāl (VN / m) exploitation
istighnā" (VN / m) doing without, laying off (workers)
istimā@ (VN / m) listening
istimrār (VN / m) continuity, continuation
bi 'stimrār always, continuously
istiqbāl (VN / m) receiving, reception
istiqlāl (VN / m) independence
istiqrār (VN / m) stability
istīrad (VN / m) importation
iswadd (v.IX) turned black
Īţālya (nf) Italy
ithnain (nm, var. **tinain)** two
ithnaināt (nf) twos
itlāf (VN / m) destruction (of documents, foodstuffs, etc.)
iţnāsh (nf) twelve
iţnāshar (nm / f) twelve in **iḑāfa** construction
ittafaq (v.VIII.1) agreed, was in harmony with
ittaşāl (v.VIII.1) called up, telephoned
iyya- (attached to pronominal suffixes) myself, himself, etc. (accusative case)
izdād (v., irreg. imp. **izdād**) increased
izraqq (v.IX) turned blue / livid

jā"iz (AP / nm, var. **jāyiz**, f. **jāyzeh**) possible, likely
jā"izeh (nf, pl. **jawā"iz**) award, prize
jāb (v.I.11) brought
jabal (nm, pl. **j(i)bāl**) mountain
jabīn (nm) forehead
jādd (adj / m, **jāddin, jāddeh, jāddāt** serious
jadd (nm, var. **jidd**, pl. **ajdād/ j(u)dūd**) grandfather, forefather
jaddeh (nf, var. **jiddeh**, pl. **jaddāt/jiddāt**) grandmother
jāhiz (AP / nm, **jāhzīn, jāhzeh, jāhzāt**) ready
jaish (nm, pl. **j(u)yūsh**) army
jakait (nm, pl. **jakaitāt**) jacket
jalāleh (nf) Majesty, king's title
jamal (nm, pl. **j(i)māl**) camel
jamārik (nf, sing. **jumruk**) customs duties
jāmi@a (nf, pl. **jāmi@āt**) university
jamīl (nm, pl. **jamāyil**) favour done to someone
jamīl (adj / m, f. **jamīleh**) beautiful
jānib (nm, pl. **jawānib**) side
jānibain (nm, dual of **jānib**) two sides
janūb (nm) south
janūbi (adj / m, **janūbiyyīn, janūbiyyeh, janūbiyyāt**) southern
jār (nm, **jīrān, jāra, jārāt**) neighbour
jara (v.I.6) happened, took place
jarīdeh (nf, pl. **jarāyid/jarā"id**) newspaper
jarīmeh (nf, pl. **jarā"im/jarāyim**) crime
jarrab (v.II.1) tried

jawhara (nf, var. **jōhara**, pl. **jawāhir**) jewel
jaww (nm) atmosphere, climate
jawwiyyeh (adj / f, m. **jawwi**) of the climate, of the upper space, of airlines
jāy (AP / nm, **jāyyīn, jāyyeh, jāyyāt**) coming
jayabān (VN / m) bringing
jāyib (AP / nm, **jāybīn, jāybeh, jāybāt**) bringing
jayyid (adj / m, f. **jayydeh**) good
jaza (nm) reward, punishment
Jazā"ir (nf) Algeria
Jazā"iri (adj / m, **Jazā"iriyyīn, Jazā"iriyyeh, Jazā"iriyyāt**) Algerian
jazīlan (adv.) very much, only in phrase **shukran jazīlan**: thank you very much
jdīd (adj / m, f. **jdīdeh**) new
jiddan (adv.) very much
jīrān (nm, sing. **jār**) neighbours
jū@ (nm) hunger
juhūd (nf, sing. **juhd**) efforts
Jum@a (nf) Friday, week; (pl.) **juma@** weeks
Jumāda 'l-ākhira (nf) 6th month of the Muslim lunar year
Jumāda 'l-ūla (nf) 5th month of the Muslim lunar year
jumleh (nf, pl. **jumal**) sentence
jundi (nm, pl. **j(u)nūd**) soldier
jur"a (nf) courage, audacity
jurḥ (nm, pl. **j(u)rūḥ/jirāḥ**) wound
juwwa (adv.) inside
juzu" (nm, pl. **ajzā"**) part, division

kā"in (AP / nm, var. **kāyin**, pl. **kā"ināt**) being
kā"in bashari human being
kabar (nm) old age
kaffa (v.II.1) was enough, sufficed
kalām (nm) talking, chatting, words
kalb (nm, pl. **k(i)lāb**) dog
kam (interr. part.) how many, how much
kamān (adv.) too, also
kāmil (AP / nm, **kāmlīn, kāmleh, kāmlāt**) complete, perfect
kāmira (nf, pl. **kāmirāt**) camera
kāmirtak your camera
kān (v.I.10) was
Kānūn awwal (nm) December
Kānūn thāni (nm) January
karafatta (nf, pl. **karafattāt**) necktie
karam (VN / m) generosity
kās (nm, pl. **kāsāt**) cup
kasar (v.I.5) broke
kāsh (nm) cash
kasir (VN / m, var. **kasr**) breaking
kāsir (AP / nm) person who breaks
kassar (v.II.1) broke deliberately and repeatedly
kātab (v.III.1) corresponded with
katab (v.I.4) wrote
kātib (AP / nm, **kuttāb, kātibeh, kātibāt**) writer
kattab (v.II.1) made someone write
kawa (v.I.6) ironed, cauterized
kāwi (AP / nm) caustic
kawi (VN / m) ironing, cauterizing
kbīr (adj / m, **kbār, kbīreh, kbār**) big, old
kidhib (nm) falsehood, prevarication
kīf (interr. part.) how
kīf ma (conj.) however
kifāyeh (nf) sufficiency, enough
kilmeh (nf, pl. **kalimāt**) word
kīlōmitir (nm, pl. **kīlōmitrāt**) kilometre
kīlu (nm, pl. **kīluwāt**) kilogramme, kilometre

kīmya (nf) chemistry
kīmyā"iyyīn (nm, sing. **kīmyā"i**) chemists
kirih (v.I.1) hated
kisil (v.I.1) felt too lazy to act
kitāb (nm, var. **ktāb**, pl. **kutub**) book
kitābeh (nf, pl. **kitābāt**) writing
kōn (nm, var. **kawn**, pl. **akwān**) universe
kthīr (adj / m, **kthīrīn, kthīreh, kthīrāt**) much, many
kūb (nm, pl. **akwāb**) cup
kull (nm / f) all
kumbyūtar (nm, pl. **kumbyūtarāt**) computer
kura (nf, pl. **kurāt**) ball
kurit el-qadam soccer
kurit es-salleh basketball
kurh (VN / m) hatred
kursi (nf, pl. **karāsi**) chair
kuttāb (nm, sing. **kātib**) writers
kutub (nf, sing. **kitāb**) books
Kuwait (nf) Kuwait
Kuwaiti (adj / m, var. **Kwaiti, K(u)waitiyyīn, K(u)waitiyyeh, K(u)waitiyyāt**) Kuwaiti
kwayyis (adj / m, **kwayysin, kwayyseh, kwayysāt**) good

khabar (nm, pl. **akhbār**) news item
khabbar (v.II.1) informed, conveyed the news
khada@ (v.I.3) cheated, fooled
khadamāt (nf, sing. **khidmeh**) services
khadd (nm, pl. **kh(u)dūd**) cheek
khāf (v.I.12) was afraid
khaffaf (v.II.1) lightened, went easy (on), slowed down
khafīf (adj / m, f. **khafīfeh**) light, not heavy
khail (nf) horses collectively
khair (nm) good in the abstract; (pl.) **khayrāt** material wealth
khair? what's up?
khajal (nm) bashfulness, shyness
khāl (nm, pl. **akhwāl**) maternal uncle
khālaf (v.III.1) acted differently, was different
khalaş (v.I.3) was exhausted
khalaţ (v.I.5) mixed
khālat (v.III.1) mixed with (usu. bad people)
khāleh (nf, pl. **khālāt**) maternal aunt
khalīj (nm, pl. **khiljān**) gulf
khalla (v.II.2) allowed, let
khāmil (AP / nm, **khāmlīn, khāmleh, khāmlāt**) inactive, idle
Khamīs (nm) Thursday
khamis (nm / f) five in **iḍāfa** constructions
khāmis (nm, f. **khāmseh**) fifth in a series
khamisţāsh (nf) fifteen
khamra (nf) alcoholic drink
khamseh (nf) five
khamsīn (nf) fifty
khān (nm, pl. **khānāt**) inn
khān (v.I.10) betrayed
khanzīr (nm, **khanazīr, khanzīreh**, f. pl. not used) pig
laḥim khanzīr pork
kharaj (v.I.4) went out
kharbaţ (v.XI) confused
kharbaţa (nf, pl. **kharbaţāt**) confusion
khārijiyyeh (adj / f, m. **khāriji**) external, foreign
wizārat el-khārijiyyeh Ministry of Foreign Affairs
kharūf (nm, pl. **khirfān**) sheep, lamb
khashab (nm, pl. **akhshāb**) wood
khashabi (adj / m, f. **khashabiyyeh**) wooden

khaṣim (nm, var **khaṣm**) discount
khaṭab (v.I.4) proposed, asked for the hand of
khaṭar (nm, pl. **akhṭār**) danger
khaṭīb (nm, f. **khaṭībeh**) fiancé / e
khaṭīr (adj / m, f. **khaṭīreh**) dangerous
khāṭir (nm) image in mind
b' khāṭrak keep us in mind, goodbye
khaṭṭ (nm, pl. **kh(u)ṭūṭ**) line
khāyif (AP / nm, **khāyfīn, khāyfeh, khāyfāt**) afraid
khayyab (v.II.1) disappointed
khilāf (nm, pl. **khilāfāt**) disagreement
khilāl (adv.) during, while
min khilāl through, by means of
khiliṣ (v.I.1) was finished, was over, (of supplies) exhausted
khisir (v.I.1) lost
khōf (VN / m) fear
khubuth (nm, var. **khubth**) slyness, wickedness
khuḍrawāt (nf, no sing.) vegetables
khuṭṭa (nf, var. **khiṭṭa**, pl. **khuṭaṭ/khiṭaṭ**) plan
khuṭweh (nf, var. **khaṭweh**, pl. **khuṭuwāt/khaṭawāt**) step

lā (adv.) no, don't
la (prep.) to, for
lā . . . wa la (conj.) neither . . . nor
lā@ib (AP / nm, pl. **lā@(i)bīn**) player
laban (nm) yoghurt; pl. **albān** dairy products
lābis (AP / nm, **lābsīn, lābseh, lābsāt**) wearing
ladūd (adj / m, used with **@aduww**) intransigent
lafaẓ (v.I.4) pronounced
laff (v.I.8) wrapped
lāhaẓ (v.III.1) observed, noticed
laḥim (nm, var. **laḥm**, pl. **luḥūm**) meat
laḥẓa (nf, pl. **laḥaẓāt**) one moment
lail (nm) night; **el-lail** night-time, darkness
laileh (nf) one night; **el-laileh** tonight
laish (interr. part.) why
lajneh (nf, pl. **lijān**) committee
lakhbaṭ (v.XI) confused
lākin (conj.) but
lamma (conj.) when
lamūn (nm, var. **laymūn**) lemons
lamūni (adj / m) lemon yellow
laṭīf(adj / m, f. **laṭīfeh**) balmy, nice, charming
law (conj.) if
lawḥa (nf, pl. **lawḥāt**) painting
lawla (conj., var. **lōla**) were it not for
lāzim (AP / n, used impersonally) should, it is necessary
li"an (conj.) because
li@beh (nf, pl. **li@bāt/al@āb**) game
li@ib (VN / m, pl. **al@āb**) playing
li@ib (v.I.1) played
Libnān (nm, var. **Lubnān**) Lebanon
Libnāni (adj / m, **Libnāniyyīn, Libnāniyyeh, Libnāniyyāt**) Lebanese
liqā" (VN / m, pl. **liqā"āt**) meeting
lōn (nm, pl. **alwān**) colour
lugha (nf, pl. **lughāt**) language

m@allim *see* **mu@allim**
mā (neg. part.) not
ma@ (prep.) with
ma@ es-salāmeh goodbye
ma@āli (nf) title of a minister (of government)

ma@īsheh (nf) living
takālīf el-ma@īsheh living costs
ma@mal (nm, pl. **ma@āmil**) factory
ma@na (nm, pl. **ma@āni**) meaning
ma@qūl (PP/nm, f. **ma@qūleh**) reasonable, logical
ma@rifeh (nf, pl. **ma@ārif**) knowledge
ma@rūf (PP/nm, **ma@rufīn, ma@rūfeh, ma@rufāt**) known, favour
mab@ūth (PP/nm, **mab@uthīn, mab@ūtheh, mab@uthāt**) sent, emissary
mabādi" (nf, sing. **mabda", m.**) principles, rudiments
mabīt (PP/nm) spending the night
mablagh (nm, pl. **mabāligh**) amount, sum
mabrūk (PP/nm, f. **mabrūkeh**, pl. **mabrukāt**) blessed; congratulations!
mad-hūn (PP/nm, **mad-hunīn, mad-hūneh, mad-hunāt**) painted
maḍa (v.I.6) went away, passed
mada (nm) extent, scope, range
madām (nf) madam; **el-madām** the wife
madd (v.I.8) extended
madfu@āt (nf, sing. **madfū@**) payments
madhalleh (nf) humiliation
mādid (AP/nm, **māddīn, māddeh, māddāt**) extending
madīneh (nf, pl. **mudun**) city
Madīneh (nf) city in Saudi Arabia to which Prophet Muḥammad emigrated from Mecca
madkhal (nm pl. **madākhil**) entrance
madraseh (nf, pl. **madāris**) school
maḍya@a (nf) waste
mafhūm (PP/nm, **mafhumīn, mafhūmeh, mafhumāt**) understood, understandable
mafrūḍ (PP/nm, **mafruḍīn, mafrūḍa, mafruḍāt**) supposed, imposed
maftūḥ (PP/nm, f. **maftūḥa**) open
maghrūr (PP/nm, **maghrurīn, maghrūra, maghrurāt**) snobbish, conceited
maghsūl (PP/nm, **maghsulīn, maghsūleh, maghsulāt**) washed, clean
maḥall (nm, pl. **maḥallāt**) place
maḥbūb (PP/nm, **maḥbubīn, maḥbūbeh, maḥbubāt**) loved, liked
maḥdhūr (PP/nm, **maḥadhīr, maḥdhūra, maḥdhurāt**) sthg expected and feared
māhir (AP/nm, **māhrīn/mahara, māhreh, māhrāt**) skilled, skilful
maḥkameh (nf, pl. **maḥākim**) court
maḥki (PP/nm, f. **maḥkiyyeh**, pl. **maḥkiyyāt**) spoken
mahma (sub. conj.) whatever
maḥsūs (PP/nm, f. **maḥsūseh**, pl. **maḥsūsāt**) tangible
maḥṭūṭ (PP/nm, **maḥṭūṭīn, maḥṭūṭa, maḥṭūṭāt**) put, placed
maḥẓūr (PP/nm, f. **maḥẓūra**, pl. **maḥẓurāt**) prohibited
majalleh (nf, pl. **majallāt**) magazine
Majar (nf) Hungary
Majari (adj/m, **Majariyyīn, Majariyyeh, Majariyyāt**) Hungarian
mājistair (nf) Master's degree

majnūn (PP / nm, **majanīn, majnūneh, majnunāt**) mad
makān (nm, pl. **amkineh**) place, vacancy (in plane, theatre, etc.)
makfūl (PP / nm, **makfulīn, makfūleh, makfulāt**) guaranteed
makhṭūb (PP / nm, **makhṭubīn, makhṭūbeh, makhṭubāt**) betrothed, engaged
Makkeh (nf) Mecca (holy city in Saudi Arabia, where Muslims perform the pilgrimage)
makrūh (adj / m, **makruhīn, makrūha, makruhāt**) hated, obnoxious
Maksīk (nf) Mexico
Maksīki (adj / m, **Maksīkiyyīn, Maksīkiyyeh, Maksīkiyyāt**) Mexican
maksūr (PP / nm, **maksurīn, maksūra, maksurāt**) broken
maktab (nm, pl. **makātib**) office
maktabeh (nf, pl. **maktabāt**) library
maktūb (PP / nm **makatīb, maktūbeh, maktubāt**) letter, written
maktūbeh (PP / nf, m. **maktūb**) written
makwi (PP / nm, **makwiyyīn, makwiyyeh, makwiyyāt**) ironed, cauterized
māl (v.I.11) inclined
māl (nm, pl. **amwāl**) possessions, wealth
malābis (nf, sing. **malbas**) clothes
malaki (adj / m) royal, monarchist
malakiyyeh (nf) monarchy, monarchism
malāyīn (nf, sing. **malyōn**) millions
mālik (adj / m, **mālikīn, mālikeh, mālikāt**) owner
malik (nm, pl. **mulūk**) king
malikeh (nf, pl. **malikāt**) queen
mall (v.I.8) became bored
malyān (adj / m, f. **malyāneh**) full
malyōn (nm) one million
malyōnain (nm, dual of **malyōn**) two million
māma (nf) mother
mamdūd (PP / nm, f. **mamdūdeh**, pl. **mamdudāt**) extended, stretched
mamlakeh (nf, pl. **mamālik**) kingdom
mamnū@ (PP / nm, **mamnu@īn, mamnū@a, mamnu@āt**) prohibited
mamshi (PP / nm, f. **mamshiyyeh**) of a track: beaten
man (rel. pron.) who
man@ (VN / m, var. **mani@**) prohibition
mana@ (v.I.3) prohibited, forbade
mandīl (nm, pl. **manadīl**) handkerchief
mansaf (nm, pl. **manāsif**) a Jordanian national dish
manshūr (PP / nm, f. **manshūra**, pl. **manshurāt**) published
mansi (PP / nm. **mansiyyīn, mansiyyeh, mansiyyāt**) forgotten
manṭiqa (nf, pl. **manāṭiq**) area, district
manẓar (nm, pl. **manāẓir**) scenes, scenery
maqfūl (PP / nm, f. **maqfūleh**) locked
maqtūl (PP / nm, **maqtulīn, maqtūleh, maqtulāt**) killed, murdered
mara (nf, var. **mar"a**, pl. **niswān/ nisā"**) woman
maraḍ (nm, pl. **amrāḍ**) illness

marḍi (PP/gender determined by pron. attached to prep. **@an**) satisfactory
mardūd (PP/nm, pl. **mardudāt**) return(s), returned
marḥaba (adv.) hello
marḥabtain (adv., dual of **marḥaba**) a double hello!
marḥaleh (nf, pl. **marāḥil**) phase, stage
marhūn (PP/nm, f. **marhūneh**) mortgaged; **marhūn bi** dependent upon
marīḍ (nm, **marḍa, marīḍa, marīḍāt**) sick
marīr (adj/m, f. **marīra**) bitter
Māris (nm) March
Mārkisi (adj/m, **Mārkisiyyīn, Mārkisiyyeh, Mārkisiyyāt**) Marxist
Mārkisiyyeh (nf) Marxism
marmi (PP/nm, **marmiyyīn, marmiyyeh, marmiyyāt**) thrown away, neglected
marr (v.I.7) passed by
marsūm (PP/nm, **marsumīn, marsūmeh, marsumāt**) drawn, portrayed
mas"aleh (nf, pl. **masā"il**) problem, question
mas"ūl (PP/nm, **mas"ulīn, mas"ūleh, mas"ulāt**) asked, responsible, in charge
masa (nm, var. **masā"**, pl. **amāsi**) evening
masa 'l-khair good evening
masā"i (adj/m, f. **masā"iyyeh**) nightly
masā@i (nf, sing. **mas@a**) effort(s)
masāfeh (nf, pl. **masāfāt**) space, distance
maṣāni@ (nf, sing. **maṣna@**) factories
maṣāri (nf/pl.) money
masdūd (PP/nm, f. **masdūdeh**, pl. **masdudāt**) closed, blocked
māsha (v.III.2) went along with
masha (v.I.6) walked
māshi (AP/nm, **māshyīn, māshyeh, māshyāt**) walking, acceptable
mashi (VN/nm) walking
mashrū@ (PP/nm, pl. **masharī@**) project
mashrūb (PP/nm, f. **mashrūbeh**) (of sthg:) drunk; pl. **mashrubāt** usu. alcoholic drinks
mashsha (v.II.2) caused someone to walk/sthg to go through
Masīḥ (nm) Christ
Masīḥi (adj/m, **Masīḥiyyīn, Masīḥiyyeh, Masīḥiyyāt**) Christian
Masīḥiyyeh (nf) Christianity
Maṣir (nf, var. **Miṣr/Maṣr**) Egypt
masjid (nm, pl. **masājid**) mosque
masjūn (PP/nm, **masjunīn/masajīn, masjūneh, masjunāt**) imprisoned, detained
maskūn (PP/nm, f. **maskūneh**, pl. **maskunāt**) inhabited, haunted
masmū@ (PP/nm, **masmu@īn, masmū@a, masmu@āt**) loud enough to be heard
masmūm (adj/m, f. **masmūmeh**) poisoned
maṣna@ (nm, pl. **maṣāni@**) factory
maṣnū@ (PP/nm, f. **maṣnū@a**) manufactured
masqi (PP/nm, **masqiyyīn, masqiyyeh, masqiyyāt**) irrigated
masraḥi (adj/m) dramatic, theatrical
masraḥiyyeh (nf, pl. **masraḥiyyāt**) play, drama
Maṣri (adj/m, **Maṣriyyīn, Maṣriyyeh, Maṣriyyāt**) Egyptian

māt (v.I.10) died
maţ@am (nm, pl. **maţā@im**) restaurant
mata (interr. part.) when
maţār (nm, pl. **maţārāt**) airport
maţar (nm, pl. **amţār**) rain
maţba@a (nf, pl. **maţābi@**) printing press
maţbūkh (PP/nm, f. **maţbūkha**) cooked
mathalan (adv.) for example
maw@id (nm, pl. **mawā@īd** appointment
mawḍū@ (nm, pl. **mawaḍī@**) subject, matter
mawjūd (PP/nm, **mawjudīn, mawjūdeh, mawjudāt**) present, available
mawqif (nm, pl. **mawāqif**) position, situation
mawwal (v.II.1) financed
mawwat (v.II.1) caused the death of
Māyō (nm) May
mayy (nf, pl. **miyāh**) water
mayyit (AP/nm, **mayytīn, mayyteh, mayytāt**) dead
mazbūţ (PP/nm, f. **mazbūţa**) correct, right
mazrū@ (PP/nm, f. **mazrū@a**, pl. **mazrū@āt**) planted
mazrū@āt (nf/pl.) crops
mbāriḥ (adv.) yesterday
mi@māri (adj/m) of an architect, architectural
miftāḥ (nm, var. **muftāḥ**, pl. **mafātīḥ**) key
mīl (nm, pl. **amyāl**) mile
mīlād (VN/m) birth
  @īd mīlād birthday
mīlādi (adj/m) of the birth (of Christ), designating the Christian calendar
min (prep.) from
mīn (interr. pron.) who, which
min shān in order that, for the sake of
minshafeh (nf, pl. **manāshif**) towel
miqtani@ (AP/nm, var. **muqtani@, miqtin@īn, miqtin@a, miqtin@āt**) convinced
miriḍ (v.I.1) became sick
mish (neg. part., var. **mush**) not
mista@jil (adj/m, **mista@ijlīn, mista@ijleh, mista@ijlāt**) in a hurry
mistanni (AP/nm, **mistannyīn, mistannyeh, mistannyāt**) waiting
mīt (nf, **miyyeh** in **iḍāfa** construction) one hundred
mitain (nf, dual of **miyyeh**) two hundred
mithil (prep.) like
mittifqīn (adj/m, sing. **mitt(a)fiq/muttafiq**, f. **mittifqa**, f. pl. **mittifqāt**) in agreement
miyyāt (nf, var. **mi"āt**, sing. **miyyeh**) hundreds
miyyeh (nf, pl. **miyyāt**) one hundred
mīzān (nm, pl. **mawāzīn**) balance
mnain *see* **wain**
mōsīqa (nf) music
mōt (nm) death
msāfir (AP/nm, **msāfrīn, msāfreh, msāfrāt**) leaving, travelling
mu"akhkharan (adv.) lately, recently
mu@ālaj (PP/nm, **m(u)@ālajīn, m(u)@ālajeh, m(u)@ālajāt**) treated
mu@ālij (AP/nm, **mu@āhlijīn, mu@ālijeh, mu@ālijāt**) giver of medical aid

mu@allim (AP / nm, **m(u)@all(i)mīn, m(u)@all(i)meh, m(u)@all(i)māt**) teacher
mu@jam (nm, pl. **ma@ājim**) dictionary
mu@ẓam (nm) the greater part of, most of
mubāhathāt (nf, sing. not used) discussions, talks
mubālagha (nf, pl. **mubalāghāt**) exaggeration
mubāsharatan (adv.) immediately
mudarras† (PP / nm, **mudarrasīn, mudarraseh, mudarrasāt**) taught
mudarris (AP / nm, **mudarrisīn, mudarr(i)seh, mudarr(i)sāt**) teacher
muddeh (nf, pl. **mudad**) period
mudhakkira (AP / nf, pl. **mudhakkirāt** memorandum
mudīr (AP / nm, **mudīrīn/ mudara, mudīreh, mudīrāt**) director, headmaster, manager
mudkhalāt (nf) input
mufīd (AP / nm, f. **mufīdeh**) useful
mufta@al (PP / nm, f. **mufta@aleh**) contrived
mufta@il (AP / nm) contriver
mughram (adj / m, **mughramīn, mughrameh, mughramāt**) fond of
muḥāḍara (nf, pl. **muḥāḍarāt**) lecture
muḥāḍathāt (nf, sing. **muḥādatheh**) talks, negotiations
muhaddad (PP / nm, var. **mhaddad, m(u)haddadīn, m(u)haddadeh, m(u)haddadāt**) threatened
muhaddid (AP / nm, pl. **muhaddidīn**) threatener
muḥāḍir (AP / nm, **muḥāḍirīn, muḥāḍira, muḥāḍirāt**) lecturer
muhājar† (PP / n, gender det. by pron. attached to prep. **min**) emigrated from
muhājara (VN / f) emigration
muhājir (AP / nm, **muhājirīn, muhājira, muhājirāt**) emigrant
muḥāmi (AP / nm, **muḥāmin, muḥāmiyeh, muḥāmiyāt**) lawyer
muhandas (PP / nm, **muhandaseh**) planned by an architect or an engineer
muhandis (AP / nm, **muhandisīn, muhandiseh, muhandisāt**) engineer, architect
muḥārab (PP / nm, **m(u)ḥārabīn, m(u)ḥārabeh, m(u)ḥārabāt**) fought against
muḥārabeh (VN / f) fighting against, resistance
muḥārib (AP / nm, **muḥāribīn, muḥāribeh, muḥāribāt**) fighter
muharrab (PP / nm, var. **mharrab, mharrabīn, mharrabeh, mharrabāt**) smuggled
Muḥarram (nm) 1st month of the Muslim lunar calendar
muḥarrar (PP / nm, **muḥarrarīn, muḥarrara, muḥarrarāt**) edited, liberated
muharrib (AP / nm, **muharribīn, muharribeh, muharribāt**) smuggler
muḥarrir (AP / nm, **muḥarrirīn, muḥarrira, muḥarrirāt)** editor, liberator
muhimm (AP / nm, **muhimmīn, muhimmeh, muhimmāt**) important

muḥmarr (AP / nm, var. **miḥmarr**, f. **miḥmarra**) turning reddish
muḥzin (AP / nm, f. **muḥzineh**) saddening
mujarrad (PP / nm, f. **mujarradeh**) abstract
mujrim (nm, **mujrimīn, mujrimeh, mujrimāt**) criminal
mukhaddirāt (nf, sing. **mukhaddir**) drugs
mukharbaṭ (PP / nm, var. **mkharbaṭ, mkharbaṭīn, mkharbaṭa, mkharbaṭāt**) confused
mukharbiṭ (AP / nm) confuser
mukhḍarr (AP / nm, var. **mikhḍarr**, f. **mikhḍarra**) covered with green
mukhkh (nm, pl. **amkhākh**) brain
mukhraj† (PP / nm) thing taken out, film or play directed
mukhrajāt (nf) output
mukhrij (AP / nm, **mukhrijīn, mukhrijeh, mukhrijāt**) film or play director
mukhtalaf (PP / n) various
mukhtārāt (PP / nf, sing. **mukhtāra**) selected, selections
mulāqa† (PP / nm) person or event met
mulaqi (AP / nm) person meeting another / facing an event
mumāsha† (PP / nm) person walked along with (lit. or fig.)
mumāshi† (AP / nm) person walking along with another (lit. or fig.)
mumaththil (AP / nm, **mumaththilīn, mumaththileh, mumaththilāt**) actor, representative
mumkin (AP / nm, f. **mumkineh**) possible
mumtadd (AP / nm, f. **mumtaddeh**) stretching, extending
mumtāz (adj / m, **mumtāzīn, mumtāzeh, mumtāzāt**) excellent
munāda (PP / nm) person called (e.g. by name), vocative
munādā (VN / f) act of calling (e.g. somebody by name)
munādi (AP / nm, **munādīn, munādyeh, munād(i)yāt**) person calling another
munāfiq (AP / nm, **munāfiqīn, munāfiqa, munāfiqāt**) flatterer
munāqashāt (nf, sing. **munāqasheh**) discussions
mundafi@ (AP / nm, **mundafi@īn, mundafi@a, mundafi@āt**) reckless
munfa@il (AP / nm, **munfa@ilīn, minfi@leh, minfi@lāt**) excited, overwrought
munha† (PP / nm) thing finished
munhi (AP / nm) person who puts an end to sthg
munjali (AP / nm, var. **minijli**) having cleared up
munkasir (AP / nm, var. **miniksir, minkisrīn, minkisreh, minkisrāt**) broken, defeated
munqaḍi (AP / nm, var. **miniqḍi**) having elapsed, reaching the end
munqalib (AP / nm, var. **miniqlib, minqilbīn, minqilbeh, minqilbāt**) overturned
muntabih (AP / nm, var. **mintabih, muntab(i)hīn, mintibha, mintibhāt**) attentive
muntaha (PP / n, gender det. by pron. attached to prep. **min**) done with, exceedingly

muntahi (AP/nm, var. **mint-hi, mint-hiyyīn, mint-hiyyeh, mint-hiyyāt**) finished
muntajāt (nf, sing. **muntaj**) products
muntaṣir (AP/nm, **muntaṣirīn/ mintiṣrīn, mintiṣreh, mintiṣrāt**) victorious
muntaẓar (PP/nm, f. **muntaẓara**) expected
muntaẓir (AP/nm, **muntaẓirīn/ mintiẓrīn, mintiẓreh, mintiẓrāt**) waiting
munzal (PP/nm) thing brought down; specifically, **Qur"ānic** revelation
munzil (AP/nm) person who gets something down
murajja@ (PP/nm, var. **mrajja@, mrajja@īn, mrajja@a, mrajja@āt**) returned
murajji@ (AP/nm, var. **mrajji@, mrajj@īn, mrajj@a, mrajj@āt**) returner
murīḥ (AP/nm, f. **murīḥa**) comfortable
murr (adj/m, f. **murra**) bitter
mus@af (PP/nm) receiver of medical aid
mus@if (AP/nm, **mus@ifīn, mus@ifeh, mus@ifāt**) giver of medical aid
musā@adeh (nf, pl. **musā@adāt**) assistance
musā@id (AP/nm, **musā@(i)dīn, musā@ideh, musā@idāt**) deputy, helper
musajjal (PP/nm, **musajjalīn, musajjaleh, musajjalāt**) recorded, registered
mushkileh (nf, pl. **mashākil/ mushkilāt**) problem
mushtadd (AP/nm, var. **mishtadd**, f. **mishtaddeh**) getting stronger/worse
mushtaha (PP/nm) desired
mushtahi (AP/nm, var. **misht-hi, misht-hiyyīn, misht-hiyyeh, misht-hiyyāt**) desiring
mūṣi (AP/nm) testator
muskirāt (nf, sing. **muskir**) intoxicants
musta@idd (AP/nm, **musta@iddīn, musta@iddeh, musta@iddāt**) willing, ready
musta@jil (AP/nm, **musta@jilīn, musta@jileh, musta@jilāt**) in a hurry
musta@mal (PP/nm, f. **musta@maleh**) used, second-hand
musta@mil (AP/nm, var. **mista@mil, musta@milīn, musta@mileh, musta@milāt**) user
mustaghall (PP/nm, **mustaghallīn, mustaghalleh, mustaghallāt**) exploited
mustaghill (AP/nm, **mustaghillīn, mustaghilleh, mustaghillāt**) exploiter
mustaghna (PP/n, gender det. by pron. attached to prep. **@an**) done without
mustaghni (AP/nm, **mustaghnīn, mustaghniyeh, mustaghniyāt**) able to do without
mustami@ (AP/nm, **mustami@īn, mustami@a, mustami@āt**) listener
mustaqbal (PP/nm) future
mustaqbil (AP/nm, **mustaqbilīn, mustaqbileh, mustaqbilāt**) receiver, receptionist
mustaqill (AP/nm, **mustaqillīn, mustaqilleh, mustaqillāt**) independent
mustashfa (nm, pl. **mustashfayāt**) hospital

mustawla (PP / n, gender det. by pron. attached to prep. **@ala**) confiscated

mustawli (AP / nm) confiscator

mustawrad (PP / nm, **mustawradāt, mustawradeh, mustawradāt**) imported

mut@a (nf, pl. **muta@**) pleasure

muta@allim (AP / nm, **muta@allimīn, muta@allimeh, muta@allimāt**) educated

muta@arrif (AP / nm, **muta@arrifīn, muta@arrifeh, muta@arrifāt**) acquainted with

mutabādal (PP / nm, f. **mutabādaleh**) mutual

mutabādil (AP / nm, var. **mitbādil**, pl. **mutabādilīn/ mitbadlīn**) exchanging

mutadhakkir (AP / nm, var. **mitdhakkir, mitdhakkrīn, mitdhakkreh, mitdhakkrāt**) remembering

mutafāhamt (PP / n, gender det. by pron. attached to prep. **@ala**) under mutual understanding

mutafahhim (AP / nm, **mutafahhimīn, mutafahhimeh, mutafahhimāt**) understanding

mutafāhim (AP / nm, var. **mitfāhim**, pl. **mutafāhimīn/ mitfāhmīn**) in mutual understanding

mutaghaddi (AP / nm, var. **mitghaddi, mitghaddyīn, mitghaddyeh, mitghaddyāt**) having had lunch

mutakhaṣṣiṣ (AP / nm, **mutakhaṣṣiṣīn, mutakhaṣṣiṣa, mutakhaṣṣiṣāt**) specializing in

mutamādi (AP / nm, var. **mitmādi, mitmadīn, mitmādyeh, mitmādyāt**) going too far

mutanāqiḍ (AP / nm, var. **mitnāqiḍ, mitnāqḍīn, mitnāqḍa, mitnāqḍāt**) contradictory

mutanāsi (AP / nm, var. **mitnāsi, mitnāsīn, mitnāsyeh, mitnāsyāt**) pretending to forget

mutaqātalt (PP / n, gender det. by pron. attached to prep. **@ala**) sthg fought for

mutaqātil (AP / nm, var. **mitqātil**, pl. **mutaqātilīn/ mitqātlīn**) fighting against each other

mutaqaṭṭi@ (AP / nm, f. **mutaqaṭṭi@a**) intermittent

mutarjam (PP / nm, **m(u)tarjamīn, m(u)tarjameh, m(u)tarjamāt**) translated

mutarjim (AP / nm, **mutarjimīn, mutarjimeh, mutarjimāt**) translator

mutasā"alt (PP / n, gender det. by pron. attached to prep. **@an**) under investigation

mutasā"il (AP / nm, var. **mitsā"il**, pl. **mutasā"ilīn/ mitsā"līn**) wondering

mutasalli (AP / nm, var. **mitsalli, mitsallyīn, mitsallyeh, mitsallyāt**) having fun

mutawaqqa@ (PP / nm, f. **mutawaqqa@a**) expected

mutlaft (PP / nm) thing destroyed

mutlif (AP / nm) person who destroys sthg

muwāfaq (PP / n, gender det. by pron. attached to prep. **@ala**) approved

muwāfaqa (nf, pl. **muwāfaqāt**) approval

muwāfiq (AP / nm, var. **mwāfiq, m(u)wāf(i)qīn, mwāfqa, mwāfqāt**) approves, agrees
muwaẓẓaf (nm, **muwaẓẓafīn, muwaẓẓafeh, muwaẓẓafāt**) employee, government official
muz@ij (nm, **muz@ijīn, muz@ijeh, muz@ijāt**) annoying
muzraqq (AP / nm, var. **mizraqq**, f. **mizraqqa**) becoming livid

na@am (adv.) yes
nā@im (AP / nm, **nā@min, nā@meh, nā@māt**) soft
nāb (nm, pl. **anyāb**) incisor
nabi (nm, pl. **anbiyā"**) prophet
nabīdh (nm) wine
nāda (v.III.2) called
nadhar (v.I.5) dedicated (himself to a cause), vowed
nādreh (adj / f, m. **nādir**) rare
nafs (nf, pl. **anfus/nufūs**) self; attached to pronominal suffixes: myself, yourself (etc.)
nafṭ (nm) oil, petroleum
nagham (nm, pl. **anghām**) tune
nahār (nm, var. **nhār**) day(time)
naḥw (prep.) towards
najāḥ (VN / m) success
najaḥ (v.I.3) succeeded
nājiḥ (AP / nm, **nāj(i)ḥīn, nāj(i)ḥa, nāj(i)ḥāt**) successful
najjaḥ (v.II.1) caused someone to succeed
nakhil (nm) date palm trees
nāl (v.I.10) won, was awarded, obtained his desire
nām (v.I.12) slept
nāqiṣ (AP / nm, **naqṣīn, nāqṣa, nāqṣāt**) incomplete, deficient, imperfect
nāqūs (nm, pl. **nawāqīs**) church bell
nās (nm) people
naṣaḥ (v.I.3) advised
naṣar (v.I.4) aided, supported, helped against enemies
nashar (v.I.4) published
nashāṭ (nm) activity
nāshir (AP / nm, pl. **nāshirīn**) publisher
nashir (VN / m, va. **nashr**) publishing
nāsi (AP / nm, **nāsyīn, nāsyeh, nāsyāt**) oblivious
naṣīb (nm) share

nassa (v.II.2) caused to forget
nathir (nm) prose
nawa (v.I.6) intended
nāwi (AP / nm, **nāwyīn, nāwyeh, nāwyāt**) intending, planning to
nāy (nm, pl. **nāyāt**) flute
nāyim (adj / m, **nāymīn, nāymeh, nāymāt**) asleep
nazaf (v.I.5) bled
naẓar (v.I.4) looked
naẓar (VN / m) looking, sight
nāzil (AP / nm, **nāzlīn, nāzleh, nāzlāt**) descending
nazzal (v.II.1) got sthg down, lowered
nihā"i (adj / m, f. **nihā"iyyeh**) final
niḥna (pron., var. **iḥna**) we
nijmeh (nf, pl. **n(u)jūm**) star
Nīl (nm) the Nile
niqāsh (VN / m) discussion
Nīsān (nm) April
nisbeh (nf, pl. **nisab**) proportion **bi 'n-nisbeh** with reference to, regarding
nisyān (VN / m) forgetting, forgetfulness
niyyeh (nf, pl. **niyyāt**) intention
nizil (v.I.1) went down
nō@ (nm, pl. **anwā@**) species, kind
nōm (VN / m) sleep, sleeping
nuqṭa (nf, pl. **nuqaṭ/nuqāṭ**) point

nūr (nm, pl. **anwār**) light
ṣabāḥ/masa" en-nūr good morning / evening
nuskha (nf, pl. **nusakh**) copy
nuṣṣ (nm, pl. **nṣaṣ**) half
Nūvambar (nm, var. **Nūvambir**) November

ōksijīn (nm) oxygen

qā"id (AP / nm, var. **qāyid**, pl. **quwwād)** leader
qā"imeh (nf, pl. **qawā"im**) list
qabil (prep. & adv.) before
qabil mā (conj.) before
qabīleh (nf, pl. **qabā"il/qabāyil**) tribe
qaḍa (v.I.6) spent his time (doing sthg)
qadam (nm, pl. **aqdām**) foot
kurit el-qadam soccer
qadar (nm, pl. **aqdār)** fate
qaddaish (interr. part.) how much
qaddam (v.II.1) he introduced somebody to, he presented
qādim (AP / nm, f. **qādmeh**) coming, next
qadīm (adj / m, **qudamā("),** **qadīmeh, qadīmāt**) old
qaḍiyyeh (nf, pl. **qaḍāya**) problem, issue, question
qahweh (nf) coffee
qāl (v.I.10) said
qalab (v.I.5) turned sthg over
qalam (nm, pl. **aqlām**) pen, pencil
qalamain (nm, dual of **qalam**) two pens or pencils
qalb (nm, pl. **q(u)lūb**) heart
qalīl (adj / m, f. **qalīleh**) little, few, not much
qalqān (adj / m, **qalqanīn,** **qalqāneh, qalqanāt**) worried
qām (v.I.10) was based on
qamar (nm, pl. **aqmār**) moon
qamar ṣinā@i man-made satellite
qamari (adj / m, f. **qamariyyeh**) of the moon, lunar
qamīṣ (nm, pl. **qumṣān**) shirt
qāmūs (nm, pl. **qawāmīs**) dictionary
qara (v.I.3, **qara"/iqra"** with hamza dropped for ease of pronunciation) read
qarḍ (nm, pl. **qurūḍ**) loan
qarīb (adj / m, f. **qarībeh**) near, recent
qarīban (adv.) shortly
qarin (nm, var. **qarn,** pl. **q(u)rūn**) century
qarrab (v.II.1) approached, came nearer
qarrar (v.II.1) decided
qās (v.I.11) measured
qaṣad (v.I.4) meant
qāsi (adj / m, **qāsyīn, qāsyeh,** **qāsyāt**) hard, cruel, harsh
qaṣīr (adj / m, f. **qaṣīreh**) short
qaṭa@ (v.I.3) cut, covered (a distance)
qātal (v.III.1) fought
qatal (v.I.4) killed
qatil (VN / m, var. **qatl**) murder, killing
qātil (AP / nm, **qatala, qātleh,** **qātlāt**) murderer, killer
qawalan (VN / m) saying
qawānīn (nf, sing. **qānūn**) laws
qaws quzaḥ (nm, pl. **aqwās** **quzaḥ**) rainbow
qāyil (AP / nm, var. **qā"il, qāylīn,** **qāyleh, qāylāt**) person who says
qibil (v.I.1) agreed, accepted
qidir (v.I.1) was able to
qilleh (nf) scarcity, paucity
qiṣṣa (nf, pl. **qiṣaṣ**) story
qiṭa@ (nf, sing. **qiṭ@a**) pieces, passages
qiyādeh (nf, pl. **qiyādāt**) leadership

qiyam (nf, sing. **qīmeh**) values (moral or mathematical)
qōl (VN / m) saying
quddām (adv.) in front of
qura (nf, sing. **qaryeh**) villages

rā"i@ (AP / nm, f. **rā"i@a**) wonderful
ra"īs (nm, pl. **ru"asa/ru"asā"**) chief, head, president
ra"san (adv.) immediately
ra"y (nm, pl. **ārā"**) opinion
ra@a (v.I.6, imp. **ir@a**) shepherded, patronized (an occasion)
rabb (nm, pl. **arbāb**) god, God, owner of
rābi@ (AP / nm, f. **rāb(i)@a**) fourth
Rabī@ el-awwal (nm) 3rd month of the Muslim lunar year
Rabī@ eth-thani (nm) 4th month of the Muslim lunar year
rabṭa (nf, pl. **rabṭāt**) necktie
rāḍa (v.III.2) tried to make it up with
radd (VN / m, pl. **r(u)dūd**) answer, response
radd (v.I.7) returned sthg, answered back
raḍḍ (nm, pl. **r(u)ḍūḍ**) bruise
rāḍi (AP / nm, **rāḍyīn, rāḍyeh, rāḍyāt**) satisfied
rādid (AP / nm) responding
rafa@ (v.I.3) raised
rafaḍ (v.I.4) refused, turned down
raff (nm, pl. **r(u)fūf**) shelf
rafi@ (VN / m) raising (e.g., of prices)
rāḥ (v.I.10) went
raḥam (v.I.3) acted mercifully
rahīneh (nf (may be m. in meaning), pl. **rahā"in/ rahāyin**) hostage
raḥmeh (nf) mercy
rajā"an (VN / m) please
Rajab (nm) 7th month of the Muslim lunar year
rāji@ (AP / nm, **rāj@īn, rāj@a, rāj@āt**) returning
rajja@ (v.II.1) returned sthg
rajul (nm, pl. **r(i)jāl**) man (the male of the species)
rakaḍ (v.I.4) ran
rakhīṣ (adj / m, var. **rkhīṣ**, f. **rkhīṣa**) cheap
rakkab (v.II.1) he caused to ride
rakkaz (v.II.1) concentrated
rama (v.I.6) threw
Ramaḍān (nm) 9th month of Muslim lunar year, month of fasting
rāmi (AP / nm) thrower, marksman
rami (VN / m) throwing
ramyeh (nf, pl. **ramyāt**) a throw
raqim (nm, var. **raqm**, pl. **arqām**) number, figure
raqīq (adj / m, f. **raqīqa**) delicate
rāqyeh (nf, pl. **rāqyāt**, m. **rāqi**, m.pl. **rāqyīn**) upper-class, top-notch
rās (nm, pl. **rūs**) head
rasā"il (nf, sing. **risāleh**) letters
rāsal (v.III.1) corresponded with
rasam (v.I.5) drew (a picture, etc.)
raṣīd (nm, pl. **arṣideh**) balance in bank account
rasim (VN / m, var. **rasm**) drawing (of pictures, etc.)
rāsim (AP / nm) drawer (of pictures, etc.); usu. replaced by: **rassām** painter
rasmiyyeh (nf, pl. **rasmiyyāt**, m. **rasmi**) official, according to protocol
rawāḥ (VN / m) going
rawaḥān (VN / m) going
rāyiḥ (AP / nm, **rāyḥīn, rāyḥa, rāyḥāt**) going to

ribiḥ (v.I.1) earned, won, profited
riḍa (VN / m) satisfaction
riḍi (v.I.2) was satisfied
riḥleh (nf, pl. **riḥlāt**) trip, journey
riji@ (v.I.1) came back
rijil (nf, pl. **arjul**) leg, (loosely:) foot
risāleh (nf, pl. **rasā"il**) letter
risāltain (nf, dual of **risāleh**) two letters
riwāyeh (nf, pl. **riwāyāt**) novel

riyāḍa (nf) sports
riyāḍi (adj / m, **riyāḍiyyīn, riyāḍiyyeh, riyāḍiyyāt**) athlete
riyāḍiyyāt (nf) mathematics
riyāḍiyyeh (adj / f, m. **riyāḍi**) mathematical
rubi@ (nm, var. **rub@**, pl. **arbā@**) quarter, one fourth
rukūb (nm) riding
rumūz (nf, sing. **ramz**) symbols
Rūsiyyeh (adj / f, pl. **Rūsiyyāt**, m. **Rūsi**, m. pl. **Rūs**) Russian
Rūsya (nf) Russia
ruzz (nm) rice

sa+ particle indicating future time
sa"al (v.I.3) asked
sā"iḥ (AP / nm, var. **sāyiḥ, suwwāḥ, sā"iḥa, sā"iḥāt**) tourist
sā"il (AP / nm, pl. **sā"ilin**) questioner
sā@a (nf, pl. **sā@āt**) hour, watch, clock
sā@ad (v.III.1) helped
sa@ādeh (nf) happiness; in **iḍāfa** construction: title of high dignitaries, Excellency
sa@al (v.I.4) sneezed
sa@īd (adj / m, **su@ada/su@adā", sa@īdeh, sa@idāt**) happy
sā@tain (nf, dual of **sā@a**) two hours
sab@īn (nf) seventy
saba@ṭāsh (nf) seventeen
saba@ṭāshar (nf / m) seventeen in **iḍāfa** construction
sabab (nm, pl. **asbāb**) reason, cause
sabaḥ (v.I.3) swam
sabi@ (nf / m) seven in **iḍāfa** construction
sābi@ (AP / nm, f. **sāb@a**) seventh
Sabt (nm, usu. attached to def. art.) Saturday
sadd (VN / m) closure, closing
sadd (v.I.8) closed
sadd (nm, pl. **s(u)dūd**) dam
saddad (v.II.1) repaid (debts)
sādid (AP / nm) closing, blocking
sādis (AP / nm, f. **sādseh**) sixth
sāfar (v.III.1) travelled, went abroad
safar (nm, pl. **asfār**) travel
safāra (nf, pl. **safārāt**) embassy
safīr (nm, pl. **sufara/sufarā"**) ambassador
sāḥil (nm, pl. **sawāḥil**) coast
sāḥir (AP / nm, pl. **saḥara**) magician
sāḥira (AP / nf, pl. **sāḥirāt**) witch, bewitching
sāhir (AP / nm) wakeful, sleepless
sahleh (adj / f) easy
sajan (v.I.5) imprisoned, incarcerated, detained
sakan (v.I.4) resided, took for a dwelling
sakhīf (adj / m, **sukhafa, sakhīfeh, sakhifāt**) silly
sākhin (AP / nm, f. **sākhneh**) warm, hot, running a temperature
sākin (AP / nm, **sāk(i)nīn, sākneh, sāknāt**) residing
sākin (AP / nm, f. **sākneh**) quiet

sakrān (adj / m, **sakranīn, sakrāneh, sakranāt**) drunk
salām (nm) peace
salāmeh (nf) safety
ma@ es-salāmeh goodbye
salamāt greetings / hello, how are you
salla (v.II.2) entertained
sallam (v.II.1) greeted, delivered sthg to someone
salleh (nf) basket
kurit es-salleh basketball
salsal (v.II.1) put in a series
sama (nf, var. **samā"**, pl. **samawāt**) sky
samā@ (VN / m) process of hearing, ability to hear
sāmaḥ (v.III.1) forgave
samaḥ (v.I. 3) allowed, permitted
samāḥ (nm) grace, forgiveness
samāwi (adj / m, f. **samāwiyyeh**) sky blue
sāmi@ (AP / nm, **sām(i)@īn, sām(i)@a, sām(i)@āt**) able to hear
Sāmiyyeh (adj / f) Semitic
samma (v.II.2) named, called
samma@ (v.II.1) caused someone to hear
sandwīsheh (nf, pl. **sand(a)wīshāt**) sandwich
saneh (nf, pl. **s(i)nīn/sanawāt**) year
saqa (v.I.6) gave a drink to
saqi (VN / m) irrigation
sāqi (AP / nm) provider of drinks, f. **sāqyeh** also: a stream
sār (v.I.11) walked
saraq (v.I.4) stole, burgled
sarī@ (adj / m, f. **sarī@a**) fast
sawfa† (particle indicating future time)
sāyiq (AP / nm, pl. **suwwāq**) driver
sayyāra (nf, pl. **sayyarāt**) car
sayyārtain (nf, dual of **sayyāra**) two cars
sayyi" (adj / m, **sayyi"īn, sayy(i)"a, sayy(i)"āt**) bad
sayyid (nm, pl. **sāda**) master, Mr
si@ir (nm, pl. **as@ār**) price
Sibtambar (nm, var. **Sibtambir**) September
sīd (nm, pl. **asyād**) master, grandfather
sijin (nm, pl. **s(u)jūn**) prison, imprisonment
simi@ (v.I.1) heard
sīnama (nf, pl. **sinamāt**) cinema
sīreh (nf) biography, story
sitār (nm, f. **sitāra**, pl. **satāyir/ satā"ir**) curtain
sitt (nf / m) six in **iḍāfa** construction
sitt (nf, pl. **sittāt**) lady, grandmother
sitṭāsh (nf) sixteen
sitteh (nf) six
sittīn (nf) sixty
siyāḥa (nf) tourism
siyāsi (adj / m, **siyāsiyyīn, siyāsiyyeh, siyāsiyyāt**) political, politician
srīrain (nm, dual of **s(a)rīr**) two beds
sū" (nm) badness, evil
su"āl (nm, pl. **as"ileh**) question
Su@ūdiyyeh (nf, var. **Sa@ūdiyyeh**) Saudi Arabia
sukkān (nm, sing. **sākin**) inhabitants
sukkari (adj / m) sweet (like sugar: **sukkar**)
sukna (nf) residence
sukūn (nm) quietness, silence
sulṭān (nm, pl. **salāṭīn**) sultan
sūq (nm, pl. **aswāq**) market, shopping complex
sūr (nm, pl. **aswār**) wall
sur@a (nf) speed

Sūriyya (nf, var. **Sūrya**) Syria
Swīsriyyeh (adj / f, m. **Swīsri**) Swiss

ṣa@b (adj / m, f. **ṣa@beh**) difficult
ṣabāḥ (nm) morning
ṣabāḥ el-khair good morning
ṣabāḥ en-nūr response to 1st greeting
ṣabāḥan (adv.) in the morning, a.m.
ṣabar (v.I.4) was patient
ṣadam (v.I.4) collided with
ṣadd (v.I.7) repulsed, repelled
ṣadd (VN / m) repulsion
ṣaddaq (v.II, I) believed what was said
ṣadīq (nm, **aṣdiqā", ṣadīqa, ṣadīqāt**) friend
ṣādirāt (nf, sing. **ṣādir**) exports
Ṣafar (nm) 2nd month of the Muslim lunar year
ṣaḥayān (VN / m) waking up, sobering up
ṣāḥi (AP / nm, **ṣāḥyīn, ṣāḥyeh, ṣāḥyāt**) wakeful, sober
ṣāḥib (nm, pl. **aṣḥāb**) friend, owner of
ṣaḥīḥ (adj / m, f. **ṣaḥīḥa**) correct, true
ṣaḥra (nf, var. **ṣaḥrā"**, pl. **ṣaḥāri**) desert
ṣaid (nm) hunting, fishing
ṣām (v.I.10) tasted
ṣandūq (nm, pl. **ṣanādīq**) box
ṣār (v.I.11) became, happened
ṣaraf (v.I.5) spent
ṣarakh (v.I.3) cried, shouted
ṣayarān (VN / m) becoming
ṣaydaleh (nf) pharmacy
ṣāyir (AP / nm, **ṣāyrīn, ṣāyreh, ṣāyrāt**) becoming
ṣayyar (v.II.1) caused to become
ṣiḥḥa (nf) health
ṣiḥi (v.I.2) waked up, sobered up
ṣinā@a (nf, pl. **ṣinā@āt**) industry, manufacture
ṣinā@iyyeh (adj / f, m. **ṣinā@i**) industrial, manufactured
Ṣīni (adj / m, **Ṣīniyyīn, Ṣīniyyeh, Ṣīniyyāt**) Chinese
ṣōfa (nf, pl. **ṣōfāt**) sofa
ṣōt (nm, pl. **aṣwāt**) voice, noise, sound
ṣu@ūbāt (nf, sing. **ṣu@ūbeh**) difficulties
ṣubiḥ (nm, var. **ṣubḥ**) morning
ṣuwar (nf sing. **ṣūra**) pictures

shā" (v.I.12) willed sthg to be
in shā" Allāh God willing
sha@ar (nm) hair
Sha@bān (nm) 8th month of the Muslim lunar year
shā@ir (AP / nm, **shu@arā", shā@ira, shā@irāt**) poet
shadd (v.I.8) tightened
wa la tshidd īdak not as good as it seems
shadīd (adj / m, **shadidīn, shadīdeh, shadidāt**) intense
shāf (v.I.10) saw
shaghghal (v.II.1) employed
shaghleh (nf, pl. **shaghlāt**) job
shahādeh (nf, pl. **shahadāt**) certificate, degree
shahar (nm, pl. **ashhur, sh(u)hūr**) month
shahrain (nm, dual of **shahar**) two months
shajar (nm) trees collectively: f. **shajara** (pl. **shajarāt**) tree
shaka (v.I.6) complained
shakk (nm, pl. **shakkāt**) cheque
shākūsh (nm, pl. **shawākīsh**) hammer
shakwa (nf, pl. **shakāwi**) complaint
shamāl (nm) north

shamāli (adj/m, **shamāliyyīn, shamāliyyeh, shamāliyyāt**) northern, left-handed
shams (nf, pl. **shumūs**) sun
shān (nm) sake
min shān in order to
@ala shān because
shanṭa (nf, pl. **shunaṭ**) suitcase
shaqqa (nf, pl. **shuqaq**) apartment
sharaf (nm) honour
shāri@ (nm, pl. **shawāri@**) street
sharīf (adj/m, **shurafa, sharīfeh, sharīfāt**) honourable
sharīṭ (nm, pl. **ashriṭa**) tape
sharikeh (nf, pl. **sharikāt**) company
sharq (nm) east
sharqi (adj/m, **sharqiyyīn, sharqiyyeh, sharqiyyāt**) eastern, oriental
sharr (nm, pl. **sh(u)rūr**) evil
sharraf (v.II.1) honoured
sharrīb (adj/m, **sharrībeh, sharrībeh, sharribāt**) drinker, heavy drinker, connoisseur
sharṭ (nm, pl. **sh(u)rūṭ**) condition
bi sharṭ provided that
shata (v.I.6) rained
shawafān (VN/m) seeing
shawwaf (v.II.1) showed, made someone see
Shawwāl (nm) 10th month of the Muslim lunar year
shāy (nm) tea
shāyif (AP/nm, **shāyfīn, shāyfeh, shāyfāt**) seeing
Shbāṭ (nm, var. **Shubāṭ**) February
shī (nm) something
shi@ir (nm, pl. **ash@ār**) poetry
shiddeh (nf) force, strictness
shirib (v.I.3) drank
shita (nm) winter, rain
shiṭranj (nm) chess
shōf (VN/m) seeing
shōk (nm) thorns
shōq (VN/m, pl. **ashwāq**) desire to see somebody/sthg
shū (interr. part.) what
shū ma (conj.) whatever
shughul (nm, var. **shughl**) work
shukran (VN/m) thank you
shukulāṭa (nf) chocolate(s)
shurb (VN/m, var. **shurub**) drinking
shurṭa (nm) policemen, the police
shurṭi (nm) policeman
shwayy (nf) a little
shwayy shwayy (adv.) gradually, easy does it!

t"akhkhar (v.V.1) was late
t"akkad (v.V.1) ascertained
t@allam (v.V.1) learned
t@āmal (v.VI.1) dealt with
t@ammad (v.V.1) did sthg deliberately
t@arraf (v.V.1) got acquainted with, recognized
t@ashsha (v.V.2) had supper
ta"kīd (VN/m) assertion
ta@@ab (v.II.1) fatigued, exhausted
ta@āl (v., irreg. imp. of **aja**) come
ta@allum (VN/m) learning sthg
ta@arruf (VN /m) recognizing, getting acquainted with
ta@āseh (nf) wretchedness, unhappiness
ta@assufiyyeh (adj/f, m. **ta@assufi**) arbitrary
ta@līm (VN/m) teaching
ta@līmiyyeh (adj/f, m. **ta@līmi)** educational
ta@yīn (VN/m) appointment (to an office or job)
tāb (v.I.10) repented
tabādul (VN/m) exchange
tadakhkhul (VN/m) interference, intrusion

tadhakkur (VN / m) remembering
tadrīs (VN / m) teaching
tafaḍḍal (v.V.1, var. **tfaḍḍal**) be good enough to (do sthg suggested by word or gesture)
tafahhum (VN / m) willingness to understand
tafāhum (VN / m) mutual understanding
tafāṣil (nf, sing. **tafṣīl)** details
tafkīr (VN / m) thinking
taghaddi (VN / m) having lunch, lunching
tahdīd (VN / m, pl. **tahdīdāt**) threat, threatening
taḥiyyeh (nf, pl. **taḥiyyāt)** greeting
taḥqīq (VN / m, pl. **taḥqīqāt**) investigation
tahrīb (VN / m) smuggling
taḥrīr (VN / m) liberation
taḥt (prep. & adv.) under, beneath, below
takālīf (nf, sing. **taklifeh**) costs
takharruj (VN / m) graduation
takhaṣṣuṣāt (nf, sing. **takhaṣṣuṣ**) specializations
taksi (nm, pl. **taksiyyāt**) taxi
talafōn (nm, pl. **talafōnāt**) telephone
talfan (v.XI) telephoned
tālyeh (AP / nf, pl. **tālyāt**, m. **tāli**, m. pl. **tālyīn**) following
tamādi (VN / m) going too far
tamāman (adv.) quite, completely
tamm (v.I.8) became complete
Tammūz (nm) July
tamwīt (VN / m) causing the death of
tanāfus (VN / m) competition
tanāquḍ (VN / m) contradiction
tanāsi (VN / m) pretending / trying to forget
taqaddum (VN / m) progress
taqātul (VN / m) mutual struggle, deadly conflict
taqrīban (adv.) nearly, almost
taqwīm (nm, pl. **taqwīmāt)** calendar
tarak (v.I.4) left, abandoned
tārīkh (nm, pl. **tawārīkh**) date (of an event), history
tarjam (v.XI) translated
tarjameh (nf, pl. **tarjamāt**) translation
tarjī@ (VN / m) returning
tasā"ul (VN / m) questioning
tasalli (VN / m) having fun, entertaining oneself
tāsi@ (AP / nm, f. **tās@a**) ninth
tasjīl (VN / m) scoring, recording
taṣwīr (nm) photographing
taṭyīr (VN / m) causing sthg to fly
tbadal (v.VI.1) exchanged
tbayyan (v.V.1) it appeared
tḍā@af (v.VI.1) doubled
tdakhkhal (v.V.1) interfered, intruded
tdhakkar (v.V.1) remembered
tfā"al (v.VI.1) acted optimistically, was hopeful
tfāham (v.VI.1) reached a mutual understanding
tghadda (v.V.2) had lunch
tghayyar (v.V.1) changed (intransitively)
tḥarrak (v.V.1) moved
tḥassan (v.V.1) improved
tijāra (nf) commerce, trade
tijāri (adj / m, f. **tijariyyeh**) commercial
tikit (nf, pl. **tiktāt**) ticket
tiknōlōgi (adj / m, f. **tiknōlōjiyyeh**) technological
tikrār (VN / m) repetition
tilif (v.I.1) became damaged
tilmīdh (nm, **talamīdh, tilmīdheh, tilmidhāt**) pupil
tīn (nm) figs
tis@a (nf) nine

tis@īn (nf) ninety
Tishrīn awwal (nm) October
Tishrīn thāni (nm) November
tisi@ (nm/f) nine in **iḍāfa** construction
tisi@ţāsh (nf) nineteen
tjāhal (v.VI.1) ignored
tkāsal (v.VI.1) acted lazily
tkassar (v.V.1) got broken, splintered into pieces
tkātab (v.VI.1) corresponded with
tmāda (v.VI.2) went too far in doing sthg
tmanna (v.V.2) wished, hoped for
tmāraḍ (v.VI.1) pretended to be sick
tnakkar (v.V.1) denied knowledge of, put on a mask
tnāsa (v.VI.2) pretended to have forgotten, tried to forget
tnāsab (v.VI.1) was proportionate to/ commensurate with
tqātal (v.VI.1) engaged in a fight with
trāḍa (v.VI.2) made it up with
tsā"al (v.VI.1) asked, wondered
tsalla (v.V.2) entertained himself; had fun
tsarra@ (v.V.1) acted hastily
tshā"am (v.VI.1) acted pessimistically, felt that things would not turn out well
Turkiyya (nf) Turkey
twassaţ (v.V.1) mediated
tẓāhar (v.VI.1) pretended
tzawwaj (v.V.1, var. **tjawwaz**) got married

ţāb (v.I.11) (of a patient:) recovered; (of life:) became pleasant
ţab@an (adv.) naturally
ţabakh (v.I.4) cooked
ţabbākh (nm, **ţabbakhīn, ţabbākha, ţabbakhāt**) cook
ţabī@iyyeh (adj/f, m. **ţabī@i**) natural
ţabīb (nm, **aţibbā", ţabībeh, ţabībāt**) physician
ţabīkh (nm) cooked food, cooking
ţābiq (nm, pl. **ţawābiq**) floor, storey
ţalab (nm, pl. **ţalabāt**) application, demand, request
ţann (nm, pl. **aţnān**) ton
ţār (v.I.11) flew
ţard (VN/m) dismissal
ţarīq (nf, pl. **ţuruq**) road, path
ţawīl (adj/m, f. **ţawīleh**) long, tall
ţāwleh (nf, pl. **ţāwlāt**) table
ţayarān (VN/m) flight, airlines
ţāyir (AP/nm, **ţāyrīn, ţāyreh, ţāyrāt**) flying
ţayyar (v.II.1) let fly, caused to fly
ţayyāra (nf, pl. **ţayyarāt**) aeroplane
ţayyib (nm, pl. **ţayyibāt**) good (thing)
ţayyib (VN/m) all right, well
ţibb (nm) medicine as a science
ţili@ (v.I.1) went up, went out
ţīn (nm) mud
ţōz (nm) dust in the Gulf area
ţūl (nm, pl. **aţwāl**) length, height
ţullāb (nm, sing. **ţālib**, f. **ţāl(i)beh**, f. pl. **ţālibāt**) students

tha@lab (nm, pl. **tha@ālib**) fox
thabat (v.I.5) stood firm, has been proved to be true
thalath (nm/f) three in **iḍāfa** construction
Thalātha (nf, var. **Thalathā"**) Tuesday
thalāthāt (nf, sing. **thalātheh**) threes

thalātheh (nf, var. **talāteh**) three
thalathīn (nf, var. **talatīn**, pl. **thalathīnāt**) thirty
thalaṭṭāsh (nf.) thirteen
thālith (nm, f. **thāltheh**) third in a sequence
thalj (nm, pl. **thulūj**) ice, snow
thaman (nm, pl. **athmān**) price
thaman (nm / f, var. **taman**) eight in **iḍāfa** construction
thamanīn (nf, var. **tamanīn**) eighty
thamanṭāsh (nf) eighteen
thamānyeh (nf) eight
thāmin (nm, var. **tāmin,** f. **thāmneh/tāmneh**) eighth in a series
thāni (nm, var. **tāni,** f. **thānyeh/ tānyeh**) second in a series, other
thānyeh (nf, pl. **thawāni**) second (unit of time), second (ordinal number)
tharawāt (nf, sing. **tharweh**) riches, resources
thintain (nf) two
thulth (nm, var. **tult/thilth/tilt**) one third
thuql (nm, var. **thuqul**, pl. **athqāl**) weight

ujra (nf) fare, rent
ukht (nf, pl. **akhawāt/khawāt**) sister
Uktōbar (nm, var. **Uktōbir**) October
ūla (nf) first
umm (nf, pl. **ummahāt**) mother
Urdun (nm, always attached to def. art.) Jordan
Urduni (adj / m, **Urduniyyīn, Urduniyyeh, Urduniyyāt**) Jordanian
usbū@ (nm, pl. **asābī@**) week
usbu@ain (nm, dual of **usbū@**) two weeks
ustādh (nm, var. **ustāz,** pl. **asātdheh/asātzeh,** f. **ustādheh**) professor; (loosely:) Mr
utail (nm, pl. **utailāt**) hotel

vīza (nf, pl. **viyaz**) visa

w (conj., var. **wa/iw**) and
wa law (= **wa** + **law**) even so, notwithstanding, that much
wā@ad (v.III.1) gave an appointment, promised to meet
wa@ad (v.I.5) promised
wā@i (AP / nm, **wā@yīn, wā@yeh, wā@yāt**) aware
wa@id (nm, var. **wa@d**, pl. **wu@ūd**) promise
wadda (v.II.2) sent
wādi (nm, pl. **widyān**) valley
waḍi@ (nm, pl. **awḍā@**) state, situation
wāḍiḥ (AP / nm, **waḍḥīn, wāḍḥa, waḍḥāt**) clear, obvious
wafa (v.I.6) fulfilled, kept a promise)
wāfaq (v.III.1) agreed
wāḥad (nm, var. **wāḥid**, f. **wāḥadeh**) one
waḥīd (adj / m, **waḥīdīn, waḥīdeh, waḥīdāt**) only, lonely
wain (interr. part.) where
min main = mnain from where
wain ma (conj.) wherever
waja@ (nm, pl. **awjā@**) pain
wajad (v.I.5) found
wājah (v.III.1) faced, confronted
wājib (AP / nm, pl. **wājibāt**) duty, moral obligation
walad (nm, pl. **awlād**) boy
wāqi@ (AP / nm) reality
el-wāqi@ actually
wāqif (AP / nm, f. **wāqfeh**) standing

waqqa@ (v.II.1) signed
waqt (nm, pl. **awqāt**) time
waraqa (nf, pl. **awrāq**) sheet of paper
waraq paper
wardi (adj/m, f. **wardiyyeh**) rosy, rose-red
warṭa (nf, pl. **warṭāt**) predicament
washa (v.I.6) informed on
wāsi@ (AP/nm, f. **wās(i)@a**) wide, spacious
wāsīleh (nf, pl. **wasā"il**) a means
wasīṭ (nm, pl. **wusaṭa**) mediator
waṭan (nm, pl. **awṭān**) homeland
waṭani (adj/m, f. **waṭaniyyeh**) national
wāthiq (AP/nm, **wāthqīn, wāthqa, wāthqāt**) certain
wathīqa (nf, pl. **wathā"iq/wathāyiq**) document
wazīr (nm, **wuzara/wuzarā", wazīreh, wazīrāt**) minister (in government)
wiḥyātak (= **w** + **ḥayāt** (life) + **-ak**) I ask you by your life, please
wijih (nm, var. **wijh**, pl. **w(u)jūh**) face
wilāyeh (nf, pl. **wilāyāt**) state
el-Wilāyāt el-Muttaḥideh the United States
willa (conj.) or
wiqi@ (v.I.1) fell down
wiqif (v.I.1) stood
wiṣil (v.I.1) arrived
wusṭā (adj/f, m. **wasīṭ**) middlemost
el-@uṣūr el-wusṭā the Middle Ages

yā (voc. part.) oh, hey
ya 'lla (= **yā** + **Allah**) hurry up, let's go
yā rait (**yā** + **rait** (corruption of Standard Arabic **lait**: would that)) I wish
yā salām (**yā** + **salām**: peace) how good, how beautiful
ya@ni (imperf. of **@ana**: he meant, used impersonally as filler) you know, I mean
Yābān (nf) Japan
Yābāni (adj/m, **Yābāniyyīn, Yābāniyyeh, Yābāniyyāt**) Japanese
Yahūd (nm) Jews
Yahūdi (adj/m, **Yahūd, Yahūdiyyeh, Yahūdiyyāt**) Jewish
Yanāyir (nm) January
yi"is (v.I.1) despaired
yimkin (imperf. of **amkan**: it was possible, used impersonally) maybe
yōm (nm, pl. **ayyām**) day
el-yōm (adv.) today
yōmain (nm, dual of **yōm**) two days
Yūlya (nm, var. **Yūlyō**) July
Yūnāni (adj/m, **Yūnāniyyīn, Yūnāniyyeh, Yūnāniyyāt**) Greek
Yūnya (nm, var. **Yūnyō**) June

za@īm (nm, **zu@ama/zu@amā", za@īmeh, za@īmāt**) leader
za@lān (adj/m, **za@lanīn, za@lāneh, za@lanāt**) angry, cross
zafāf (nm) wedding ceremony
zakhārif (nf, sing. **zukhruf**) arabesques
zakhraf (v.XI) decorated with arabesques
zāki (adj/m, f. **zākyeh**) delicious, tasty
zāl (v.I.10) was removed, no longer existed
zalameh (nm, pl. **zlām**) man, the male of the species
zaman (nm, pl. **azmān**) time
zār (v.I.10) visited

zara@ (v.I.3) planted
zāri@ (AP / nm, **zār@īn, zār@a, zār@āt**) planter
zawāj (nm) marriage
zawj (nm, var. **zōj**, pl. **azwāj**) husband
zawjeh (nf, var. **zōjeh**, pl. **zawjāt/ zōjāt**) wife
zaytūn (nm) olives, olive trees
zaytūni (adj / m) olive in colour
zghīr (adj / m, **zghār, zghīreh, zghirāt**) small
zirā@a (VN / f) planting, agriculture
zirā@i (adj / m, f. **zirā@iyyeh**) agricultural
ziyāra (nf, pl. **ziyārāt**) visit
ẓāhir (AP / nm, **ẓāhrīn, ẓāhreh, ẓāhrāt**) appearing, exposed
eẓ-ẓāhir it seems
ẓahr (nm, var. **ẓahir**) back (of person), top (of car)
ẓālil (AP / nm, **ẓallīn, ẓālleh, ẓāllat**) remaining
ẓalīl (adj / m, f. **ẓalīleh**) shady
ẓall (v.I.9) remained, continued to be
ẓann (v.I.7) supposed, surmised
ẓuhur (nm, var. **ẓuhr**) noon
ẓuhūr (nm) appearance
ẓulman (adv.) unjustly
ẓulum (nm, var. **ẓulm**) injustice

Picture Credits
Jacket: Robert Harding Picture Library: D. Kraus, Bildagentur Schuster top right and bottom spine; Rolf Richardson top left; Dr. A. C. Waltham centre right above; Hutchison Library: top centre, bottom centre; Carlos Freire centre far right and back jacket; J. Horner centre far left; Tony Souter bottom left; Christopher Tordai bottom right; Telegraph Colour Library: G. Brightling centre left and top spine; Steve Dunning, Colorific centre right.